INT
SO
MW01717567
A quarterly journal of socialist theory

Spring 1992
Contents

Issue 54 of INTERNATIONAL SOCIALISM, quarterly journal of the Socialist Workers Party (Britain)

Published March 1992

Distribution/subscriptions: International Socialism, PO Box 82, London E3.
American distribution/subscriptions: PO Box 16085, Chicago Illinois 60616
Editorial and production: 071-538 1626/071-538 3307
Sales and subscriptions: 071-538 5821 x133
American sales: 312 666 7337

ISBN 0-906224-69-1

Printed by BPCC Wheatons Ltd, Exeter, England
Typeset by East End Offset, London E3

Cover: Edward Hopper, *Gas* (1940); cover design by Ian Goodyer

For details of back copies see the end pages of this book

Subscription rates for one year (four issues) are:

Britain and overseas (surface):	individual	£12.00 ($20)
	institutional	£20.00
Air speeded supplement:	North America	nil
	Europe/South America	£1.00
	elsewhere	£2.00

Note to contributors

The deadline for articles intended for issue 56 of *International Socialism* is 1 July 1992

All contributions should be double-spaced with wide margins. Please submit two copies. If you write your contribution using a computer, please also supply a disk, together with details of the computer and programme used.

INTERNATIONAL SOCIALISM

A quarterly journal of socialist theory

AMERICAN WORKERS once dreamt that every generation would see its children grow up more prosperous, better housed, better educated and healthier than those who went before. Now that dream lies in ruins as the US economy pitches into a recession so deep that many are comparing it to the Depression of the 1930s.

Sharon Smith of the American International Socialist Organisation examines the social crisis in the US—the poverty and sinking wages, the inner city decay and the inadequate health service, the racism and the attack on the labour movement. 'Twilight of the American Dream' shows how class is re-entering the vocabulary of US politics as George Bush, only a year ago the hero of the Gulf War, sees his presidency begin to unravel.

BUSH'S PROBLEM is, in part, that the New World Order of free market prosperity which he so loudly proclaimed is turning into a disaster—and nowhere more so than in eastern Europe. Mike Haynes' 'Class and crisis' uses original material to present a comprehensive analysis of how the market has already failed the ordinary people of eastern Europe. He concludes by looking at how the growing threat of nationalism and fascism can be met by socialist politics.

JAPANESE CAPITALISM may look like the part of the system that crisis has not reached but, argues Costas Kossis, appearances are deceptive. He looks beneath the surface to trace the fractures in the Japanese economic miracle.

EXPERIMENTAL BIOLOGIST Steven Rose looks at the question raised by the Green movement, 'Do animals have rights?' in an article based on his lecture at Marxism 91.

ALEX CALLINICOS' reply to Nigel Harris' defence of his book *National Liberation*, printed in our last issue, plus reviews of Peter Linebaugh's *The London Hanged* and Helmut Gruber's *Red Vienna* conclude this issue.

Twilight of the American Dream

SHARON SMITH

'What's good for General Motors is good for America' is the slogan which exemplified the American Dream of the 1950s and 1960s. Once the world's richest company, GM manufactured one out of every two cars bought in the US. But today few people still harbour illusions in the American Dream—least of all GM's workers. At the end of 1991, after a decade of extracting concessions from its workforce, GM announced plans to cut 74,000 jobs, on top of 130,000 already cut since 1986. The transformations at General Motors have come to symbolise the dramatic changes that have occurred in US society since the heyday of American capitalism. This article is an attempt to explain the nature of these changes and what they mean for the future.

The affluence of the US working class during the post Second World War economic boom is well known: during the same period in which the US rose as the world's main superpower, American workers achieved wages and living standards that were unmatched elsewhere. Average weekly earnings for US manufacturing workers rose by 84 percent between 1950 and 1965, while prices rose by only 31 percent during the same period.[1] And the American Dream was clearly something to which vast numbers of workers aspired, demonstrated by the large portion of the US population which considered itself to be middle class. In 1964, 44 percent of respondents to a survey saw themselves as middle class or higher, compared with 37 percent in 1952.[2] The economic and political stability of US society in this period prompted many on the right and the left to conclude that US capitalism had discovered a way to buy itself out of class conflict.

In 1951 the editors of *Fortune* magazine congratulated US capital in finding a uniquely 'American' solution to the 'problems of class struggle and proletarian consciousness'.[3] Sociologist Daniel Bell proclaimed 'the end of ideology' in 1960, adding later, 'Abundance . . . was the American surrogate for socialism.'[4] The left echoed these conclusions, both within and outside US borders. The working class in the heart of the beast was regarded as a part of the problem, rather than a potentially powerful part of the struggle for world socialism. The central tenet of Marxism was thrown out by left wing writers who theorised that the promise of some day owning a house in the suburbs had permanently subverted the class interests of US workers. The German-American philosopher Herbert Marcuse, the guru of many radicals in the 1960s, argued that the system provided a 'comfortable smooth reasonable democratic unfreedom' in which '"the people", previously the ferment of social change, have "moved up" to become the ferment of social cohesion.'[5]

But while the relative affluence of US workers was undeniable, it was by no means uniform. Even in 1959 more than one in five people lived below the official poverty line.[6] Wages for unorganised workers rose much less quickly than for those in unions. And the gap between black and white workers was dramatic. Throughout the 1950s and 1960s, the median income of black workers remained at about 55 percent of white workers' income. Even in Detroit, the centre for world auto production, the median black family income was only two thirds that of white families in 1954.[7]

Even for those workers whose living standards did not rise, their expectations did. This is perhaps the most important reason why the Civil Rights Movement began in the mid-1950s. Masses of black soldiers returned from fighting in the Second World War to face Jim Crow segregation in the South and *de facto* segregation in the North. Three million blacks left their farms in the South between 1940 and 1960 and moved to relocate in the ten largest industrial cities in what eventually became known as the 'rust belt', in the hopes of finding good paying industrial jobs. But by 1962 about 70 percent of black workers were employed in blue collar and service work, the vast majority in unskilled or semi-skilled jobs. And two thirds of all Northern blacks found themselves living in urban slums.[8]

Unionised white workers in particular experienced dramatic improvements in their living standards, but they paid the price of a drastic rise in the rate of exploitation. Output per worker more than doubled between 1947 and 1972. And while the number of manufacturing workers grew by 28.8 percent between 1950 and 1968, manufacturing output grew by 91 percent.[9] In 1950 US steel mills produced half the world's steel; US auto companies were responsible for 76 percent of world vehicle production.[10] So the real beneficiaries sat on the boards of directors of the biggest US corporations, willing to grant workers higher wages in order to pre-empt or shorten strikes and other interruptions in production.

Nevertheless, they were not entirely successful at winning labour peace, even among the best paid union members. Even at the height of the boom years, steel workers, for example, struck for 45 days in 1949, for 59 days in 1952, for 36 days in 1956 and for 110 days during a bitter battle in the recession of 1959. And in 1957 a rank and file slate challenged union leaders' 'tuxedo unionism' and demanded more democracy within the United Steel Workers of America (USWA).[11] In the auto industry the 1950s and 1960s were not characterised by amicable relations between capital and labour. United Auto Workers (UAW) officials negotiated a five year contract in 1950 which set the trend for decades to come: in return for higher wages, they agreed to a no-strike pledge and higher productivity.[12] The shopfloor grievance procedure became a bureaucratic nightmare for workers, and grievances were left unresolved for long periods by an increasingly remote union leadership. Frustrations erupted in periodic wildcat strikes during this entire period—so much so that UAW president Walter Reuther was forced to shorten the length of the contract to three years in 1955 and even authorised occasional local strikes over working conditions. As Stanley Weir described the situation in 1967:

> *The General Motors Corporation employs as many workers as all other auto manufacturers combined. In 1955, United Automobile Workers' president, Walter Reuther, signed a contract with GM which did not check the speedup or speed the settlement of local shop grievances. Over 70 percent of GM workers went on strike immediately after Reuther announced the terms of his agreement. A larger percentage 'wildcatted' after signing the 1958 contract because Reuther had again refused to do anything to combat speedup. For the same reason the auto workers walked off their jobs again in 1961. The strike closed every GM and a number of large Ford plants.*[13]

The number of strikes across all US industries in the 1950s was only slightly lower than during the strike wave which marked the second half of the 1940s. But strikes tended to be shorter and involved fewer workers in the 1950s, and still fewer in the first half of the 1960s.[14] The resolve which had typified earlier Congress of Industrial Organisations (CIO) picket lines was gradually replaced by passivity, as workers became accustomed to waiting out strikes, rather than playing any meaningful role. This was bound to have an effect on the class consciousness of white workers, who formed a politically conservative block which had little sympathy for either the civil rights movement or the anti-war movement throughout most of the 1960s.

The upsurge of the late 1960s and early 1970s

Stagnation had set in by the late 1960s. This stagnation, combined with growing frustration at speedup and a bloated and disinterested union bureaucracy, coincided with the height of the anti-war and black power movements as well as the wave of ghetto riots which swept across every major city in the late 1960s. The result was a massive shift in working class sentiment against the Vietnam War, and a series of working class revolts which began as the 1960s came to a close. These revolts were led initially by workers who were influenced by the movements and by the atmosphere of radicalisation of the period.

Black auto workers led the most overtly political struggles. But most importantly, these struggles are significant because black and white workers joined together to fight against racism as well as to raise economic demands. Specifically, black auto workers raised demands against what came to be known as 'niggermation'— the combination of speedup and racial discrimination. Black workers were almost completely excluded from the higher paying skilled trades at all of the Big Three auto plants: in 1968 Chrysler had 3 percent blacks in skilled trades jobs, Ford had 3 percent, and General Motors had 1.3 percent. And the union, for its part, was equally racist: while blacks made up a fourth of the UAW's total membership, they found themselves shut out of its leadership. Only six black delegates attended the UAW's 1968 convention and of the union's top 26 officers, only one was black.[15] The Dodge Revolutionary Union Movement (DRUM) was formed by a group of black revolutionaries at the Dodge Main Chrysler plant in Detroit after a wildcat strike in May 1968 led by black workers:

> *On May 2, 1968, 4,000 workers shut down Dodge Main in the first wildcat strike to hit that factory in 14 years. The immediate cause of the strike was speed-up and both black and white workers took part, but the driving force was . . . DRUM. The activities and ideas of DRUM were to inspire black workers throughout the United States. No less an authority than the* ***Wall Street Journal*** *took them very seriously from the day of the first wildcat, for the* ***Wall Street Journal*** *understood something most of the white student radicals did not yet understand: the black revolution of the sixties had finally arrived at one of the most vulnerable links of the American economic system—the point of mass production, the assembly line.*[16]

DRUM's successes at Dodge Main resulted in a number of spin off RUMs at other Detroit auto plants and even a Black Panther Caucus at the Fremont, California GM plant. The RUMs came together to form the League of Revolutionary Black Workers in 1969. The RUMs maintained a formal policy of discouraging white support which no doubt blunted the real potential which existed for building black and white unity. Nevertheless, a significant minority of white workers supported the strikes led by the RUMs. The United Black Brothers, who led a wildcat strike at the Ford plant in Mahwah, New Jersey, in 1969, is lesser known but in some ways even more impressive than DRUM, because the Mahwah workers understood the need to build solidarity with white workers at the plant. The United Black Brothers was formed out of a wildcat strike in 1967, when 500 black workers walked out after a foreman called a black worker a 'black bastard'. In 1969, when it organised a strike against racism at the Ford plant, whose workforce was one third black, it issued an appeal to white workers to join the strike:

> *Why do we ask your support? Because the same thing can happen to you. The company has been laying off men by the dozens, but the lines have not slowed up a bit. You have been given more work, and if you can't do it, you lose your job or get time off. The supervisors are harassing the men and calling them all kinds of names such as 'Dirty Guinea Bastard,' 'Black SOB' and 'Stinking Spick,' to name a few . . . We ask that all of you stay out and support us in this fight!* [17]

The number of wildcat strikes across all industries doubled, from 1,000 to 2,000 between 1960 and 1969. The year 1970 witnessed a veritable strike wave. General Motors experienced a 67 day strike. Some 40,000 coal miners struck in three states to demand benefits for disabled miners. New York postal workers led postal workers on strike across the country, closing down the postal service in 200 cities. When the government brought in the National Guard they expressed sympathy with the strikers. After two weeks, postal workers, who are legally prohibited from striking, won a 14 percent wage increase. On 1 April, Teamsters went out on strike and many stayed out for up to a month after Teamster president Frank Fitzsimmons ordered them back to work.[18]

While 1970 was the high point, the rank and file upsurge continued. In 1972 the Miners for Democracy elected a reform candidate for union president. In 1975 the Teamsters for a Decent Contract (which later became Teamsters for a Democratic Union) was formed, and in 1976 a national Teamsters strike paralysed the freight trucking industry. Also in 1972 the 8,000 mostly white workers at the Lordstown, Ohio, GM plant voted to strike by a margin of 97 percent. Led by youthful 'long-hairs' and a sprinkling of Vietnam veterans, the Lordstown strike was a result of sheer alienation. Through a combination of automation and speeding up the assembly line, the Lordstown plant raised its output from 66 cars per hour in 1966 to over 100 per hour in 1971. The 29 year old UAW local (branch) president told reporter Studs Terkel in *Working*:

> *If the guys didn't stand up and fight, they'd become robots too. They're interested in being able to smoke a cigarette, bullshit a little bit with the guy next to 'em, open a book, look at something, just daydream if nothing else. You can't do that if you become a machine.*[19]

The rank and file upsurge of the late 1960s and early 1970s showed the potential for even the highest paid US workers to struggle as part of their class against the employers. But the upsurge came to an abrupt halt in the late 1970s. When the New Left emerged in the late 1960s among a new generation of students who had been radicalised by the anti-war and black movements, the US working class was widely regarded as 'bought off'. The 'old left' had all but vanished under the impact of the McCarthyite witchhunts and the mass defections of Communists from the party after Russian leader Nikita Khrushchev's 1956 speech denouncing Stalin. The bulk of student radicals joined various Maoist and Stalinist organisations, which looked primarily to the Third World for revolutionary struggle.[20] Thus, while the Maoist left numbered thousands by the early 1970s, it quickly disintegrated along with the Maoist left internationally by the decade's end.

Even when the upsurge in workers' struggle began in the late 1960s, the student left largely ignored it, or dismissed workers' struggles as 'economistic'. Smaller sections of the left did develop a working class orientation, but the recession of 1973-5 produced a retreat rather than an explosion of struggle, as many had predicted.

The decline in workers' struggles and the end of the mass movements of the 1960s produced a crisis in the ranks of the left. A section of the left disintegrated completely, while others refused to acknowledge that any significant developments had taken place to merit a change of perspective and orientation. The lesson drawn by many of the 1960s radicals who had been convinced of the need to build a revolutionary party (albeit of a Stalinist/Maoist variety), now rejected such efforts. In the decade that followed, they built single issue campaigns and 'movements', abandoning revolutionary change for reform and eventually rejecting Marxism altogether. The main beneficiary of the left's 'new realism' was the Democratic Party—largely via the Jesse Jackson presidential campaigns.

Layers of the left maintained a political commitment and orientation to the working class, but all too often believed that dropping socialist politics was a precondition for success in the trade union movement. As the years of retreat of the late 1970s stretched into a decade of Reaganism, trade union reformism had replaced revolutionary politics for the bulk of the left.

Reaganism before Reagan

Ronald Reagan and the Republican Party have received most of the credit for implementing tax cuts for the rich and slashing social spending for the poor which have greatly increased inequality inside the US in the 1990s. But, while Reagan certainly deserves any amount of contempt slung his way, these policies originated years before Reagan took office.

The 'Great Society' of the 1960s, during which Presidents Kennedy and Johnson increased welfare spending to attract black votes, was short lived. In inflation adjusted terms, welfare (known as Aid to Families with Dependent Children, or AFDC) payments fell by 29 percent between 1969 and 1981, the year Reagan took office.[21] Taxes followed a regressive route over roughly the same period: between 1965 and 1975 corporate income taxes declined as a percentage of gross federal receipts from 21.8 percent to 14.6 percent, while personal income taxes for the bottom tenth of the population tripled and the next lowest tenth more than doubled.[22]

Wages had risen steadily throughout most of the 1960s. The gap between rich and poor had continued to close throughout the boom until 1967, when wages began to stagnate and trends started to reverse.[23] In the early 1970s this process began to accelerate. The US ruling class had reached a turning point. Having just been defeated in Vietnam and humiliated by a massive anti-war movement at home, the recession of 1973 signalled the onset of decline and long term economic crisis for US capital:

> *While it was highlighted by the 1973-75 recession, the economic deterioration that drove this process began before, and continued after, that catastrophic event . . . At the bottom line, profits of US firms declined after 1965 and failed throughout the next 15 years to regain their early 1960s levels. Annual net investment in plant and equipment followed suit, falling from an average 4 percent of GNP during 1966-70 to 3.1 percent over 1971-75 and 2.9 percent over 1976-80 . . . Productivity suffered in turn, as the annual growth of output per worker employed in non-residential business fell from 2.45 percent over 1948-73 to 0.08 percent over 1973-79.*[24]

Internationally, the US share of world trade and world GNP continued to fall throughout the 1970s. The US trade balance moved into negative territory in 1971 for the first time since 1893, marking the beginning of a trade deficit that would grow to mammoth proportions during the Reagan administration. By 1979 US auto companies produced only 28 percent of world car output. By 1981 the US share of world steel production dropped to 15 percent.[25] Jimmy Carter, a Democrat, took office in time to oversee the first stage of the employers' offensive. In many ways Carter's presidency followed the familiar course of Democrats in the White House since Roosevelt. During his campaign he sincerely pledged to look out for the interests of blacks, workers and the poor, and then proceeded to thumb his nose at them once he had taken office.

The so called 'New Deal Coalition', a block of Southern segregationists ('Dixiecrats'), and banking and capital intensive business interests had provided the backing for the Democratic Party since the 1930s. Since the New Deal the Democrats had succeeded in containing social upheaval by promoting certain reforms and implementing still fewer. By the late 1970s there were no social forces to contain, and the Democrats joined forces with their Republican counterparts in clamouring for a new social programme: one which would sharply attack workers' living standards and organisation. During Carter's presidency the ruling class united on the need to reverse the gains made by sections of the working class in the 1960s.

Thus during his tenure Carter instituted key policies which set the stage for Reagan's more draconian measures. For example, Carter, not Reagan, took the first stab at deregulation, which in the 1980s would leave big business and banking unencumbered by environmental or other 'social' restraints, such as worker safety. In 1978 he signed legislation deregulating the airline industry and in 1980 he began deregulating trucking. Carter also began the military build up which was completed by Reagan, especially after the fall of the Shah of Iran, when he made a trade off between military and social spending, authorising a whopping 5 percent annual increase in military spending coupled with massive cuts in poverty programmes.[26]

In 1978 Congress passed a tax reform bill which cut the top capital gains rate for businesses by more than 40 percent, from 48 to 28 percent, while the social security tax, a regressive tax in which the same rate is paid by everyone, no matter what their income, increased dramatically.[27] Meanwhile, Carter did nothing to intervene on behalf of workers when employers began union busting in earnest in the late 1970s. The number of charges of unfair labour practices filed against employers swelled by 750 percent between 1957 and 1980, at a time when union representation elections had increased by only 54 percent.[28] During this same period union membership fell to 23 percent of the labour force—a drop of 10 percentage points since the mid-1950s. The

AFL-CIO estimated that more than 1,000 union busting consultant firms were operating across the US in 1979. According to the *Economist* they were collectively making over 100 million dollars a year, issuing promises like these to employers:

> *we will show you how to screw your employees (before they screw you)—and how to keep them smiling on low pay—how to manoeuvre them into low-paying jobs they are afraid to walk away from—how to hire and fire so you always make money.*[29]

In 1979 the Carter administration intervened to rescue the smallest of the Big Three automakers, Chrysler, from bankruptcy. Although the UAW agreed to concessions amounting to 200 million dollars, Congress refused to give Chrysler its 1.2 billion dollar loan guarantee unless workers gave concessions totalling 462 million dollars. This included a wage freeze and giving up 17 days paid vacation. But a year later Chrysler chairman Lee Iacocca was back demanding further concessions, which this time totalled 673 million dollars, and involved a pay cut of 1.15 dollars per hour and the loss of three more vacation days. Yet by 1985, when Chrysler had been restored to profitability, Iacocca had risen to the second highest paid US executive, with a salary of 11.4 million dollars.[30] The Chrysler bail out marked the beginning of a new era in collective bargaining.

In addition, during the Carter administration the ruling class was able to score two important ideological victories against the right to abortion and affirmative action. These fired the opening shots in what would become a relentless attack on all the victories of the movements of the 1960s and early 1970s.[31] No sooner had Carter taken office than he endorsed a recent amendment passed by Congress which cut off federal funding for poor women's abortions. Carter's response?

> *there are many things in life that are not fair, that wealthy people can afford and poor people can't. But I don't believe the federal government should take action to try to make these opportunities exactly equal, particularly when there is a moral factor involved.*[32]

In 1978 the US Supreme Court made its landmark Bakke decision, which set in motion a decade of attacks on affirmative action programmes. The Court ruled that Allan Bakke, a white male, had been denied a place at the University of California at Davis medical school due to 'reverse discrimination' policies which victimised white males. The medical school's policy of setting aside 16 of its 100 annual openings for non-white students was found to be discriminatory against 'better qualified' whites. But several important facts about the Bakke case never surfaced in the mass media. The first is that the medical school at Davis also set aside a certain number of places each year for the sons and daughters of wealthy (white) alumni. Secondly, 36 of the 84 white students admitted the year Bakke applied had lower test scores than Bakke. Bakke, moreover, had been turned down by ten other medical schools.[33]

But most importantly, as late as 1948, 26 of the 27 medical schools in the US openly practised racial segregation. In the year that Bakke applied to medical school, blacks made up about 12 percent of the US population, but just over 2 percent were doctors and under 3 percent were medical students. Racial quotas were needed because segregation was alive and well.[34] Nevertheless, the Bakke case firmly established 'reverse racism' as the basis for undermining affirmative action programmes.

By the time he left office, Jimmy Carter had achieved the shift necessary to pave the way for Ronald Reagan's success.

The looting decade

In 1981, just as the economy entered a new recession, the employers' offensive took a qualitative leap. Business interests set aside their differences and united as a class in order to make Reaganism work for them. The Business Roundtable, which brought together both Republicans and Democrats, including most of the top officers of the biggest US companies, was an organisation dedicated to this process. Formed in the 1970s, the Business Roundtable played an activist role in shaping the policies of Reaganism.

Unemployment broke the 10 percent barrier at the height of the 1981-2 recession. But that was part of the plan. As Reagan's Budget Director David Stockman explained to a Chamber of Commerce breakfast meeting in 1982, a period of sustained unemployment was 'part of the cure, not the problem' for the US economy.[35] By 1983 more than 15 percent of the population was living below the official poverty level.[36]

But Reagan was throwing a party for the rich, and the poor weren't invited. Behind Reagan's 'trickle down' theory was an economic plan for a massive arms build up, an attack on social spending and working class living standards, and huge tax breaks for the rich. One of Reagan's first moves upon taking office in 1981 was to announce plans for major tax cuts for corporations. As Thomas Ferguson and Joel Rogers describe in *Right Turn*:

> *big business mobilised rapidly. Immediately after the Administration's announcement, the Business Roundtable called an emergency meeting. Executives of America's top firms descended on Washington in droves, for an orgy of lobbying that became known as the 'Lear Jet Weekend.'*[37]

Democrats and Republicans set out on a bidding war, each party trying to outdo the other in inventing tax breaks, including special breaks for oil, real estate, and high tech firms, to ingratiate themselves to the business leaders. As David Stockman later described the scene, 'The hogs were really feeding. The greed level, the level of opportunism, just got out of control.'[38] Business tax rates were effectively halved, from 33 percent to 16 percent between the Economic Recovery Tax Act passed in 1981 and the 1982 Tax Equity and Fiscal Responsibility Tax Act. These reforms were widely supported by Democrats in both Houses of Congress. More than half of House Democrats voted in favour, as did more than 80 percent of Democrats in the Senate.[39]

Meanwhile the capital gains tax was capped at 20 percent, down still further from Carter's cuts. The 1986 Tax Reform Act cut tax rates for the richest individuals from 70 percent in 1981 to 28 percent for 1988—a low not seen since the Roaring Twenties. Yet between 1982 and 1984 the working poor, those earning under 10,000 dollars, saw their taxes rise by 22 percent.[40] As Kevin Phillips put it in *The Politics of Rich and Poor:*

> *By the middle of Reagan's second term, official data had begun to show that America's broadly defined 'rich'—the top half of 1 percent of the US population—had never been richer. Federal policy favoured the accumulation of wealth and rewarded financial assets, and the concentration of income that began in the mid-1970s was accelerating . . .* ***No parallel upsurge of riches had been seen since the late 19th century, the era of the Vanderbilts, Morgans and Rockefellers*** (his emphasis).[41]

According to official government figures, the number of US taxpayers reporting more than 1 million dollars gross income increased fourteen-fold between 1980 and 1989. As a group, their total income grew by 1,630 percent. And the number of taxpayers reporting more than half a million dollars rose more than tenfold.[42]

Reagan, again with barely a peep from the Democratic Congress, massively increased military spending. Under Reagan, like Carter before him, defence spending rose commensurate with falling social spending. Social spending went down from 28 percent of the federal budget to 22 percent between 1980 and 1987; military spending, on the other hand, rose from 23 percent to 28 percent in this period. This was not how Reagan explained it, of course. He conjured up images of 'welfare queens' driving around in fancy cars as he dropped millions from welfare rolls and slashed programmes for pre-natal care for poor women. He argued that the government should only fund programmes for the 'truly needy' while his administration cut millions of poor children from school lunch programmes. To reduce costs further, Reagan's Food and Nutrition Service even reclassified ketchup as a vegetable in poor children's school lunches.[43]

By the end of the 1980s, while the US was still the richest nation in the world, by a number of measurements it was also among the most unequal, leading among major industrial countries in the gap between the richest and the poorest fifths of the population. A recent report on salaries in ten leading companies showed that, while the average CEO earned 34 times more than the typical worker in his employ in the mid-1970s, that figure had jumped to 110 times by the late 1980s. In February 1992, *Business Week* reported that, on average, US executives earn 160 times the pay of their employees and three to six times the salary of their European and Japanese counterparts.[44]

But the rich didn't get richer only because of tax breaks. They gambled their money. Even after the economy had been pulled out of recession in 1983 and productivity began to rise, the temptation was to use profits for speculation, which was much more lucrative than investment. Nowhere was this more true than in the savings and loan (S&L) industry. Here again the stage was set during the Carter administration. In 1980 Congress voted to provide federal insurance to any and all S&L deposits up to 100,000 dollars apiece, up from a 40,000 dollar cap voted in 1974. In 1982 Congress did the S&Ls another favour: they deregulated, removing all limits on interest rates. This meant that corporations and wealthy individuals could divide up their fortunes into 100,000 dollar deposits and park them in S&Ls all over the country, at exorbitantly high interest rates—all of it completely insured with taxpayers' money:

> *To complete the felonious scene, the new law (1) permitted* [real estate] *developers to own S&Ls and (2) permitted the owners of S&Ls to lend to themselves. In short, the vault was not only opened to the crooks, it could be owned by them. No wonder, then, at the Rose Garden signing of the bill, President Reagan, with his customary talent for the unconscious confession, chortled, 'All in all, I think we've hit the jackpot.'*[45]

If the S&Ls had been shut down as soon as they became insolvent, there would have been no need for a colossal bail out. But federal regulators waited years, while insolvent thrifts went on losing billions of dollars before they stepped in. By the end of the process, which will be years from now, the working class will have spent an estimated 300 billion dollars bailing out the savings and loan industry. And many of the same problems which brought down the S&Ls also plague commercial banks.

Charles Keating's fairy tale existence at the helm of American Continental and Lincoln Savings gives an accurate picture of the wealth and power enjoyed by the crooks running the savings and loan industry. Over a period of five years Keating paid himself and his family almost 39 million dollars, not including stocks and options. The whole family flew to Europe 15 times in a corporate jet which had gold plated trim, leather seats, a wet bar and the best audio and video equipment money could buy. One Christmas the family planned a celebration for top corporate employees, for which they flew in an entire orchestra from New York. Meanwhile, when American Continental and Lincoln Savings became insolvent, 17,000 bondholders, most of them elderly depositors, lost 200 million dollars. Many of them were thrown into poverty.[46]

Bush's own son Neil is one of the crooks. Neil Bush sat on the board of the Silverado, a Denver S&L, which will cost taxpayers 1 billion dollars to bail out. A phone call from the White House to federal examiners in mid-1988 convinced them to hold off from seizing Silverado's assets until after the 1988 presidential elections. They did, and Silverado was seized on 9 December, just one month after Bush was elected President.[47]

The fruits of the S&L swindle extended far beyond those running the S&Ls. The fate of the S&L industry was closely bound to that of junk bonds: by 1989 S&Ls owned 14 billion dollars worth of junk bonds.[48] And in both Houses of Congress generous campaign contributions (read 'payoffs') kept Congress from blowing the whistle. The 'Keating Five', the five senators accused of fronting for Charles Keating, represent only the tip of the iceberg. It has been estimated that members of Congress officially received 11 million dollars, and unofficially twice that amount, from S&L interests in the 1980s.[49]

The working class under attack

For many years the government tried to cloak statistics on rapidly falling real wages by focusing on the fact that median family incomes had remained stable in the 1980s. But median measurements can be extremely misleading, especially when you have the likes of Charles Keating weighing down one end of the spectrum. Family income statistics are further misleading because they hide the fact that most families now have two adult earners rather than one, due to the huge influx of women into the workforce since the 1960s. In 1989, nearly 60 percent of women were in the labour force, compared with under 40 percent in the 1960s. The figures are similar even for married women with children under age 6, whose labour force participation rose from 36.7 percent to 58.4 percent in 1989. But even two earner families couldn't keep pace; a recent Joint Economic Committee report showed that adults in 80 percent of two-parent families with children worked longer hours in 1989 than in 1979, but their incomes didn't rise commensurately. Real hourly pay for husbands fell in 60 percent of families, while women's wages average only 65 percent of men's. Only families in the top income quintile showed 'clear gains in their standard of living.'[50]

But even median family incomes have dropped for those under the age of 30. Families in this age group had a median income in 1991 that was 13 percent lower in inflation adjusted terms than such families earned in 1973. And more than one third of all single parent families, which made up one in every four families in 1987, live below the poverty line. For the nearly one in two black families headed by women, two thirds live in poverty.[51]

The 'working poor' multiplied during Reagan's two terms in office. The minimum wage of 3.35 dollars an hour remained the same from 1981 until 1989, a drop in real income of 36 percent. In 1986 workers received the same disposable income as in 1961, and 20 percent less than in 1972. Real hourly wages in constant dollars were no higher in 1989 than they had been in 1966.[52] And, thanks to the cuts of the Reagan era which halved the duration of unemployment benefits from 52 to 26 weeks, only one in three of the unemployed were entitled to collect benefits in 1990, compared with two in three in 1981. But even these statistics don't describe the drastic decline in working and living standards that has taken place. Close to 40 million Americans have no health insurance coverage whatsoever. But these are not the poorest of the poor: more than 85 percent of the uninsured are workers or their dependants. The US government provides only two forms of medical care: Medicaid, for those on welfare (although Medicaid covers fewer than half of all the poor); and Medicare, which covers those over the age of 65. Employers, moreover, are not required to provide medical coverage to their employees—an option exercised by fewer and fewer firms in the last decade.[53] Thus, while health care spending amounts to more than 12 percent of the GNP in the US, the highest rate in the world, the US still ranks twenty second in infant mortality internationally.

Like the S&L debacle, the sorry state of health care in the US is the story of greed gone mad. For decades a conglomeration of insurance companies, drug companies, doctors and hospitals that make up the nearly 700 billion dollar a year medical industry have ensured that neither the laws of competition nor state intervention will interfere with profits. And, like the S&Ls, the health care giants are willing to pay Congress generously not to meddle. More than 200 political lobbying groups (known as 'political action committees', or PACs) representing the various wings of the medical industry together contributed more than 60 million dollars in campaign contributions to members of Congress between 1980 and 1991.[54]

The results have been catastrophic for millions of workers. Insurance companies are given a free hand to choose who they will and won't cover and to refuse to pay for 'pre-existing conditions'. Most insurance companies, for example, are allowed to test for the HIV virus and to exclude those who test positive on the grounds that they have a 'pre-existing condition'. In other words, health insurance companies may reject people who are sick. Other companies put a cap on how much they will pay towards treating AIDS—some as low as 5,000 dollars towards a disease which costs an estimated 32,000 dollars per year to treat. Occupational safety and health also deteriorated in the 1980s. Workplace injury rates doubled thanks to speedup: more overtime, smaller work crews and faster assembly lines are all the ingredients for workplace accidents. Today the US has by far the highest occupational fatality rate of any Western industrialised nation. A 1991 fire at a poultry processing plant highlighted the turn of the century working conditions experienced by factory workers all over the country. When fire broke out at a North Carolina poultry processing plant in September 1991, the 90 workers inside rushed to the exits, but only one of the nine doors would open. The owner had blocked or padlocked the other doors to prevent workers from stealing his chickens.[55] The plant had only one fire extinguisher and no sprinkler system. Passers by reported hearing workers screaming and beating on plant doors, but it was too late. Of the 90 workers, mostly black women, 25 died in the fire, and 53 more were injured. There was no union. After the fire an agricultural inspector told a Congressional committee that he had received phone calls from colleagues in the poultry industry from as far away as Texas 'going around with bolt cutters the day after the fire unlocking doors' in their own plants.[56]

It was also revealed in the aftermath of the fire that North Carolina has only enough occupational safety inspectors to visit each workplace once every 75 years. Nationally, there are only 1,200 inspectors for 5 million workplaces. But it is questionable whether safety inspectors, who routinely call ahead to employers to warn that they are coming, make much difference at all.[57]

Race and class

Ever since slavery, racism has been the key division inside the US working class. In exploiting this division, the US ruling class has historically resorted to the most vicious racism itself in order to deflect class solidarity on the part of black and white workers. Jim Crow laws which segregated blacks from whites across the Southern states during the first half of this century, for example, were a result of ruling class fear of a multi-racial sharecroppers' revolt.

There have, however, been important glimpses of racial unity during the 20th century especially at high points of class struggle. Thousands of black and white workers fought side by side during the CIO strike waves in the 1930s, and the US Communist Party claimed black membership was 9 percent of its total in the late 1930s, representing a small but significant step towards building a multi-racial working class party. And, as described earlier, the black auto workers' revolts such as DRUM got real support from a minority of white workers in the late 1960s upsurge. Reaganism as practised by both political parties aimed to deepen the wedge between white workers and those of all other races, blacks in particular. The degree of racism emanating from the White House was frequently staggering. Reagan courted the white racist vote in 1980 by repeatedly assuring audiences that he had consistently opposed civil rights and even resurrected the slogan of Southern segregationists, 'The South will rise again!'[58]

Nearly every social spending cutback was justified with a racist stereotype. 'Welfare', 'drugs' and 'crime' have been the racist code words scapegoating poor blacks for over a decade. Despite the fact that two thirds of welfare recipients are white, the welfare cheats Reagan complained about were always depicted as black. When Bush ran for President in 1988, he ran a television advertising campaign against crime which consisted of a police photograph of a black convict, Willie Horton. In a 1988 survey of blacks which asked whether the Reagan administration 'tended more to help blacks or . . . to keep blacks down', an overwhelming 78 percent answered 'keep blacks down'.[59]

Every aspect of life got worse for the vast majority of black Americans under Reaganism. Whereas in 1975 the average annual income of blacks was 63 percent that of whites, by 1991 the figure had fallen to 56 percent—the same as before the 'Great Society' programmes of the 1960s. One in every three blacks lives below the poverty line. The poverty rate for all Latinos stands only slightly lower, at 26.8 percent, but more than 40 percent of Puerto Ricans live in poverty. Black infant mortality rates are double that for white children. Black unemployment has remained double that of whites for decades, but unemployment rates for young blacks have skyrocketed in recent years—the national rate stood at 34 percent by 1987 and ranged as high as 50 percent in some cities.[60]

In 1988 life expectancy for US blacks fell for the fourth year in a row. The homicide rate among young black men nearly doubled between 1984 and 1988 and in some areas exceeds the casualty rate among US soldiers in the Vietnam War. The *New England Journal of Medicine* recently reported that a young black man in Harlem has less chance of living to the age of 65 than a man in Bangladesh. The homicide rate was the leading cause of death.[61] While racial segregation doesn't legally exist any more in any part of the US, *de facto* segregation by neighbourhood and by suburb exists almost everywhere. In fact, 86 percent of suburban whites live in suburbs that are less than 1 percent black. Police brutality and harassment are a fact of life in black neighbourhoods all across the country, and even affluent blacks find themselves routinely stopped and searched when they are in white areas. More than 8 percent of the black population is arrested each year. The sheriff of Jefferson Parish, Louisiana, an all white suburb of New Orleans, called a press conference in 1986 specifically to announce that he was instructing his police force to arrest any young black males seen in the area after dark.[62] And once arrested the US 'justice' system does the rest:

> *someone poor and black tried for stealing a few hundred dollars has a 90 percent likelihood of being convicted of robbery with a sentence averaging between 94 and 138 months. A white business executive who has embezzled hundreds of thousands of dollars has only a 20 percent likelihood of conviction with a sentence averaging about 20 to 48 months.*[63]

Largely because of statistics like these, the notion of a black 'underclass' has caught on in recent years. But the idea that a growing proportion of blacks belong to a substratum of society, permanently removed from the job market, is wrong. Most importantly, it is unduly pessimistic about the possibility for blacks to win real gains in the future. For while blacks suffer grossly disproportionate poverty and unemployment levels, the vast majority of blacks are a key part of the working class.

The ruling class has tried to use black workers both as a cheap labour pool *and* to foster racist divisions within the working class in order to drive down the living standards of all workers. It was a deliberate policy of many employers, especially from the 1880s through the 1910s, to recruit black workers from the South to replace striking white workers in the North. Employers also hired newly-arrived European immigrants in efforts to divide and rule. While some employers refused to employ blacks and insisted on an all white workforce, others like the Ford Motor Company as a policy made sure that blacks were at least 5 percent of the workforce in an effort to fuel racial friction. The antagonisms between blacks and whites created by such divide and rule tactics was one of the factors behind the wave of race riots that swept the US in 1919. Racism is used for the same purpose by the ruling class to this day. The legacy of racism and low unionisation in the South is that wages for *both* black and white workers are lower there than in the North. And while 'anti-welfare' agitation is a racist rallying cry of the right wing, the reality is that two thirds of welfare recipients are white.

Black unemployment rates remain steadily double those of whites, but they rise and fall in the same patterns as whites', in syncronisation with the business cycle. According to a recent study on work patterns among young black men, the group with the highest unemployment rate, half of black male teenage unemployment is concentrated within 7 percent of this population. Thus, while the layer of chronically unemployed undoubtedly grew during the 1980s, chronic unemployment, which leads young blacks to resort to a lumpen existence of petty theft and drug dealing, is still the exception rather than the rule. 'The pattern among young blacks is to have short term employment followed by long spells of being out of work. In fact, among central city black youth, a year of non-employment is not unusual.' The same study showed young black workers are less likely than young whites to voluntarily quit a job.[64]

But all blacks have not suffered equally. The black middle class grew in size and income in the 1970s and 1980s, thanks mainly to the gains of the civil rights movement, like affirmative action programmes. Before affirmative action the black middle class consisted of a small number of small business owners and professionals who oriented mainly to the black ghetto. Affirmative action programmes opened the doors for blacks to enter businesses and professions outside the black ghetto economy. By and large, blacks continue to be shut out of the ruling class—as of 1985 no black owned business had made the *Fortune* 500 list, and only one black businessman, John Johnson publisher of *Ebony* and *Jet*, had made it onto the lower end of the *Forbes* 400 List.[65] Still, class polarisation among blacks has surpassed that of whites. As Manning Marable wrote recently:

> *Now, in the post civil rights era of the 1980s and 1990s, even the definition of the term 'black community' is up for debate. The net result of affirmative action and civil rights initiatives was to expand the potential base of the African-American middle class, which was located primarily outside the neighbourhood confines of the old ghetto. By 1989, one out of seven African-American families had incomes exceeding 50,000 dollars annually, compared to less than 22,000 dollars for the average black household. Black college educated married couples currently earn 93 percent of the family income of comparable white couples.*[66]

The gap is more than financial. There is a gap in consciousness as well. Although middle class blacks experience racism in their daily lives, as a group they have chosen to make a deal with the system rather than fight against it. So, while the black middle class has been the main beneficiary of the civil rights movement, it has moved far to the right since then. This even includes veterans of the civil rights movement. In part, the growing conservatism of the black middle class simply mirrors the trend of the entire US middle class—regardless of race—during the 1970s and 1980s. But it is also a reflection of the profound changes that have taken place since the days of the civil rights movement. Prior to the 1960s, the small black middle class that did exist *had an interest in joining the fight for civil rights.* So while the vast majority of participants in the civil rights and black power movements were black workers, its leadership was middle class—and the aims it set for the movement reflected this. The black middle class joined with black workers to demand the right to vote and an end to legal segregation in the 1960s, but they sought to remove the barriers to their advance within the system, not to transform it.

So while the demand for the right of blacks to vote was at the centre of the struggle, the election of thousands of black politicians since then has achieved little for black workers. While working class blacks became increasingly alienated from the Democrats during the Reagan era, the black middle class threw their weight behind the Democratic Party throughout the 1970s and 1980s.

But the Democratic Party route has been spent as a strategy for social change. By January 1990 there were 7,335 black elected officials, the vast majority of them Democrats, across the country. Most major cities have black mayors, who have found themselves carrying out the very same programmes as their white counterparts, with the same net result: greater poverty and unemployment for the black population, a continuation of segregation and police brutality.

This has been the record of all black mayors since Carl Stokes became the first mayor of a major city in 1967. While solidly Democrat, the National Conference of Black Mayors went so far as to support a 1985 Reagan proposal to reduce black youth unemployment through the establishment of a sub-minimum wage for teenagers. Explained Johnny Ford of Tuskeegee, Alabama: 'If 2.50 dollars an hour is all we can go with at this time, we'll take whatever we can.' In some cases, black mayors were able to carry out attacks on black workers which would have produced explosions if implemented by a white mayor. The most shocking example came in 1985, when Wilson Goode, the black mayor of Philadelphia, ordered a bomb dropped on a residential neighbourhood. The victims were members of a counter-cultural black group, MOVE, who refused to allow city officials into their homes. From the tragic to the comic, Tom Bradley, mayor of Los Angeles, posed for photographs by the *South African Digest*—presenting the key to the city of Los Angeles to the South African General Consul.[67]

Even Jesse Jackson's Rainbow Coalition, which gave the Democratic Party a left wing cover, was dissolved by Jackson after the

1988 election. Unlike many on the left who saw the Rainbow Coalition as a springboard to a 'new movement', Jackson made clear his loyalty to the Democratic Party—and to US capitalism. His aim was to increase black representation within the system, not to challenge it. Meanwhile, black voter turnout dipped to new lows in this same period. Recent evidence suggests that the presence of a black candidate on the ballot is no longer enough to guarantee a strong black turnout for an election. As a result, the black middle class can lay no claim to leadership of the masses of blacks, even in a limited, formal sense. The NAACP, the traditional middle class black organisation, saw its membership plunge from 550,000 in the mid-1970s to about 150,000 ten years later.[68]

But this is nothing to worry about for some of today's black politicans. Typical of the new 'post-black' politicos is Douglas Wilder, the governor of Virginia. He declares proudly: 'I never viewed myself as an activist . . . Of course, everybody says they marched on Washington now. I was not there. I didn't even participate in pickets here in Richmond, but I felt I had to make my contribution in other ways.' As black sociologist Manning Marable has noted:

> *These charlatans rely on the old nationalist rhetoric of racial solidarity, but lack any progressive content because they are detached from any social protest movement for empowerment or resistance . . Most of us have not anticipated an ideological shift among many African-Americans or Latino politicans, using racial solidarity to ensure minority voter loyalty, but gradually embracing more moderate to conservative public policy positions, especially on economic issues.*[69]

Some sections of the black middle class have even become Republican—as have a larger number of black voters. In 1990, Republican candidates received the highest percentage of black votes Republicans have received since the late 1950s. Fully 22 percent of black voters voted Republican in 1990. Thirty two percent of blacks between the ages of 45-59 voted Republican.

This vacuum of leadership left by traditional black civil rights leaders has yet to be filled. It has allowed less mainstream figures, like Rev Al Sharpton, a black nationalist with no coherent programme, to step in and lead some important anti-racist struggles since the mid-1980s. Sharpton's somewhat dubious past (he was once an FBI informant), combined with his sharp nationalist rhetoric, had kept him outside the black middle class establishment. Sharpton took the lead in organising protests involving thousands of blacks after two young blacks were murdered by white racists in New York. In late 1986, 23 year old Michael Griffith was killed when racists chased him into a moving car in the all white Howard Beach neighbourhood in Queens. Then in 1989 another young black, Yusuf Hawkins, was murdered in Bensonhurst, another all white neighbourhood. If Sharpton hadn't organised the protests, which included angry marches through the all white neighbourhoods, in all likelihood no mass protests would have taken place.

At the same time, however, the vacuum of leadership had important negative consequences at the beginning of the 1990s. Just as frustrations with day to day poverty and racism pushed many living in black ghettoes to the boiling point, expressions of anger sometimes turned into misdirected explosions. During the long hot summer of 1991 in New York, for example, a car driven by a Hasidic Jew hit several small black children, killing a seven year old boy in Brooklyn's Crown Heights section of New York. After clashing with the police all summer, hundreds of outraged blacks rioted against the police, but also against Crown Heights' Jews. In 'retaliation' for the child's death, a group of young blacks murdered a Hasidic Jewish rabbinical student. Al Sharpton led a march through Crown Heights on the Sabbath, with clear anti-semitic overtones. Legitimate outrage against racism had been channelled towards the nearest visible targets—Hasidic Jews—while the real enemy, the New York Police Department, used it as yet another excuse to storm a black neighbourhood.

The labour movement in retreat

Within a few months of taking office Ronald Reagan came to a showdown with the labour movement for which the working class was ill prepared. He even chose one of the very few unions which had supported his candidacy for President as his first target. The 12,000 members of the Professional Air Traffic Controllers Organization (PATCO) walked off their jobs on 3 August 1981. Within four hours, President Ronald Reagan was on national television, warning the controllers that if they didn't return to work within 48 hours, they 'will have forfeited their jobs and will be terminated'. Reagan was perfectly ready to carry out this threat. Jimmy Carter had planned ahead: 12 months before the PATCO contract was due to expire, Carter set up the Management Strike Contingency Force, which prepared a plan to run air traffic without the controllers if they went on strike.[70]

The union leaders talked tough, but did nothing to build solidarity with the PATCO strikers. AFL-CIO president Lane Kirkland called Reagan 'harsh and vindictive', and then sent out a letter to all AFL-CIO locals urging them not to join in a nationwide job action to support the strike. Kirkland wrote, 'I personally do not think that the trade union movement should undertake anything that would represent punishing, injuring or inconveniencing the public at large for the sins or the transgressions of the Reagan administration.'[71] The president of the International Association of Machinists (IAM), the union representing airline machinists, refused to call his members out on strike to support PATCO, arguing, 'It should be recognized the IAM has a no-strike clause with the airlines'.[72]

Thus, although US labour unions had already planned a massive 'Solidarity Day' march in Washington, DC, a few weeks after the strike began, PATCO barely got a mention in speeches to the half million workers who marched. Instead speaker after speaker urged workers to vote for the Democrats next time around. Left to fight alone, the 12,000 striking air traffic controllers lost their jobs. PATCO had been crushed.

The PATCO strike represented a turning point from which the labour movement has yet to recover. Reagan's crushing of the air traffic controllers' union, played out on national television, signalled a go ahead to business to engage in union busting on a massive scale. But the labour unions, with their bloated union bureaucracies, had no intention of fighting back. Years of conservatism had made them believe they could negotiate a deal with employers and rely on the election of 'friends of labour' to Congress. They feared the prospect of rank and file activism more than they feared the employers' attacks. Rather than lead any kind of fightback, they searched for ways to salvage the comfortable relationships they had nurtured with the employers for decades.

Ties between the US labour bureaucracy and the government date back to the 1930s Depression when the leaders of the CIO, which would grow into the main industrial union federation, threw their support behind Roosevelt and the Democratic Party. Thanks to the bankruptcy of Stalinism, at the height of the CIO sitdown strikes the Communist Party also endorsed Roosevelt, drawing in thousands of the most militant workers behind them. The best possibility in US history for workers to form their own political party had been lost.

Collaboration between labour and capital was strengthened during the Second World War when, except for the United Mine Workers, all major unions, including again all the CP led unions, agreed to a no-strike pledge for the duration of the war. Since the war the union leaders' loyalty has never wavered, despite occasional rhetoric to the contrary. It continued even after the 1947 Taft-Hartley Act became law. Taft-Hartley gave the government the right to delay or prevent workers from striking, and to send in the National Guard if workers went on strike anyway. No Congress since has seen fit to repeal Taft-Hartley, as it has come in handy plenty of times. Democratic President Harry Truman used the Taft-Hartley Act 12 times to break strikes during his presidency.

The CIO demonstrated its support for the McCarthyite anti-communist purges by expelling 11 CP led unions in 1949, which together accounted for over 500,000 union members. By the time the two rival federations of the union movement, the American Federation of Labor (AFL) and the CIO, merged to form the AFL-CIO in 1955, business unionism was already entrenched in the executive suites of the Federation's top officials. As George Meany, the AFL-CIO's first president said, 'We believe in the American profit system.'[73] In the 1950s and 1960s the AFL-CIO extended its allegiance to US imperialism's aims abroad. In 1985 the AFL-CIO had operations in 83 countries, with a total international budget of 43 million dollars.[74]

All union bureaucrats share interests separate from the members they represent, because they are relieved of real contact with the shop floor and because their own jobs are unaffected by layoffs and contract language. But the US version, though not qualitatively different, is a somewhat unique breed. For example, Meany once bragged to the National Association of Manufacturers, 'I never went on strike in my life, never ran a strike in my life, never ordered anyone else to run a strike in my life, never had anything to do with a picket line.'[75]

One difference is that US workers have never formed a major labour or social democratic party. With workers themselves providing a mass voting base for the Democratic Party, the AFL-CIO feels no organised pressure to the left of the Democrats. The AFL-CIO's expansive bureaucracy and close ties to the US government only increase the pressure toward conservatism. Since it was founded in 1955, the AFL-CIO has had only two leaders: George Meany and Lane Kirkland. The AFL-CIO presidency is more a coronation than an election.

And while union membership has been in steady decline since the mid-1950s, the AFL-CIO felt no urgency to shift its strategy. Through the mid-1980s it maintained its dues base at a steady 13 million members. As Meany aptly put it in 1972: 'Frankly, I used to worry about the membership, about the size of the membership. But quite a few years ago, I just stopped worrying about it, because to me it doesn't make any difference.'[76] The union leaders' only response to the employers' offensive was more of the same. Labour unions' financial contributions to political candidates' election campaigns increased more than threefold between 1974 and 1982. The AFL-CIO supported Democrats while the Teamsters and a few others supported Republicans, but the strategy was the same: collaboration, rather than any form of confrontation. The full implication of this approach was revealed when, after UAW president Doug Fraser agreed to massive concessions in the 1979 Chrysler bail out, he was awarded a seat on Chrysler's board of directors. One local UAW official had warned workers who hesitated to grant concessions, 'Those of you who don't want to take a wage cut, go out and find another job. No one's stopping you from leaving this organisation.'[77]

While initially firms claimed they needed concessions to stay afloat, once Reagan had crushed PATCO in 1981, concessions and union busting became the order of the day. In a 1982 *Business Week* survey of 400 executives nearly one in five said, 'Although we don't need concessions, we are taking advantage of the bargaining climate to ask for them.' In 1983, one third of all workers with new contracts had agreed to wage cuts. By 1987, in the midst of the Reagan boom, almost three quarters of all contracts covering 1,000 or more workers included concessions. For manufacturing workers the figure was 90 percent.[78] After extracting huge demands from workers desperate to save their jobs, many plants closed down anyway. In fact, employers often used the savings they squeezed out of workers to finance their plans for rationalisation. As Kim Moody put it:

> *In 1983, the same year that it received concessions from the USW, US Steel announced plans to close one third of its remaining steel capacity as well as various finishing and fabricating mills. Chrysler, of course, closed several plants as part of the bail out operation and continued closing plants after returning to profitability. In March 1987 Chrysler announced that it would buy AMC (American Motors Corporation) from Renault for 1 billion dollars; in that same week, it also announced that it would close a parts plant in Indiana.*[79]

Gone were the days when industry standards were negotiated into a single industry wide contract. Here too union leaders allowed contract negotiations to set groups of workers in competition with those from other plants, companies and other countries. Union leaders' only response when plants closed down in search of cheaper labour was to clamour for protectionism. Many employers forced their workforces on strike with proposals for drastic wage cuts, and then hired scabs as permanent replacements as soon as the strikes began. In US law after 12 months the scabs could legally have an election to decertify the union. About 200,000 workers became non-union thanks to decertification elections in the 1980s. Other employers chose to simply lock out their workers, effectively forcing them to strike.[80] By 1989 union membership had fallen to 16 percent of the workforce. Current estimates for private industry put unionisation rates at just under 10 percent.

Strike levels in 1987 had fallen to their lowest point since the Second World War no-strike pledge. This figure is an important gauge of the level of demoralisation felt by most workers, but it tells us little about those workers who did struggle. Groups of workers fought back against the employers' offensive in the 1980s, but they often found themselves engaged in long term, bitter disputes which pitted them against their own union leaders as well as their employers. Evidence suggests that, while the number of strikes fell in the early 1980s, the number of workers involved and the workdays lost actually rose, indicating longer walkouts.[81] Rather than lasting days or weeks, many strikes lasted months or even years during the 1980s, and, with few exceptions, ended in defeat.[82]

Union leaders deserve little or no credit for the few examples of workers' militancy and solidarity in the 1980s. For example, machinists' union president William Winpisinger pledged his support to the machinists at Brown and Sharpe during their 1981 strike. When they battled with police on their picket line, he proclaimed, 'Labour history is being written' in Rhode Island. Yet in two years he never even bothered to visit the picket line of one of the longest strikes in US labour history.[83] In fact, union leaders consistently played the role of discouraging, forbidding or even sabotaging militancy and solidarity.

The Hormel meatpackers' strike which began in 1985 and stretched into 1986 brought the most bitter clash between striking workers and their union leaders during the Reagan era. Workers at Hormel's Austin, Minnesota, meatpacking plant had already agreed to an eight year concessions contract in 1978. The profitable *Fortune* 500 company wanted more, and unilaterally imposed a wage cut. But when the 1,500 members of Local P-9 of the United Food and Commercial Workers (UFCW) finally voted to strike in August 1985, their national union wasn't behind them. In fact, UFCW leaders did everything they could to undermine the strike. In a perverse twist of logic, UFCW president William Wynn argued, in a letter sent to every AFL-CIO local in the country, that because P-9 workers were demanding wages higher than the concessions contracts UFCW had negotiated for the rest of the industry,

> *The P-9 story is not one of 'solidarity' in action. It is the converse of that honoured union principle. Local P-9's leaders refused to act in solidarity with other Hormel workers. Instead of acting together with other Hormel workers to accomplish the most good for the greatest number of Hormel workers, Local P-9 leaders sought a better deal for Austin alone.*[84]

When P-9 organised roving pickets to call out nearby Hormel plants in solidarity, Wynn sent out a telegram to union locals, urging them to have no part of the 'plague' from P-9. Finally, after eight months on strike the national union revoked even its formal sanction of the strike and stopped all strike benefits. Meanwhile, the company forced the city of Austin, a company town, to declare martial law and call in the National Guard.[85] Although the Hormel strikers continued to fight on for another six months, the national union took over their union local and negotiated a contract for the scabs who stole their jobs.

Workers who attempted to defend their living standards in the 1980s had neither a political party nor a labour movement to bolster their struggles. Wages in 1990, which stood at 346 dollars per week before taxes were almost 20 percent lower than in 1972 when adjusted for inflation. Average hourly wages of US production workers in manufacturing are now surpassed by workers in Germany, Norway, Switzerland, Sweden, Netherlands, Denmark, Belgium, and Finland, and are nearly matched by those in Japan, Canada, France and Italy.[86] As Vicente Navarro described:

> *The average worker in the US, for example, works longer hours and has less paid vacation than workers in the majority of advanced capitalist countries. The average workweek for full time US workers in 1986 was 42.3 hours, compared with 37 in Denmark, 37.5 in Norway and Finland and 39 in France and Britain and 37 in West Germany . . . The level of disposable income of US workers is lower than that of workers in the majority of advanced capitalist countries. Disposable income as percentage of gross earnings is 78.9 percent in the US, lower than in France (98.72 percent), Japan (89.10 percent), Canada (88.03 percent), Italy (86.19 percent), West Germany (79.22 percent), and the United Kingdom (78.98 percent).*[87]

The party's over

As the 1980s came to a close so did the Reagan boom. George Bush was sworn in as president in 1989, when the economy first hit the doldrums. But as the economy again buckled for what turned out to be the longest recession since the Second World War, there was little fat left on the system. Millions of workers are only a paycheck away from poverty. Millions more are already there. The vast majority of workers long ago figured out that, although Reagan had promised that wealth would 'trickle down,' instead it flooded in the other direction.

To the chagrin of the ruling class, Reagan's supply side boom had been built upon quicksand: in order to fund the tax cuts for the rich and the massive military build up, the Reagan administration needed to borrow huge sums of money at high interest rates. In 1985, the US became a debtor nation for the first time since 1914. The annual deficit had already reached the 200 billion dollar range when he left office. Just funding the interest on the debt cost 129 billion dollars in 1983, 178 billion dollars in 1985 and 216 billion dollars in 1988.[88] Furthermore, the Reagan boom had failed to prevent the continued global decline of US capital. Voices of dissent began emanating from sections of the ruling class by the decade's end. They argued that Reagan's policies had actually contributed further to declining US hegemony. Kevin Phillips, a Republican and former chief political analyst for Richard Nixon's Presidential campaign, lamented in *The Politics of Rich and Poor*:

> *the Reagan years, and especially the President's debt ridden second term, saw an indisputable shift of comparative wealth and economic leverage away from the United States: assets began to migrate along a pathway blazed by debt. Friedman and other economists acknowledged that the implications for the future might have been different if Americans had productively invested most of these foreign borrowings. But much of the borrowed money wound up in financial restructuring, paper entrepreneurialism and lavish consumption, as well as in millions of attendant low-productivity service jobs. These and other dislocations within the late 1980s US domestic economy only aggravated the global redistribution of wealth.*[89]

Rising right wing criticisms of the US's relative share of world military spending grew in the 1980s and rose to a feverish pitch during the 1991 US war against Iraq. The complaints centred around comparisons between the US share of military spending and that of its main economic competitors, Germany and, with particular acrimony, Japan. Among the top five most advanced economies in 1983 (the US, Britain, France, West Germany and Japan), the US share of combined defence spending amounted to 56.7 percent, while Japan's stood at only 3.3 percent.[90]

In 1987 a *Wall Street Journal* article summarised the gloomy outlook for US imperialism:

> *The US now sits in the bottom corner, where Britain was from 1926 to 1944. Such nations live on past credit, suck in foreign capital and can't save enough to finance domestic investment. Two rankings higher stands Japan: a strong country with a trade surplus, saving more than it spends and sending excess money abroad. That puts Japan among other nations at the height of their strength, including the US from 1946 to 1970 and Britain from 1851 to 1890.*[91]

The Reagan Revolution is over, but Bush hasn't found anything to replace it. His administration has pursued familiar supply side policies, with the result of an even bigger deficit, which is expected to reach 350 billion dollars in 1991.[92] At the same time the scale of poverty has reached crisis proportions in the second recession in a decade. A recent Florida study reported that among 16 percent of families there at least one family member goes to bed hungry. Unemployment topped 7 percent in December 1991, and by 1989, total consumer credit had risen to 775 billion dollars, equal to almost one-fifth of total personal income. The number of personal bankruptcies in 1991 was triple the annual rate during the 1981-2 recession. Yet Bush wondered aloud why 'consumer confidence' was so low during the 1991 holiday shopping season, since the 1981-2 recession was 'deeper'.[93]

Whereas the federal government slashed social spending ten years ago, local city and state budgets are doing so now. The newest trend has been for individual states to cut welfare spending, removing the last cushion available to millions of the poor. Sixteen of the 50 states have made cuts already. Michigan completely eliminated its general welfare programme in the autumn of 1991, leaving 90,000 of the state's poorest citizens without an income. Homeless organisations expect Detroit's homeless, who numbered about 50,000 before the cuts, to double. The first casualties of Michigan's cuts came in November. Two men died of carbon monoxide poisoning in an abandoned building where they were using a charcoal grill for heat. A spokesman for Michigan's governor issued this icy statement in response to the deaths: 'They had a shelter available to them. Instead, they chose to remain in this abandoned home. Any death is tragic.'[94]

New York, which has suffered massive job losses, now has an estimated 90,000 homeless, one third of whom are HIV positive. Mayor Dinkins' response? Periodic police sweeps to remove them from subways, so commuters can be spared undue unpleasantness. New York has seen a resurgence of tuberculosis, a disease supposed cured long ago. Yet due to poverty doctors reported in 1991 that roughly one in seven New Yorkers has developed tuberculosis, including a new drug-resistant strain. By early 1992, federal health officials had declared the spread of tuberculosis 'out of control' as they reported outbreaks in 12 states.[95]

Many of the cuts have been justified with vicious scapegoating of the poor. The typical California welfare family lives 30 percent below the poverty line. But California's governor, Pete Wilson, claimed the state's welfare payments, which are the highest in the nation, are 'not fair to the working men and women of California'. He has proposed a 'Taxpayers' Protection Act', which would immediately cut payments by 10 percent, and would be followed by a 15 percent cut in six months. Women on welfare who have any more children would be denied any additional payments. Teenage mothers would be required to live with their parents.[96]

The overconfident ruling class

When Bush was running for President in 1988, he promised to be a 'kinder, gentler' president. He fooled no one. Within his first two years in office he invaded Panama and carpet bombed Iraq—ostensibly to rid the world of two 'madmen', Manuel Noriega and Saddam Hussein. Through strict control over the news media, who gave their full co-operation, Bush managed to keep the public from finding out about the thousands of Panamanians and hundreds of thousands of Iraqis killed in these two wars. Even the 150,000 anti-war protesters who marched in Washington, DC, during the war against Iraq never appeared on the national news.

For the US ruling class, the war against Iraq wasn't just another war. It was the largest US military intervention since its defeat in Vietnam. US planes dropped more explosives onto Iraq each day than were dropped on Hiroshima and Nagasaki. Bush could proclaim at the end of the war, 'The Vietnam Syndrome is over.' Moreover, Bush's triumph over Iraq showed that, even if US imperialism was slipping as the world's main economic superpower, it still remained the world's main military power. As he said towards the end of the war, 'When we win, and we will, we will have taught a dangerous dictator, and any tyrant tempted to follow in his footsteps that the US has a new credibility, and that what we say goes . . .'[97]

As wars have been known to do in the short term, the six week triumph against Iraq sent Bush's popularity soaring to 90 percent. But it soon became apparent that the long term US aims in the war were unsatisfied: Saddam Hussein remained in power, stability was not forthcoming anywhere in the Middle East and, most importantly, the massive military victory over Iraq did nothing to arrest the US's continued economic decline. At the height of his popularity, Bush made a miscalculation, a not uncommon one among rulers. With the balance of class forces skewed decisively in favour of capital, he got carried away and tried to push things a step too far. No sooner had the war ended overseas than Bush resumed the war at home. Having made great strides towards eliminating the Vietnam Syndrome, he set his sights on finishing off the other reminders of the 1960s social movements, escalating attacks on blacks, women, and lesbians and gays under way since the late 1970s.

But Bush's strategy backfired. His own overconfidence caused him to overlook the possibility of provoking a response from below. After the unification of Germany and the collapse of Stalinism, he didn't predict that his own chest beating about the wonders of the free market would focus Americans' attention on the S&L bail out or the lack of health care. And, in his efforts to finally erase the nation's memory of the 1960s era of struggle, he merely set the stage for the next period of social upheaval, by straining social relations to the breaking point. Bush launched his new attack when he made a speech, excerpts of which were later televised, to a University of Michigan graduation ceremony. The new enemy, he told students, was 'political correctness':

> *political extremists roam the land, abusing the privilege of free speech, setting citizens against one another on the basis of their class or race . . . The notion of 'political correctness' has ignited controversy across the land. Although the movement arises from the laudable desire to sweep away racism and sexism and hatred, it replaces old prejudices with new ones. It declares certain topics off-limits, certain expressions off-limits, even certain gestures off-limits.*[98]

Nothing could have been further from the truth. Since the late 1970s all the gains won by the movements of the 1960s, abortion and affirmative action in particular, had been severely eroded. But that didn't stop Bush from jumping on the bandwagon of right wingers who were already leading a crusade against feminists, black activists and gays in the name of stamping out the tyranny of 'political correctness'. Thanks to cover stories in *Newsweek*, *Time* and other major news sources echoing Bush's sentiments, 'political correctness' ('PC') had become a household word by the summer of 1991. Bush's diatribes against political correctness were completely transparent, for those who cared to look. Abortion funding for poor women has never been restored since it was cut in the late 1970s. It has been estimated that since funding was cut 20 percent of poor women have been forced to bear unwanted children.[99] The government renewed its attack on abortion in 1989, beginning with a Supreme Court ruling that allowed individual states to severely restrict abortion within their borders. A Missouri law, for example, now bars any publicly funded facility from either performing abortions or providing abortion counselling. Other states have passed laws which challenge the very right to legal abortion. Pennsylvania passed a law in 1989 requiring married women to notify their husbands before they could have an abortion. In 1991 Louisiana and Utah passed laws which virtually ban abortion.

It is now up to the Supreme Court, stacked with Reagan and Bush anti-abortion conservatives, to decide the future of legal abortion. During the summer of 1991, as if to give a sneak preview of what might be in store, the Supreme Court upheld a law from the Reagan era which forbids any employee in federally funded birth control clinics from even mentioning the option of abortion. For this reason, it has been called the 'gag' rule. Even if a woman asks where she can get an abortion, clinic staff are required to repeat this phrase: 'This project does not consider abortion an appropriate method of family planning.' Four million poor women will be affected by this new law. Their confidence boosted by the turn of events, Operation Rescue anti-abortion protesters appeared at abortion clinics all around the country in the summer and fall—only to find themselves outnumbered by pro-choice supporters in most cities.

Lesbians and gays have fared no better during the Reagan and Bush years. In 1986 the Supreme Court upheld archaic 'sodomy' laws, stating that there is no fundamental right to homosexual sex. In their written decision, the Court compared gay sex to 'adultery, incest and other sex crimes.'[100] In September 1991, cashing in on the anti-PC atmosphere, California Governor Pete Wilson vetoed a gay rights bill that would simply have extended anti-discrimination protection to lesbians and gays. He said the legislation would unfairly burden businesses. Californians had approved of the bill by a two to one margin. The response was immediate: thousands of lesbians and gays took to the streets the night of the veto in mass protests. The next night 7,000 gay rights activists marched through San Francisco, many throwing rocks and breaking windows, chanting, 'Gays bash back.'[101]

But racism has been at the centre of Bush's attacks. Affirmative action programmes were effectively gutted by 1989. It was no coincidence that Clarence Thomas was picked to be Bush's nominee to the Supreme Court last year. Thomas, a black conservative opposed to affirmative action, had earlier proven his loyalty to Reaganism as head of the Equal Employment Opportunity Commission (EEOC), the federal programme set up to rectify job discrimination. During his years as chairman of the EEOC whites complaining of 'reverse racism' got more of a hearing than blacks and other minorities. In 1989 a series of Supreme Court decisions wiped out affirmative action as a tool for black workers. This didn't stop Bush from taking one last swipe at affirmative action. In 1990 he vetoed a civil rights bill aimed at restoring some aspects of affirmative action because it required 'quotas'. He vowed to do the same thing to the 1991 civil rights bill, which was a watered down version of the 1990 bill.

But Bush was stopped in his tracks. In the fall of 1991 Bush's own racist code words, 'welfare', 'crime' and 'drugs' began emanating from the ultra right. Neo-Nazi David Duke had entered the fray, running for Governor of Louisiana—*as a Republican*. Duke did not become Governor of Louisiana in November 1991, but he did win 55 percent of the white vote. And within weeks he announced that he would be running for President in 1992, again as a Republican. Duke, a long time Nazi and former Ku Klux Klan leader, now leads the National Association for the Advancement of White People (NAAWP), which is, in Duke's words, 'more of a high class thing' than the Klan. The NAAWP, for example, calls cross burnings 'illuminations' and his own title is 'national director' rather than the Klan's preferred 'Grand Wizard'. But in all crucial respects, Duke's world outlook comes directly from Hitler. Duke's only criticism of apartheid in South Africa is that it doesn't go far enough because blacks are allowed to live within South Africa's borders.[102]

Like Bush and Reagan, however, Duke has zeroed in on affirmative action and welfare as campaign issues. Duke also opposes affirmative action quotas. And carrying Bush's attacks on welfare recipients a step further, Duke has argued, 'There's no reason why we shouldn't give incentives to welfare recipients, criminals, and the mentally defective to go childless.'[103] The comparisons were obvious, even though Bush denounced Duke as a 'charlatan'. He quickly signed the 1991 civil rights bill in the hope of distancing himself from Duke. But Vice-President Dan Quayle botched the effort when he stated on national television:

> *The message of David Duke is . . . anti-big government, get out of my pocketbook, cut my taxes, put welfare people back to work. That's a very popular message. The problem is the messenger. . .*[104]

Then another right winger jumped into the 1992 Presidential race. Pat Buchanan, who had opposed the US war against Iraq from the right, is campaigning on an 'America First' isolationist platform, in which he calls for protectionism, an end to foreign aid, and closing US borders to Third World immigrants. Buchanan has no hopes of winning the Presidency, but he raises the pressure on Bush from the right. Bush's popularity plunged to 46 percent by November 1991. Moreover, only one in four approved of Bush's handling of the economy, a level of discontent not approached since the final days of Jimmy Carter.[105]

More polls further jolted the Bush administration. Health care was the main issue on voters' minds—an issue which Bush had all but ignored, claiming that the US health care system didn't need reform because it was the best in the world. In a *Time*/CNN news survey, 91 percent of the respondents said, 'our health care system needs fundamental change.' And 70 percent said they would be willing to pay higher taxes to guarantee that all Americans have health coverage. Another survey showed a majority opposes further capital gains cuts for the rich, something Bush proposed to Congress. In yet another poll 71 percent agreed with the statement that the US government is run by 'a few big interests'.[106]

In the face of a deepening recession Bush faced comparisons with Herbert Hoover, the Republican President who refused to acknowledge the Crash of 1929. Bush finally admitted that the recession wasn't over. With pressure coming from both the left and the right, Bush was forced to backtrack at the end of 1991, but he couldn't figure out in which direction he should go—giving the White House the appearance of panic and disarray. Bush signed a bill temporarily extending workers' unemployment payments by 20 weeks—the same bill he'd vetoed only a month earlier, claiming workers didn't need additional benefits because the recession would be 'short and shallow'. Then, after opposing tax cuts called by Democrats and many Republicans, Bush did an about face and announced that he liked the tax cuts 'enthusiastically'.[107] He then prepared his own set of proposed tax cuts.

Then Bush sent the stock market reeling when in a speech to a Republican fundraising luncheon he suggested that banks should lower credit card interest rates from their present 18 to 20 percent charge. The very next day the Senate took Bush at his word and passed legislation capping credit card interest rates at 14 percent. Two days later the Dow Jones index plunged 120 points, the fifth largest point drop in Wall Street history. Bank lobbyists swarmed to Congress, threatening that if the law were enacted, as the *New York Times* put it, 'shaky banks might go under and millions of Americans whose credit ratings are less than ideal would have their credit cards recalled.' Bush's own staff denounced him. Treasury Secretary Brady said the proposal was 'wacky'. Richard Darman, Director of the Office of Management and Budget, said it was 'preposterous'. Even Dan Quayle thought it was stupid. Bush had no choice but to request that Congress reject his request.[108]

Bush's blunders did not sit well with business interests, to whom it was apparent that he had no plan for jump starting the economy. Corporate giants, saddled with rising health care costs, raised the demand for a national health care plan. GM, for example, claims that for every car produced on its assembly lines, management pays out 600 dollars in health care costs. *Business Week* announced, 'We're for a Universal Health Care System', and issued a six page proposal for one.[109] When Bush loaded up a plane with corporate executives to barter with Japan, he was likened to a travelling salesman. The business weekly *Barron's* quipped, 'Bush returned from his arduous undertaking with nothing to show but bad publicity and solemn promises (which, close inspection revealed, were dated 1987.)'[110]

The Republocrats

Although the winds of change are blowing, the vacuum to Bush's left has yet to be filled. The most obvious possibility, of course, is that the Democrats will come forward. But while a host of unknowns joined the presidential race, those with name recognition, like New York's Governor Cuomo and even Jesse Jackson, decided to sit this election out. Even with the writing on the wall, the party which dissolved its 'New Deal Coalition' during Reagan's first term has forgotten how to mouth the rhetoric. Besides, the Democratic Party's leadership abandoned its appeals to blacks and workers, otherwise known as 'special interest groups', after the Democrats' resounding defeat to

Reagan in the 1984 Presidential election. Democratic leader Robert Strauss put it bluntly:

> *Women, blacks, teachers, Hispanics. They have more power, more money than ever before. Do you think these groups are going to turn the party loose? Do you think labour is going to turn the party loose? Jesse Jackson? The others? Forget it.*[111]

The prospects for a major shake up in 1992 are slim. None of the major Democratic candidates, for example, has called for a national health service even as minimal as the Canadian plan. One Democratic candidate, Tom Harkin, was touted as a 'populist' when he decided to run. Dubbed the 'working man's friend', he does call for the federal government to set up a Works Project Administration to create jobs, modelled after Roosevelt's New Deal. But Harkin mixes in a strong dose of xenophobia: he considers the 'real enemies' of working people to include the Japanese, along with rich Republicans and big corporations. And, however low Bush's popularity has dipped, few consider the Democrats to be an alternative. According to a December 1991 *Newsweek* poll, while only 31 percent of US adults approved of Bush's 'economic management', only 28 percent believed the Democrats would do a better job. In fact, some opinion polls show Congress, which is dominated by Democrats, is held in even greater disdain than Bush: 49 percent blamed Congress for major problems, while 29 percent held Bush responsible.[112]

Thus the majority of workers sit out most elections. In a typical presidential election half of the voting age population participates. And turnout rates have been in steady decline over the last three decades. Reagan and Bush could each boast a 'mandate' from about 26 percent of eligible voters. The chronically low voter turnout rates are an unmistakable expression of alienation. When asked recently whether they agreed with the statement, 'I don't think that public officials care much about what people like me think', 59 percent agreed.[113]

The bottom line for Bush is the state of the economy. As one White House aide said of his re-election prospects in late 1991, 'If the economy comes back in six months, nothing else matters. If it doesn't nothing else matters.'[114] And whether or not Bush is re-elected, his problems are not likely to go away. The factors underlying the economic crisis for US capital remain in place. Most importantly, the rate of growth has not exceeded 1.7 percent since Bush took office, compared with an average of 3 percent under Reagan and an average of 2.1 percent during the 1930s Depression. Even after the recession ends, mainstream economists paint a gloomy picture for the 1990s. In early 1992 a survey of 48 US economists predicted growth of only

1.6 percent this year—revised downward by a full percentage point from what they predicted three months earlier. Unemployment is expected to hover around 6 percent for years to come.[115]

The manufacturing sector restored its productivity during the 1980s, in some fields surpassing even the rates of Japan. But even after more than a decade of concessions and lay offs, US manufacturing has not been able to reverse its global decline. Moreover, productivity in the service sector has remained stagnant. Many are now predicting that a new 'white collar recession' is in the offing. Already at the end of 1991, with unemployment ranging higher than 10 percent in some white collar non-supervisory job categories, IBM, the personal computer giant, announced it plans to cut 20,000 jobs.[116]

And from workers' point of view, even a period of extended recovery only promises a further sharpening of class contradictions. After all, the Reagan boom produced the biggest transfer of wealth upwards since the Roaring Twenties. Recovery or not, the only hope for US workers is to begin to shift the balance of class forces, and that can only happen through struggle.

The way forward

One of Reagan's aims had been to restore the dominance of US imperialism on a world scale, primarily through a massive military budget and slashing social spending. The collapse of the Eastern European regimes convinced many that Reaganism had achieved its aims. And to many on the left Bush's success in the Gulf War confirmed the view that the US was at the beginning of yet another period of global domination. But this view is clearly mistaken. It ignores the significant problems facing the ruling class internationally, and—what has been the focus here—the domestic price of Reaganism. US employers have been successful in forcing workers to pay the cost of restructuring. But in the process they have also greatly increased the bitterness and anger of millions of working class people. No longer can it be said that US workers think of themselves as middle class. That is the reality behind all the opinion polls.

The US working class is not what it was in 1950. For most workers then, expectations of higher living standards were in part matched by reality. The US ruling class claimed conditions would only continue to improve and that the 'American way' stood in the face of 'totalitarianism'. Workers today have been stripped of such illusions. Whether black, white or Latino, male or female, employed or unemployed, conditions for *all* workers have declined markedly. The economic expansion of the 1980s added hundreds of thousands to the ranks of the working class, but 85 percent of the jobs created were in low pay, part-time service work. Almost 20 percent of all workers have no health insurance, and 40 percent have no pension coverage. Those workers who have a job are unlikely to belong to a union, and two thirds of those who don't have a job get no government assistance. For the first time since the end of the Second World War, this generation of American workers faces a lower living standard than that of their parents. Already 22 percent of children in the US live in poverty. Bitterness and anger has been building for close to 20 years among every section of the working class. For most workers, the election of either the Democrats or the Republicans is an event not worth participating in.

But this anger and bitterness will soon find political expression. The evidence that it exists is easy to find. In February 1991, 58 percent of those polled believed the US was headed in the right direction, with 39 percent saying it was on the wrong track. By October, the proportion of Americans who said the country was headed in the right direction had dropped to 26 percent. The shift in working class consciousness—and what this represents—has not been lost on some of the more astute political analysts of the ruling class. Kevin Phillips, whose 1969 book *The Emerging Republican Majority* was described by *Newsweek* as 'the political bible of the Nixon era', now worries that the past decade has laid the basis for an explosion of class conflict. This, he argues, has been the historical pattern of the US—a period of unrelenting ruling class assault on workers followed by an eruption of working class resistance, as happened in the 1890s-1910s and 1930s. He quotes the warnings of one sociologist: 'When you talk to people, you get an awful lot of this kind of generalised anger. From a political point of view, I think the potential for a lot of very difficult and dangerous things is there, but it hasn't been happening yet.'[117]

It will probably take years for US workers to rebuild their confidence to struggle after two decades of retreat. But there are signs that the tide may be starting to turn. While the number of strikes has remained low, some strikes which have taken place in the last two or three years have ended in partial or outright victory. The Pittston miners' 11 month strike of 1989-90 is the most notable: after a three day occupation and solidarity strikes, which at one point involved 30,000 miners from seven states, the miners kept the company from busting their union or getting major concessions. And workers scored an important victory in 1991. For the first time in the history of the Teamsters union, the rank and file democratically elected its leadership, and an entire reform slate was voted in. The Teamsters, with 1.5 million members, has a long history of embezzlement, corruption, and mafia involvement with its top officials. For example, three of its last five presidents wound up in prison. A fourth, Jackie Presser, died before his case was tried. Finally, in 1989 the US government—no doubt for dubious motives—used racketeering statutes to intervene in the union, setting up, among other things, elections.

In the past, Teamster conventions, held once every five years, were mainly restricted to fulltime union officials and, usually held in Las Vegas, were known mainly for their lavish social gatherings, which typically began around 4pm. At the last convention Joseph Trerotola, a New York Teamster leader, threw a party costing 648,000 dollars.[118] But at the 1991 convention union delegates booed outgoing union president William McCarthy. They also booed George Bush's videotaped message. Discontent has been brewing inside the Teamsters for many years. The reform slate, headed by New York Teamster official Ron Carey, also includes members of the Teamsters for a Democratic Union (TDU), a union reform organisation that has built a presence inside the union for 15 years. And, while Carey himself is no left winger (he is a former Republican), he at least breaks the trail of corruption stretching back for generations of Teamster leaders.

But the most important aspect of this reformer's victory is the effect on the morale of rank and file workers inside and outside the Teamsters. Only hours after news of Carey's victory, former UAW president Doug Fraser stepped forward to emphasise that the Teamsters union is a special case, and denied that the Teamster victory could set an example for workers in other unions.[117] Fraser's response is evidence enough that it well could. In fact, the New Directions reform caucus inside the UAW is already planning to run its own candidate, Jerry Tucker, for union president.

There are more than a few parallels between the balance of class forces today and that which existed in the late 1920s. Then also, union membership had fallen to skeletal levels, working class struggles were largely defensive, and the left was quite small. Yet with the onset of mass struggle in the mid-1930s the left was able to grow massively. The key weakness of the US left since that time has been the dominance of Stalinism in its various forms. In the 1930s Stalinists led workers into the Democratic Party at the high point of struggle. In the 1960s and 1970s Maoists either discounted the working class or were pulled toward reformism. In the 1980s Maoists and ex-Maoists entered the Democratic Party *en masse* via Jesse Jackson's Rainbow Coalition. The collapse of Stalinism internationally, along with the overwhelming US victory against Iraq, demoralised the tiny fragmented socialist movement which still existed at the beginning of the 1990s.

Revolutionary socialists are in short supply in the US. But the left is finally free of Stalinism, leaving open the real possibility that the socialist movement can be reborn in the 1990s. Our numbers are small, but the potential is huge. The myth of the American Dream is over.

Notes

Thanks to John Rees, Ahmed Shawki, Alan Maass, Bill Roberts and Lance Selfa for comments on the first draft.

1 K Moody, 'The American Working Class in Transition', *International Socialism* (Old Series), October/November 1969, p13.
2 F Levy, *Dollars and Dreams* (New York, 1987) p59n.
3 Quoted in M Davis, *Prisoners of the American Dream* (London, 1986) p102.
4 D Bell, *The End of Ideology* (Illinois, 1960) p84. D Bell, *The Cultural Contradictions of Capitalism* (New York, 1976) p251.
5 Quoted in S Aronowitz, *False Promises* (New York, 1973) p327, and C Harman, *The Fire Last Time: 1968 and After* (London, 1988) p3.
6 F Levy, op cit, p47.
7 J Jacobson, *The Negro and the American Labor Movement* (New York, 1968), pp218-219. P Foner, *Organized Labor and the Black Worker* 1619-1981 (New York, 1981) p295n.
8 J Jacobson, op cit, pp212-213.
9 T Ferguson and J Rogers, *Right Turn: The Decline of the Democrats and the Future of American Politics* (New York, 1986) p49. K Moody, op cit, p13.
10 N Harris, *The End of the Third World: Newly Industrializing Countries and an End of an Ideology* (London, 1986) pp106, 111.
11 S Weir, *USA: The Labor Revolt* (Boston, 1967) p284. J R Green, *The World of the Worker: Labor in Twentieth Century America* (New York, 1980) p213.
12 Until 1948 the standard UAW contract lasted only one year. In 1948 the UAW agreed to the employers' demand for a two year contract.
13 S Weir, op cit, p280.
14 K Moody, *An Injury to All: The Decline of American Unionism* (London, 1988) p68.
15 P Foner, op cit, pp411-412.
16 D Georgakas and M Surkin, *Detroit I Do Mind Dying* (New York,1975) p24.
17 P Foner, op cit, p423.
18 K Moody, *An Injury to All*, op cit, pp86-87.
19 S Terkel, *Working* (New York, 1972) pp261-262. See also J Green, op cit, pp219-220, and S Aronowitz, op cit, pp21-50.
20 The Maoist organisations' success at recruitment during the anti Vietnam War movement can also be partly explained by the weakness of the two wings of Trotskyism in the US during this period. See C Harman, op cit, pp177-181.
21 K Stallard, B Ehrenreich, H Sklar, *Poverty in the American Dream: Women and Children First* (Boston, 1983) p31.
22 T Ferguson and J Rogers, op cit, p67.
23 P Matera, *Prosperity Lost* (Reading, Massachusetts, 1990) p15.
24 T Ferguson and J Rogers, op cit, pp79-80.
25 J Cohen and J Rogers, 'Reaganism After Reagan', in *Socialist Register 1988* (London, 1988) p390. N Harris, op cit, pp106 and 111.
26 T Ferguson and J Rogers, op cit, p111.
27 Ibid, p109.
28 P Matera, op cit, p107.
29 M Goldfield, *The Decline of Organized Labor in the United States* (Chicago, 1987) pp109, 193.
30 K Moody, *An Injury to All*, op cit, pp155 and 165-166.
31 The right to legal abortion was granted in the US Supreme Court's *Roe v Wade* ruling, issued in January 1973. Affirmative Action programmes were established to redress racial discrimination in employment and education in the wake of the

1964 Civil Rights Act. Quotas were established in many firms and government agencies to set guidelines for minimum compliance, but have rarely been adequately enforced.

32 See L Tribe, *Abortion: The Clash of Absolutes* (New York, 1990) p154. Federal funding for abortion for poor women has never been restored. By 1990, only 13 of the 50 states provided for poor women's abortions, and 32 states denied funding even to victims of rape or incest.

33 A Pinkney, *The Myth of Black Progress* (Cambridge, 1984) pp153-154.

34 J H Wilkinson III, *From Brown to Bakke—The Supreme Court and School Integration: 1954-1978* (New York, 1979) pp267 and 275.

35 T Ferguson and J Rogers, op cit, p119.

36 K Phillips, *The Politics of Rich and Poor* (New York, 1990) p53.

37 T Ferguson and J Rogers, op cit, p121. See also K Moody, 'Reagan, the Business Agenda and the Collapse of Labour,' in *Socialist Register 1987* (London, 1987) pp165-166.

38 Ibid, p122.

39 J Cohen and J Rogers, op cit, pp395-396.

40 K Phillips, op cit, p80, T Ferguson and J Rogers, op cit, p123.

41 K Phillips, op cit, p10.

42 *Washington Post Weekly Edition*, 4-10 November 1991.

43 K Phillips, op cit, p87. K Stallard, B Ehrenreich, H Sklar, op cit, p42.

44 Ibid, pp8 and 180. *Chicago Sun Times*, 1 January 1992. See also Labor Research Association, *Economic Clips*, November-December 1990, *Business Week*, 3 February 1992, p29.

45 R Sherrill, 'The Looting Decade: S&Ls, Big Banks and Other Triumphs of Capitalism', in *The Nation 251:17*, 19 November 1990.

46 *Chicago Tribune*, 5 January 1992.

47 R Sherrill, op cit, pp609-610.

48 Ibid, p599.

49 The five Democratic Senators who made up four of the "Keating Five" include Senators Alan Cranston of California, Donald Riegle of Michigan, Dennis DeConcini of Arizona and John Glenn of Ohio. The Republican Senator is John McCain of Arizona. R Sherrill, op cit, p590.

50 US Dept of Commerce, Bureau of the Census, *Statistical Abstract of the United States, 1991,* (Washington DC, 1991) p391. *Wall Street Journal*, 21 January 1992.

51 *Business Week*, 19 August 1991, p80. P Matera, op cit, p139. M Marable, 'Black Politics in Crisis', in *The Progressive*, January 1987, p20.

52 V Navarro, op cit, p437. P Matera, op cit, p18.

53 *Business Week*, 7 October 1991, p59.

54 *The Washington Post Weekly Edition*, 28 October-3 November 1991, p28.

55 M Feinberg, 'Warning: Work is Hazardous to Your Health', in *The Progressive*, January 1992, p26.

56 M L Kerr, 'Chickens Come Home to Roost', in *The Progressive*, January 1992, p29.

57 *Chicago Sun Times*, 1 January 1992.

58 M Marable, 'Race and Realignment in American Politics', M David, F Pfeil, M Sprinker, eds in *The Year Left* (London, 1985) p19.

59 L Sigelman and S Welch, *Black Americans; Views of Racial Inequality: The Dream Deferred* (Cambridge, 1991) p36.

60 M Marable, 'Black America in Search of Itself', in *The Progressive*, November 1991, p22. *Los Angeles Times*, 16 December 1989. J T Gibbs, *Young, Black and Male in America: An Endangered Species* (Westport, 1988) p7.

61 *The Washington Post*, 18 December 1990.

62 D R Judd, 'Segregation Forever?' in *The Nation,* 9 December 1991, p742. M Marable, *How Capitalism Underdeveloped Black America* (Boston, 1983) p127. J T Gibbs, op cit, p3.
63 Ibid, p127 quote from former director of the National Conference of Black Lawyers.
64 J T Gibbs, op cit, pp100, 102.
65 Landry, The New Black Middle Class, (Berkeley, 1987) p229.
66 M Marable, 'Black America in Search of Itself', op cit, p22.
67 L Brenner, The Lesser Evil: The Democratic Party. (Seacaucus, NJ, 1988) pp278-279, 188.
68 M Marable, 'The Contradictory Contours of Black Political Culture', in *The Year Left 2: Toward a Rainbow Socialism*, M Davis, M Marable, F Pfeil, M Sprinkler, eds (London, 1987) p6.
69 Quoted in 'The Crisis in Black Politics', in *Socialist Worker* (US), October 1990.
70 K Moody, *An Injury to All*, op cit, pp139-141.
71 Editorial, *Socialist Worker* (US), September 1981.
72 'Solidarity Forever', ibid, October, 1981.
73 K Moody, *An Injury to All*, op cit, p56.
74 A Weinrub and W Bollinger, *The AFL-CIO in Central America* (Oakland, 1987), p16. With a budget that is 90 percent paid for by the US Government the AFL-CIO has worked with the US State Department to set up anti-Communist unions through Latin America, Asia and Africa.
75 A Preis, *Labor's Giant Step* (New York, 1964), p85.
76 K Moody, *An Injury to All*, op cit, p125.
77 Ibid, pp148, 154, 166.
78 P Matera, op cit, pp112-113.
79 K Moody, *An Injury to All*, op cit, pp185.
80 Ibid, pp116-117.
81 M Goldfield, op cit, p46. Statistics are much harder to measure for the 1980s, since during the Reagan administration, the Bureau of Labor Statistics stopped including strikes involving fewer than 1,000 workers in its strike statistics.
82 An important exception is the Watsonville Cannery strike which began in 1985. Of the 1,000 workers who struck against Watsonville, most of whom were Latino women, not one union member crossed the picket line during the entire 18 month strike. The company did not succeed in busting the union.
83 'Brown and Sharpe: How Not to Win', in *Socialist Worker* (US), February 1983 and November 1983.
84 'Victory to the P-9 Strike!' in *Socialist Worker* (US), April 1986.
85 'War in Austin', in *Socialist Worker* (US), March 1986.
86 Labor Research Association, *Economic Notes*, May-June 1991, January-February 1990.
87 V Navarro, op cit, p429.
88 K Phillips, op cit, p89-90.
89 Ibid, p142.
90 Ibid, p133.
91 Ibid.
92. *Business Week*, 25 November 1991.
93 *St Petersberg Times*, 26 December 1991. Matera, op cit, p22. *Chicago Tribune*, 5 January 1992.
94 C Colastosi, 'Governor Shreds Michigan Safety Net', in the *Guardian*, 4 December 1991, p3. *Newsweek*, 2 December 1991, pp26-27. *Wall Street Journal*, 11 December 1991.
95 B Day, 'Drug-Resistant TB Strains NYC Health', *Guardian*, 4 December 1991, p7. *Chicago Tribune*, 24 January 1992.

96 *Wall Street Journal*, 11 December 1991. *New York Times*, 18 December 1991.
97 J Jacobson, 'Pax Americana: The New World Order', in *New Politics* 111:3 (New Series) Summer 1991, p18.
98 L Selfa and A Maass, *What's Behind the Attack on Politically Correct?* (Chicago, 1991), p2.
99 This figure is from the Alan Guttmacher Institute. Quoted in S Smith, *Abortion: Every Woman's Right* (Chicago, 1987), p5.
100 'Defend Gay and Lesbian Rights', in *Socialist Worker* (US), August 1986.
101 See 'California Lesbians and Gays Take to the Streets', in *Socialist Worker* (US), October 1991.
102 See 'Setback for Master Race', *Socialist Review*, December 1991, p22.
103 L Hill, 'The Influence of National Socialist Political Theory in the Contemporary Political Thought of David Duke' (unpublished paper, distributed by the Louisiana Coalition, 1990), p16.
104 *Socialist Worker* (US), December 1991.
105 *Newsweek*, 9 December 1991, p45. *New York Times*, 26 November 1991.
106 *Time*, 25 November 1991, p36. *Business Week*, 2 December 1991, p32. *The Washington Post National Weekly Edition*, 11-17 November 1991.
107 *Newsweek*, 9 December 1991, p45.
108 Quoted in H Gold, 'Bush's Credit Bulimia: Gorge Big Banks, Starve Customers', *The Nation*, 23 December 1991, pp807-808.
109 *Business Week*, 7 October 1991.
110 *Barron's*, 13 January 1992, p31.
111 T Ferguson, J Rogers, op cit, p9.
112 *Newsweek*, 9 December 1991, p45. *The Washington Post National Weekly Edition*, 11-17 November 1991, p8.
113 *Washington Post National Weekly Edition*, 11-17 November, p7.
114 *New York Times*, 22 November 1991.
115 *The Wall Street Journal*, 13 January 1991. *New York Times*, 2 January 1992.
116 For productivity comparisons, see *Monthly Labor Review*, May 1991, p98. *New York Times*, 2 January 1992. *Newsweek*, 9 December 1991, p50.
117 *The Washington Post National Weekly Edition*, 20-26 January 1992. K Phillips, op cit, p209.
118 W Serrin, 'The Teamsters' Toughest Contract', *The Nation*, 29 July/5 August 1991, p151.

Class and crisis—the transition in eastern Europe

MIKE HAYNES

Popular power in Eastern Europe in 1989 lasted no longer than the length of a smile, according to the Czechoslovak president, Vaclav Havel. For the length of that smile everything seemed to be possible. Speaking to an audience of American bankers in the autumn of 1989 Lech Walesa told them, 'There will not be any unemployment because there is so much to do'.[1] The picture is very different today. The smile has now gone as crisis has intensified throughout the region. Where austerity programmes have been put in place, standards of living have fallen and unemployment has risen. But in countries like Romania, Bulgaria and Albania, where change has been more halting, the development of the crisis has been no less intense—undercutting the idea that there was any salvation in the old ways.

As the pain has intensified enthusiasm has melted away. In Poland and Hungary in particular the result has been astonishing levels of apathy and alienation from the political systems. Elsewhere the main beneficiary has been nationalism. The Yugoslav example is a dreadful warning of what might lie down that road. For Haval now 'the happiness is gone. The second act is called crisis. The crisis will be chronic and then the catastrophe will happen. Finally the catharsis will come and after that everything will go well'.[2] He may be right, but a look at the real conditions in eastern Europe suggests that his hope is based rather more on a literary model of life than on a cool assessment of the objective possibilities in the foreseeable future.

The aim of this article is to try to make such an assessment. It is an urgent task because the disorientation produced by the collapse of eastern Europe has affected the left across the world. At the same time the ideologists of the right are trying to maintain the initiative by presenting bullishly optimistic accounts of the change. But their promises of brighter tomorrows and visions of newly liberated peoples advancing towards the rising sun, after the temporary difficulties of transition, have as much basis in reality as some of the worst excesses of Stalin's propaganda about the promised land.

The events of 1989 in East Germany, Poland, Hungary and Czechoslovakia and the ongoing pressures for change in the former Soviet Union, Romania, Bulgaria and Albania reflect the coming together of two distinct movements. At one level they have been an expression of popular pressure from below and they could not have developed without this. But, as in any revolutionary crisis, there was a second movement, this time at the top of the system. The existing ruling classes in order to maintain the core of their power shifted their ground, accommodated to the popular mood, sacrificed their most hated representatives and recomposed themselves so as to be better able to maintain themselves in the future. They were able to do this the more easily in this case because the demonstrating crowds and striking workers in Eastern Europe posed primarily political demands. They left the question of the social base of power of those who ruled them largely untouched except insofar as it was partially expressed through the role of the Communist Parties. It is this that accounts for the apparent paradox of the 'revolutions' in these societies.

The state is being dismantled to some degree, planning is giving way to more market control but the same social group, shorn of its figureheads and old secret police, is still in control. What it has succeeded in doing has been to partly shift the institutional base of its power out of a 'state pocket' and into a 'private pocket'. In the process there has been some upward mobility within the ruling class and the occasional new entrant. There has also been a change in the balance of power within the ruling class between its sections. But, contrary to those who claim that what was at stake was the substitution of a socialist mode of production or a new form of class society by a capitalist society, there is no evidence that a fundamental change has taken place in the nature of the ruling class. What is striking is how little change has actually occurred. To sack a general and promote a colonel hardly constitutes a social revolution any more than selling off a state enterprise to its managers does or renationalising it with a similar group of people in control. Rather it suggests that what is at stake is an internal transformation within a mode of production, in this instance a shift in the form of capitalism from one of strong state capitalism to more mixed state and market forms.

There will be many people who will try to resist this conclusion, so in order to support our argument we will later explore in more detail how the ruling class in eastern Europe has shifted the base of its power. But a full understanding of how and why this has happened requires us first to explore how the Eastern European crisis developed and then to tie down the real possibilities of a market transition in the 1990s. We will then be better able to see what has been at stake socially and how this relates to the internal class character of these societies.

Rationality and irrationality under the old regime

In the wake of the collapse in eastern Europe and the revelations of corruption, waste and inefficiency many commentators have marvelled that these regimes could have survived so long. But the fact that they did points to an important issue—for a long period these systems were both dynamic and viable. Their dynamism was frequently overestimated but it was nevertheless real. Just as it makes no sense to judge a bankrupt company's past performance on the basis of its final winding up balance sheet of devalued stocks and assets so in eastern Europe and the former Soviet Union the enormous scale of the collapse should not blind us to past achievements. The fears of the Cold War for all their exaggerations were based on the threat of something real.

This reality did not lie in the achievements of 'socialism' for these societies were based on the enormous exploitation and oppression of the working class which led to periodic revolt. Rather the reality lay in a period of successful state directed competitive industrialisation which lasted in the Soviet Union from 1928-1929 to the 1970s and in Eastern Europe from 1948 to the 1970s. What lay behind this was the attempt of the different ruling groups in these societies to break out of their relative economic backwardness so as to be better able to cope with the military and economic pressures of the world economy.

Past reliance on the market to achieve this had proved spectacularly unsuccessful. For Eastern Europe (excluding the former East Germany and the Soviet Union after 1917) the most recent calculations show that the economies of the area were failing to make any significant impression on the gap that had developed with advanced capitalism before 1945.[3] The region as a whole was especially badly hit by the inter-war economic crisis which led to a final collapse of faith in market forces. At the same time piecemeal and pragmatic state intervention, whose content was a prisoner of narrow vested interests within the existing ruling class, also proved unable to deal with the area's difficulties. Here was a section of world capitalism that was characterised by 'complete economic chaos, almost inextricable confusion and a state of utter hopelessness', say two of the area's leading historians. For an American commentator 'a gigantic backlog of backwardness, increasing demographic pressures, consistently erroneous economic policies, insuperable nationalistic barriers to fruitful co-operation in the area all but arrested the process of economic growth'.[4]

Thus although the particular forms of development after 1945 were not predetermined, the history of past failures and the immediate post-1945 pressures within the world economy were pushing towards industrialisation drives involving substantial state elements irrespective of the precise political forms that developed. It is worth recalling, for example, that the original ideas in 'Third World' development economics that became so influential in the three decades after 1945 of state directed growth were actually formulated as a response to the inability of these eastern European states to break out of the vicious circles of backwardness and stunted growth within the capitalist world economy.[5]

In the event the circumstances of war, Cold War and Stalinist control dictated that the ruling classes in these societies after 1948 would pursue policies of state directed industrialisation that paralleled those of the Soviet Union after 1928-29. The particular circumstances that led to the adoption of this pattern and the more detailed logic of these moves in terms of the pressures of the world economy and the needs of the Soviet ruling class and the recomposed eastern European ruling classes have been discussed elsewhere and need not detain us here.[6] The important thing is that the new policies worked for a long period *in terms of their own objectives*. The costs were enormous, but the previous barriers were broken and these states did move forward at a pace that for a time gave rise to real concern amongst their competitors in the advanced West. The basis of this is shown in Table 1 below.

TABLE 1

ANNUAL AVERAGE PER CAPITA GROWTH RATES 1950-1980[7]

World average	*2.7*
Centrally planned economies	*3.6*
Industrialised economies	*3.1*
Middle income market economies	*3.0*
Low income group	*1.5*

As a result of these growth rates there was some closing of the gap with the advanced West as well as some convergence within the Eastern bloc itself as the weaker economies grew slightly faster.

This was what the ruling classes in eastern Europe had hoped for. But over time growth slowed and by the late 1970s and early 1980s the

Eastern European economies were stagnating and the gap between them and the advanced West was growing again. For our purposes what is important is the way in which this emerging crisis gradually exposed the limitations of the long run strategies that had been adopted in order to compete with the West.

The industrialisation drives (as with the earlier Soviet one) had been based upon attempts to compete in a world dominated by the imperatives of accumulation and commodity production. To compete here economies had to be built whose structures were in direct competition (both militarily and economically) with the states of the advanced West. Army was set against army, nuclear missile against nuclear missile, steel industry against steel industry and so on. In the Soviet Union in the 1930s the impact of the world crisis forced the economy to turn inward, reducing the importance of foreign trade and therefore of direct commodity competition. The main competitive drive came indirectly through the military sector. This continued to be a major axis of competition forcing the process of accumulation ever onward, but over time it was supplemented more and more by the direct pressure of competition through trade. In the case of eastern Europe this latter form of competition has always been more important. But in both instances trade relations were controlled to some degree in order to be better able to build the economic base in the face of superior Western competition. In other words, in order to better compete with the most advanced military and economic powers in the *world economy* the integration of these weaker economies into the *world market* had to be limited.

Over time this pattern began to break down under the pressure of growth and integration tendencies in the world economy. But integration and specialisation remained weak compared to what existed elsewhere. In particular there was relatively less movement of labour as the migration of both skilled and unskilled workers was restricted. Without these restrictions Eastern Europe would have been a major exporter of migrant labour in the post-war world, as indeed Yugoslavia became. Secondly, there was also relatively little movement of capital with limited direct investment and penetration by Western multinationals. Thirdly, trade, the international exchange of commodities and services, was much less integrated. Trade shares rose substantially over time, but production specialisation and integration was limited.[8] The Eastern European bloc and the states within it tried instead to duplicate the structures that they were competing with, but they lacked the levels of development and the market sizes to do this successfully and this became especially so as the pace of integration in the rest of the world economy intensified in the most recent decades. Since an understanding of this is important for any appreciation of the impact of transition it is worth exploring the dimensions of these structures more precisely.

The first was that these economies developed overlarge industrial sectors which gave them the base for military and great power competition but which made little sense from the view of the world market as a whole. This contradiction between the global logic of capitalism and its particular national form in Eastern Europe meant that industries could only be kept going by large subsidies which imposed considerable strains on these economies. The problem became even more evident in the 1970s and 1980s when the pressure of competition forced a shift towards more high technology industries such as computers. The result was a series of weak 'low tech-high tech' industries reflected best perhaps in the East German computer industry—advanced in bloc terms but nowhere in world terms.

Within these industrial sectors, because of the smaller markets, it was impossible to develop full economies of scale or to have the level of diversification and product competition apparent in the West. Although these features were accentuated by planning decisions and preferences, the relative weaknesses of the Eastern European economies dictated that if they were to have a whole range of industries within their borders then this would have to be on the basis of higher levels of vertical integration, a smaller number of producers and higher levels of plant size than in the West. Table 2 shows one aspect of this, the large size of plant in Eastern Europe as production concentration developed to a much higher degree than in the West.

TABLE 2
PERCENTAGE CONCENTRATION OF THE LABOUR FORCE BY PLANT SIZE IN THE 1980S[9]

No of workers in plant	*Sample West**	*West Germany*	*East Germany*	*Poland (total)*	*Poland (state)*	*Poland (co-ops)*
100 or less	*35*	*17*	*10*	*2*	*6*	*42*
101 - 500	*33*	*30*	*25*	*13*	*21*	*54*
501 - 1000	*13*	*13*	*15*	*12*	*16*	*4*
1000 or more	*19*	*40*	*51*	*73*	*58*	*1*

** average for Austria, Belgium, France, Italy, Japan and Sweden*

The other side of this concentration was that most of these large plants were in effect monopoly producers of their products within these economies (and sometimes the bloc at large). In the USSR, for example, an examination of production by industry has shown that of nearly 6,000 separate items produced in the engineering industry 87 percent are produced by single firms with an absolute internal monopoly—over a further 8 percent of the product range only two to three firms are involved in the production of each item. This reliance on the concentration of the production of individual products in individual plants is extreme in this industry but reflects the basic pattern across the Soviet and eastern European economies. In Soviet metal production, for example, 28 percent of the product range is made in firms with an absolute monopoly but for a further 49 percent of the range there are only 2 to 6 producers for each item. It is the same story for chemicals where 47 percent of the product range is made by single producers and a further 40 percent by 2 to 6 producers for each item.[10]

Opening these economies further to the world market has therefore led to the beginnings of a radical restructuring. In particular, the share of industry in output is being cut both relatively and (in the short term) absolutely. The relative cut reflects the expansion of the service sector which had been suppressed to encourage the competitive industrial base as well as some more minor swing back towards agriculture. The absolute cut reflects the inability of key sections of industry to withstand the world competition they are now being *directly* exposed to rather than in the more state mediated forms of the past. This is also producing a slimming down of plant size and a disintegration of production within the economies to allow more specialisation and integration with the world market. What it is not doing, however, is producing intensified internal market competition in the economic cores because over a wide range of industries there is no basis for such competition and, as the restructuring proceeds, the dependence on a limited number of producers is likely to be maintained because only a limited number will survive.[11]

The question that has to be posed, therefore, is why an attempt to shift to a more market based structure with a higher level of integration with the world market appealed to the Eastern European ruling classes at all?

Did they jump or were they pushed?

The answer to the question of whether the ruling classes jumped or were pushed is a little of both. They jumped in the sense that they made the first moves and established a basic momentum. They were pushed in the sense that pressure from below drove them to make their own great leap in the dark in 1989. There were a number of factors alongside the longer term economic contradictions that we have just noted that pushed key sections of the ruling class in this direction.

The first was the growing internal dissatisfaction of the ruling class with its own position. One aspect of this was that as the system stagnated so its ideological strength withered and with it the willingness to accept less than their counterparts in the West. Indeed as the crisis developed it even began to cut directly into the privileges of the ruling class itself. In Poland Adam Michnik has expressed this well in what has been called the 'doctrine of the radiators':

> *Three years ago all of the radiators stopped working ... Shivering in his apartment ...[Michnik]...thought that at least the Party officials were warm in their* ***dachas****. Then he met the wife of the former Polish premier at a friend's wedding. She was shivering, 'Why are you so cold?', he asked. She said, 'My husband is sitting at home wearing the fur hat given to him by Kosygin'. The country's heaters were on a 'permanent strike'.*[12]

A second element was the way in which the growing crisis of the 1980s intensified the short term contradictions of the bloc. One aspect of this was the growing debt burden which was built up as attempts were made to draw on Western capital to provide the means of rescue from falling rates of growth. This proved unsuccessful and by the late 1980s the bloc had some of the highest rates of capital accumulation in the world but negative or low rates of profit and growth. The result was that the chickens very quickly came home to roost. In particular the debt burden began to become critical. Table 3 sets out its basic dimensions.

TABLE 3
THE GROWTH OF NET DEBT IN EASTERN EUROPE[13]
$ billions

	1985	*1986*	*1987*	*1988*	*1989*	*1990*
Bulgaria	*1.6*	*3.6*	*5.1*	*6.1*	*8.0*	*9.8*
Czecho-slovakia	*3.6*	*4.3*	*5.1*	*5.6*	*5.7*	*6.3*
Hungary	*11.5*	*14.7*	*18.1*	*18.2*	*19.4*	*20.3*
Poland	*28.2*	*31.9*	*35.8*	*34.1*	*37.5*	*41.8*
Romania	*6.5*	*6.3*	*5.1*	*2.0*	*-1.3*	*1.3*
USSR	*15.8*	*16.6*	*25.1*	*27.7*	*39.3*	*43.4*
Total	*67.3*	*77.5*	*94.3*	*93.8*	*108.9*	*122.9*

Subsequently it became increasingly difficult to penetrate Western markets to generate the foreign exchange needed to maintain the debt burden and to take advantage of the growth that did exist in the world economy. In the case of Poland, for example, between 1978 and 1989 exports to the West rose by only 19 percent while world trade as a whole expanded by 60 percent and exports in Western Europe by 50 percent.[14] The paradoxical result was that as a growing recognition dawned of the importance of integration with the world economy what was taking place in practice was a forced and unwanted inward retreat in the pattern of trade of these countries. This is reflected in Table 4. Although some conservatives took satisfaction in this in the mid-1980s they were a minority and for reformers the need to halt the trend only became more evident.

TABLE 4
THE CHANGING REGIONAL STRUCTURE OF EASTERN EUROPEAN TRADE IN THE 1980S CRISIS[15]

	1980	1985	1988
Exports to			
Eastern Europe	*42.1*	*46.8*	*49.0*
Developed Countries	*32.0*	*25.6*	*21.9*
Developing World	*13.8*	*13.2*	*14.3*
Other 'Socialist'	*12.1*	*14.4*	*14.8*
Imports from			
Eastern Europe	*42.9*	*47.6*	*54.0*
Developed Countries	*35.4*	*27.8*	*25.1*
Developing World	*11.5*	*11.0*	*8.2*
Other 'Socialist'	*10.2*	*13.6*	*12.7*

The third element was that the ruling class itself began to adjust its social position before 1989 (and especially in Poland and Hungary) so as to place one foot in the new emerging order. In the case of Hungary the process was trenchantly observed by the sociologist Elemer Hankiss:

> *it is not unusual today [1988] to meet a family belonging to the Kadariste oligarchy where the father is a high ranking party or state official, the daughter owns a town centre clothes shop, the eldest son represents a Western company in Hungary, the son in law is the chairman of a recently created company or a Western bank and a grandmother owns a family hotel on the edge of Lake Balaton.*[16]

For Hankiss what was happening was the 'migration of the bureaucracy' into new positions of power. We would rather describe this as a partial shift in the social base of the ruling class, but its political implications were the same either way. Even before 1989 there was already a movement towards a new system which prepared the way for the rapid acceptance of change under popular pressure in 1989.

This is not to say that the final destination was clearly understood. Instead Hankiss calls the process only 'semi-conscious'. Most people's assumption was that moderate levels of reorganisation would be capable of producing the desired result and in some states reorganisation could probably be avoided completely. Early in the process of restructuring in the Soviet Union, Gorbachev's then adviser Abel Aganbegyan was promising that with perestroika 'the Soviet national income by 2000 would closely approach that of the United

States'.[17] But once embarked on this road, the pre-1989 subterranean social and ideological shift of the base of the ruling class strengthened its ability to make its eventual jump from the middle of 1989 as pressure mounted. At the start of that year the then Hungarian Communist Party reformer Imre Pozsgay expressed the situation in the following terms,

> *I think that we have got to a river, a very steep and very quick river, that you can only cross by stepping from one stone to another and you need a certain speed, because if you stop on one stone you will lose your balance and fall into the river. And this is the state of affairs in Hungary. But a quick run through the river might be successful.*[18]

In the event the run was even quicker than Pozsgay imagined, but the analogy is a useful one. What happened is that the ruling class had already achieved enough momentum so that, when it realised that it could not turn back and there was safe ground on the other side, it could continue its run across the stones.

What caused them to speed up their run was the pressure from below that erupted in the autumn of 1989. The history of the Eastern European societies had been punctuated by major and minor revolts from below. Now, in the autumn of 1989, as the grip of the ruling groups weakened, people began to first vote with their feet by trying to migrate from East Germany and then, as confidence grew, to demonstrate, protest and strike. The whole process began spilling over national borders, as it had done before in the great revolutionary turning points in the history of capitalism.

Faced with this situation the ruling groups within the ruling class wobbled visibly. Some looked to repression, others to compromise and their indecision—sometimes forced, sometimes deliberate, paralysed the police and the army in the face of the swelling clamour for change. The scale of the protests and the obvious weakness of the state machine stiffened the resolve of those at the top looking for compromise and change. The ruling class as a whole began to run to keep up with the pressure from below.

Once again it was Hankiss who captured the essence of the situation. In the midst of the turmoil of the autumn of 1989 he wrote an article posing the question, 'Why did they not shoot?'. Earlier that year in China the rulers had suppressed a popular revolt by force, but this had not happened in Eastern Europe. Hankiss's answer remains at the core of any understanding of the transition,

> *A section of the elite in power recognised that it could quite easily, and without losing anything, transform its authority from the bureaucratic party where it was founded on compulsion into a political and economic power capable of functioning in a new system which integrates both the market economy and democracy. The party-state could then sink peacefully beneath the waves of history.*[19]

In the light of our own insistence that we are dealing with a ruling class we might prefer a slightly different terminology but it would be hard to better this as a contemporaneous insight into what was at stake in 1989. And, as we shall see later, by one of those ironical tricks that history often plays, Hankiss was to come to embody a part of the process he was describing.

Eastern Europe and the general crisis of the weak state economies

Most accounts of the transition in eastern Europe have been written as if the process of crisis there is specific to the area—a part of the collapse of some supposed 'socialist' mode of production. There are, of course, specific elements in any situation but in the case of eastern Europe the specific problems of its crisis serve more to differentiate what has happened quantitatively rather than qualitatively from the crisis that hit much of the world economy in the 1980s. In fact unless an attempt is made to understand the tendencies of development in the world economy at large and the particular way in which problems have arisen in the recent past it becomes impossible to understand the particular manifestations of crisis in eastern Europe.

Put at its crudest, any long run analysis of the development of the world economy shows two basic tendencies. One has been towards integration as trade and flows of capital and labour have tied the production process closer together on a world scale. The result has been the increasing multinationalisation or globalisation of the world economy. The second tendency has been towards an extension of state control which has varied in degree but been a universal long run tendency in world capitalism. Charting the scale of this is difficult because state ownership, regulation and control cannot easily be reduced to a common denominator and measured. But Table 5 shows one measure of this tendency—government expenditure growth which reflects both the way that the state produces itself and the way it draws in and redirects resources from the 'private sector'.

TABLE 5
GOVERNMENT EXPENDITURE AS A PERCENTAGE OF GDP AT CURRENT PRICES 1880-1986[20]

	1880*	1913	1929	1938	1950	1973	1986
USA	n.a.	8.0	10.0	19.8	21.4	30.7	37.1
UK	9.9	13.3	23.8	28.8	34.2	41.5	45.9
Germany	10.0	17.7	30.6	42.4	30.4	41.2	47.8
France	11.2	8.9	12.4	23.2	27.4	38.8	53.2
Holland	n.a.	8.2	11.2	21.7	26.8	49.1	58.0
Japan	9.0	14.2	18.8	30.3	19.8	22.9	35.5
Average	n.a.	11.7	17.8	27.7	26.7	37.4	46.3

** figure for Germany for 1881 and Japan for 1885*

Depending on their form these two tendencies can contradict or complement one another and their precise relationship and balance have varied in the past in important ways.[21] Most recently the first impact of the growing difficulties in the world economy in the 1970s was to increase the level of state action especially, but not exclusively as is evident in Table 5, in the weaker parts of the world economy.

The pattern that emerged presented uncomfortable problems for those who wanted to draw a sharp distinction between capital and the state and to argue that state domination, as in Eastern Europe, in some way implied the negation of capitalism. Comparing the level of state control is notoriously difficult because competing measures give competing results. But on any measure it is certainly true that Eastern Europe has experienced some of the highest measures of *peacetime* state control anywhere in the world economy. What is often insufficiently appreciated, however, is that if we put all the world's economies on a scale of state control measuring from 0 percent to 100 percent then virtually all the economies would cluster in the middle to third quarter. Table 6, for example, shows one measure of state control in Eastern Europe in terms of the share of central government expenditure in output (net material product). The unwary should be warned that Table 6 cannot simply be compared with Table 5 as a measure of state control. But the tables well illustrate our main point which is that the gaps between the two blocs have frequently been overstated because of an under-appreciation of the role of the state in the advanced West and an overestimation of its role in the former Eastern bloc.

TABLE 6
CENTRAL GOVERNMENT EXPENDITURES IN EASTERN EUROPE AND THE USSR AS A PERCENT OF OUTPUT[22]

	1982	*1985*	*1989*
Bulgaria	*54.7*	*55.2*	*61.9*
Czechoslovakia	*67.0*	*69.8*	*76.6*
Hungary	*61.2*	*61.1*	*59.0*
Poland	*52.2*	*48.2*	*48.1*
USSR	*49.3*	*49.8*	*51.4*

Under the impact of crisis in the world economy that gap has frequently diminished still further. Take the way in which the crisis at the turn of the 1980s affected Latin America. In Peru there was an increase of public expenditure from 24 percent to 60 percent of GDP from 1970 to 1982; in Mexico the increase was from 22 percent to 46 percent in the same period; in Argentina and Venezuela by 1980 public expenditure had risen to more than half of GDP and so on.[23]

With the expansion of state control also came an intensification in the West of features normally associated with the Eastern European system. Consider, for example, a set of economies characterised by

> *massive centralisation of decisions on the mobilisation and use of resources, on pricing, investments, and on the relationship between management and labour ... Public agencies and enterprises ... hosts to inefficiency, waste and vested interests.*

Eastern Europe? No. This is a World Bank Vice-President for Latin America writing on the region in 1989.[24] Of course, he was writing to highlight what the World Bank believes needs changing but even allowing for an element of exaggeration the question remains of whether we are really dealing with qualitatively different forms to those which existed in Eastern Europe. And exactly the same question must be posed about the nature of the crisis. As the general difficulties of the world economy continued and the build up of state measures grew, often financed by foreign debt, the differential impact of the crisis began to increasingly expose some of the weaknesses of state driven attempts at salvation.

Overall the crisis caused the whole rate of expansion in the world economy to slow (subject to the ups and downs of the economic cycle). But the sharpest impact was perhaps felt in terms of a growing differentiation of performance. If the world economy on average grew more slowly, its weakest and most exposed parts grew not at all or fell back. In the 1960s only 15 countries had experienced such economic difficulties that over the decade their per capita income fell. In the

1970s the figure was 27, and 62 in the 1980s. Table 7 shows what this meant if we look not at states but the shares of the world's population experiencing the problems of the world economy.

TABLE 7
PROPORTION OF THE WORLD POPULATION LIVING IN STATES BY TYPE OF ECONOMIC PERFORMANCE[25]

	percentage of world population living			
	in advanced states	in states closing gap	in states falling behind relatively	in states with falling output per head
1960s	28.5	25.2	43.3	3.0
1980s	22.6	2.6	51.1	23.7

The result of this was the development of external pressures on the weaker countries to restructure and these were given shape by institutions like the IMF and the World Bank as well as in the foreign policies of advanced capitalist states. These policies found uneven acceptance within many of the ruling classes and the result was the implementation of a whole series of IMF backed austerity programmes in Latin America, Africa and Asia. These programmes were direct forerunners of what is now being constructed in eastern Europe:

> *a typical programme in Latin America embodies a variety of policies—devaluation, limits on banking credit and public borrowing, removal of price subsidies, reduction of tariffs and elimination of some import controls, encouragement of foreign investment, and financial resistance to nominal wage increases.*[26]

The logic underlying these programmes has been to restore the rate of profit and the ability of these countries to repay their debt. The general impact on inflation before 1981 was limited, although policy has been more successful since then. Austerity programmes have also had a variable impact on growth, weakening it in some cases but not in others. Their two unambiguous achievements have been 'improvements in balance of payments' and 'the strongest and most consistent effect of Fund programmes: absolute and relative reductions in [the] labour force share of income'.[27] What this means is that such austerity programmes have been designed to achieve particular ends at the cost of growing poverty on a scale that even the IMF and World Bank economists have not been able to ignore.[28]

What is now happening in eastern Europe is a particular development of this whole logic of crisis and austerity response. Indeed in the IMF and World Bank community it is often the same people who are constructing programmes for eastern Europe who in the mid and late 1980s cut their teeth on Latin America. The most notorious example of this has been Jeffrey Sachs who has been called 'the Indiana Jones of economics'.[29] Sachs was the architect of the 'Bolivian miracle' who became an adviser to Solidarity and the Solidarity government and who is now working on one of the many reform programmes for the USSR.

It is therefore instructive to see what happened in Bolivia itself and how this relates to the Latin Americanisation of Poland and eastern Europe more generally.

The Bolivian model and the logic of austerity

Landlocked Bolivia with a population of only 6.4 million is the poorest Latin American country. But in the late 1980s it replaced Chile as the model testing ground for the 'free market'.[30] Bolivia's past history had been built around the mining of silver, antimony, copper, wolfram and especially tin. Despite its small size and general backwardness the development of mining in Bolivia welded together a labour force of miners and peasants partly engaged in both mining and agriculture who in 1952 helped to create the basis of one of the three great revolutions of modern Latin American history alongside those of Mexico and Cuba.[31] Despite its failure this revolution left Bolivia with one of the strongest trade union organisations in Latin America, the Central Obrera Boliviania, as well as helping to consolidate a tradition of state capitalism that meant that by 1985 *some 70 percent of the economy was in state hands*. Bolivia, however, remained trapped in its backwardness and a prisoner of tendencies in the world economy despite a series of swings from left to right in the decades after the 1952 revolution.

For the Bolivian economy the growing crisis in the world economy in the first half of the 1980s culminated in 1985 when the tin market crashed and hyperinflation hit 25,000 percent. Backed by the IMF, a section of the ruling class seized the opportunity to impose a vicious austerity package designed by Jeffrey Sachs. The core of this programme was financial discipline, massive state cutbacks and the abandonment of much of the regulatory role of the state.

Sachs was disconcertingly frank about what this strategy would achieve: 'What you have is a miserable, poor economy with hyperinflation, if you are brave, if you are gutsy, if you do everything right, you will end up with a miserable, poor economy with stable prices'.[32] In the long run, however, he insisted that such a strategy would be the basis for sustained growth. This is what the IMF, Sachs and the World Bank claim has now been achieved and it has been these claims that have helped to sustain the credentials of Sachs and his acolytes as gurus of Poland's market strategy and now more widely that of the former Soviet Union and eastern Europe. It is important, therefore, to understand what has really happened in Bolivia.

As an anti-inflationary strategy Sachs' plan was spectacularly successful. By 1987 inflation had come down to 15 percent and it was still only 18 percent in 1990—an outstanding record in Latin American terms. But Sachs had been rather immodest in his prediction, for what the plan had achieved was not 'a miserable, poor economy with stable prices' but 'a miserably poorer economy with almost stable prices'. It is true that once the austerity programme was introduced there was some growth in the economy in the late 1980s but the standard of living had been falling before 1985 and on one estimate it fell a further 60 percent in 1985.[33] Thus for all of the propaganda of success the key issue for ordinary Bolivians would be when their standard of living would return to 1978 levels. On the basis of the growth rates after 1985 the answer would appear to be that it will take up to 40 years! Moreover, much of the growth that was achieved after 1985 has been based on something that Sachs did not anticipate—cocaine. Coca production is now estimated to directly employ 75,000 people and creates some 10 percent of Bolivian GNP, providing between a third and a half of its export earnings—a testament to the virtues of profit and the logic of the free market.

Prior to 1985, Bolivian state policy had been directed towards subsidised development of modern sectors and exports. As in Chile in the 1970s, the removal of protection and wholesale liberalisation combined with tight financial discipline and a reduction in state expenditure all led to a sharp restructuring of the economy in line with the logic of the world market. Much of the small industrial sector, although relatively modern in Latin American terms, could not survive. But agriculture also suffered because imports at world market prices frequently undercut peasant production. Mining also contracted as world market prices remained low.

The economy therefore experienced not only a fall in output per head but a degree of deindustrialisation leading to a distorted swing to the primary sector and services. The losers in this were the core modern sectors. But the peasants also began to increasingly turn to coca production and the continued development of the drugs trade was also assisted by the financial liberalisation which made it easier to hide drug profits. At the same time the urban population had to turn more and more to the informal sector which rapidly increased in size, sucking in not only men but large numbers of women and children desperate to survive by small scale production and trade.

The strategists had promised a private enterprise boom and saw the growth of the informal sector as evidence of the development of entrepreneurial virtues. To Sachs it was a demonstration of what could happen in Poland and eastern Europe. If 'the peasant Indians in the Bolivian market' could operate this way what was to stop the 'cultured Poles' rapidly learning the logic of the market. This is, of course, a fairy tale. Even if it were true that the informal sector was a spawning ground for entrepreneurship and capital accumulation it would take decades for it to form the basis of anything substantial. In reality the standard of living in the informal sector fell too as the austerity programme hit, worsening the prospects of any serious capital accumulation there. The other part of the promised free enterprise boom was to come through privatisation. The objective was to sell off the 158 state companies to the private sector both nationally and internationally. But nothing has materialised. In fact by the middle of 1991 not a single one of these companies had been fully privatised.

This is the underside of the Bolivian miracle that is omitted from the glossy publicity. But the problems are not hard to find, and they raise an obvious question—if this is the cost of moving from one state of miserable poverty to another, what is the point? Are we not looking at a world where market zealots are imposing their ideas, blind to the reality of what is happening?

From the point of view of the economists themselves there is a considerable truth in this type of judgment. Market economic theory has a compelling simplicity which, if the falseness and restricted nature of its assumptions are ignored, is incapable of refutation because every practical refutation is explained away by the fact that some evil force—the state, monopoly, the left—is preventing the market from working as it should. For Sachs and his supporters, politics and economics are separate spheres in which there is always a danger that the political sphere will invade the economic one making 'smooth, professional solutions to problems...impossible'.[34] The remedy for this then becomes that of giving an even greater role to the market.

Market economists become like those Victorian doctors who believed in bleeding their patients with leeches and who, when the patient stubbornly refused to get better, drew the conclusion that even more bleeding was necessary. And, of course, those patients who had confidence in their doctors accepted the 'cure' even to their dying breaths. It was perhaps Keynes who best captured the 'irrational rationality' of the market theorists when he noted of a work by Friedrich Hayek, the grandfather of post Second World War free market economics, that it was an example 'of how, starting with a mistake, a remorseless logician can end up in Bedlam'.

But this is only a partial explanation. The market is such a powerful weapon not only because of its ideological content but because behind this other objectives are being secured which are partially recognised by some theorists but at a tangent to their general discussions, just as the real world of capitalism is at a tangent to their models.

What has been at stake in Bolivia has been a restoration of economic and political order. The benefits and gains have been made by those who try to control world capitalism and its Bolivian branch. The losses have been experienced by someone else—some sections of the ruling class in Bolivia have certainly suffered but in general it has been the working class and the peasantry that have been made to pay the price of order.

The first of these objectives is to discipline weak states financially and politically in the interests of advanced capitalism. What successful austerity programmes achieve in the first instance is confidence in the world financial community—'the IMF seal of approval'. This denotes that economies are being restructured so as to maintain their debt repayments through internal financial discipline and the turning round of balance of trade deficits. This is both an economic and a political task.

The political task is the most fundamental in as much as it is necessary to defeat those internal forces that might try to buck the interests of the world's financial markets. Once these have been brought into line it may then be possible for Western banks and states to be more generous in economic concessions, confident that advantage will not be taken of such 'generosity'. In addition such generosity, even though there is no chance of it being generalised, can help model economies (Bolivia, Poland) to succeed as an example for others to follow. Occasionally such programmes can have unintended consequences for advanced capital, as the expansion of cocaine in Bolivia shows. But even here it is possible to turn such consequences to advantage and to strengthen international discipline as the United States has done by effectively militarising the drugs war in this area of Latin America.

The second of these objectives relates particularly to the internal issue of state authority. The crises that preceded the introduction of IMF backed shock programmes have usually involved social disintegration. This has partly been reflected in the way that states have proved incapable of arbitrating between the demands of different groups and imposing order. The clearest expression of this is inflation being let rip in an attempt to satisfy everyone and, of course, no one. To eliminate this the internal authority of the state has to be recreated and imposed on the competing factions. This is how a Bolivian Finance Minister put it: 'rather than a strictly economic programme, the New Economic Policy is a political plan... The first political task consists of restoring the state's authority over society at large'.[35]

The third objective flows specifically from the second, for while the spiralling competition of warring groups in general is a threat, the underlying internal problem tends to be that of bringing the organised working class as a whole under control. Restructuring achieves this politically by forcing or winning working class leaderships over to the acceptance of austerity programmes and socially through the way that these programmes cut into the bases of the organised working class through industrial restructuring and unemployment. If the social process is sufficiently sharp this itself can be sufficient to achieve acquiescence even without the formal complicity of the old working class leadership. This is substantially what happened in Bolivia, where the combined effect of crisis and austerity ripped apart much of the tin industry, leading to the dismissal of 80 percent of its 75,000 workforce and so destroying one of the core groups of the COB.

The seductive appeal of the market model

> *It is not that we are unwilling to put our own house in order. It is that we want to keep our house and not let it go up in flames.*
> Dominican Republic Planning Minister in the early 1980s after riots induced by IMF austerity plans.[36]

> *The degree of consensus in eastern Europe in favour of establishing a Western style market economy exceeds the levels of consensus found in Latin America and other parts of the developing world.*
> David Lipton and Jeffrey Sachs, Solidarity's American Economic Advisers.[37]

As the Western advisers began to flood into eastern Europe they were genuinely astonished at the lack of resistance to their ideas from people whom they had imagined to be Marxists. Everywhere it seemed that the more right wing the idea the more approval with which it was met. This consensus had and has two aspects—one is suggested by the planning minister of the Dominican Republic—there was little or no resistance from below in eastern Europe which was formulated either as resistance to the Stalinism of old or to the new style market reforms. This meant that it was easier for the ruling class to swing behind the market because it had only to worry about the diminishing opposition of its weaker and more bureaucratic sections. Unlike some Latin American countries there was less need to worry so much about the whole house going up in flames because of resistance from below.

The second aspect has been the widespread seduction of the larger part of the ruling class and most of the opposition by the market, as Lipton and Sachs suggest. The nature of this ideological volte face—the shift from a belief in the efficacy of the state to that of the market—can be traced especially sharply in the influential work of the Hungarian economist Janos Kornai. Kornai has deliberately avoided direct entanglement with the old or new regimes in Hungary and eastern Europe but his work has provided much of the theoretical structure for orthodox accounts in both East and West of the way the old economies of Eastern Europe functioned and is now at the heart of discussions of the most brutal forms of 'shock therapy'.[38] Kornai originally tried to stand between what he once called holding 'a belief in the almightiness of planning' and 'trusting the perfection of the market'. So far as the former was concerned Kornai emphasised that in Eastern Europe enterprises necessarily performed badly because they had 'soft budget constraints'—essentially there was no fear of bankruptcy to discipline and encourage managers. This inefficiency was further accentuated by 'the shortage economy', 'a social relationship in which the buyer is at the mercy of the seller—and feels himself to be so'.[39] But at the same time Kornai also saw himself as a critic of the market and did indeed have penetrating insights into its tendency to unemployment and the unreality of theories that the market could produce balance and equilibrium.

In the light of this it might have been thought that Kornai was ideally placed intellectually to be the theorist of some middle way of a social democratic kind. Yet by the early 1990s even Alec Nove could condemn him as a supporter of 'capitalism with an inhuman face'. 'It is probably inevitable', wrote Kornai, 'that history moves not in a straight line, but like a pendulum...it is now time to take great steps in the direction of a minimal state'.[40]

The resonance of the phrase 'minimal state' is clearly intended by Kornai who has been a frequent visitor to the West. It reflects his own disillusion with previous attempts to reform the Eastern European economies and particularly that of Hungary where all that happened was (as he saw it) a shift from 'direct bureaucratic regulation' to 'indirect bureaucratic regulation', '20 years of muddling through with...partial changes'. Kornai now argues that there is no way in which the state can be made efficient and while this does not mean that mass privatisation could be undertaken tomorrow (quite the contrary, the continuing inefficiency of the state sector prevents this) it does mean that 'it is time to abandon hope that the budget constraint can be hardened'. State bureaucratic inefficiency is inevitable, 'there are certain problems that have no solution, one of them being the efficient operation of a large state owned sector'. As a result 'the basic idea of market socialism simply fizzled out'. For Kornai:

> *bureaucratic subordination is as much the* ***spontaneous*** *effect and natural mode of state property's existence as market co-ordination is of private property. This is no longer a debating point, but simply a* ***fact*** *that must be accepted.*[41]

Since our interest is to understand the evolution of Kornai's thinking as perhaps the single most influential eastern European economist we will simply note our view that what Kornai asserts as 'fact' is far from that and both aspects of this statement are wrong. What is more interesting is how this argument simply echoes the conventional wisdom of the right. Its logic, however, has led Kornai to be a major influence on the 'shock therapy' imposed on Poland and to formulate plans for a similar dose of medicine in Hungary. The former Solidarity's two American economic advisers note that their conclusions 'run parallel to those of Janos Kornai...We have benefited enormously from detailed discussions with Professor Kornai' and Kornai has returned the compliment—'the policy proposals David Lipton and Jeffrey Sachs advance...will get no criticism here. Sachs and I discussed these issues several times, and we are in complete agreement on all basic principles'.[42]

So far as Hungary is concerned Kornai has agreed in support of his proposals that the Hungarian population is like a patient who in desperation is finally ready to risk an operation.

> *I feel that the Hungarian population is approaching a point where it cannot tolerate further suffering...I believe they are ready to take the risks of a radical operation. And for all the temporary trauma troubles it would cause, the operation at least holds out the promise of genuine order and calm.*[43]

What we see here is the comfortable ideology of the 'doctor's mandate'. Not only does the doctor not feel the pain but he deliberately blinds himself to what is at stake. For even if the operation is a success it can hardly lead to 'genuine order and calm', for that is not the way of the market. Moreover in the process of trying to achieve this illusory state of good health the suffering is likely to increase. But once arguments are developed in this way it is but a short step to blaming the patient for his lack of effort to assist any recovery. Thus for Kornai, 'if someone becomes unemployed, his first duty is to help himself'. Of course government assistance can help the unemployed to help themselves but in a phrase redolent with 19th century assumptions

Kornai advises that 'a complete demoralisation of the able bodied and healthy unemployed' should be avoided through too much indiscriminate aid.[44]

For those who imagined that what existed in Eastern Europe was a non-capitalist society the alacrity with which such arguments have been taken up has come as an enormous shock. How has it come to be that the market exercises such a powerful sway on the minds of reformers in eastern Europe? The most obvious explanation is that the West has had the power to enforce its ideological vision in Eastern Europe on such a scale that it has simply marginalised any alternative account from the Western or Eastern left who themselves have been disoriented by the last decade and even more by the rapidity of collapse in Eastern Europe.

In fact the Western left, although hampered by confusion in its analysis of the nature of Eastern Europe, did not have a bad record in supporting dissent under the old regime.[45] No doubt more could and should have been done but real support on the basis of limited resources was forthcoming whereas the Western ruling classes, for all their rhetoric, preferred deals with the existing ruling classes of Eastern Europe. The notorious romance with the Ceausescu regime, despite its long history of internal repression, because it was apparently a thorn in the Soviet side was only the most visible and repulsive expression of this. But when the tactics of the Western states changed to encouraging a market transition their power swamped any past history of commitment except amongst a small honourable minority of socialist oppositionists.

The base of the advanced West's power here lay in the reality of its superior economic performance to that of Eastern Europe in the recent past. This superiority was attributed to the magic of the market in order to help sell it to the reformers in the East. 'Today leaders around the world are turning to market forces to meet the needs of their peoples... the jury is no longer out. History has decided', George Bush has insisted on a number of occasions.[46] History, of course, demonstrates nothing of the sort. During the 1980s the importance of the state to Western capitalism has not generally diminished despite the claims of the right. This has been especially so in the United States where state intervention has kept crucial parts of the economy going. But such realities have not been allowed to disturb the mythologies of the marketeers. Their ideas, given the added authority of national governments, the IMF, the World Bank and the OECD and backed by assistance funds, have appeared to most commentators in eastern Europe to contain the secret of the success.

But it is not enough to simply look to the power of the West to explain the attraction of these ideas. Two aspects of the ideological pattern in Eastern Europe and the former USSR predisposed their opinion makers and reformers, and the larger part of the opposition, to accept market economics as an explanation of their past failures and a mechanism of future successes. The first has been the widespread illusion that what has determined the way in which the Eastern European societies have developed has been a monstrous ideological imposition in the form of 'socialism'. So long as these economies seemed to work, 'socialism' was not seen as a problem. Once they faltered, the insistence that 'socialism' had been at the root of their successes was turned on its head and 'socialism' became the cause of their difficulties.

What socialism meant here was simply *state control,* but when economic reformers tried to vary the degree of state control and still failed to turn these economies around a degree of disillusion set in. The lurch to the market was under way. In fact, as with the stress on the market in the West, this whole conception was at a tangent to the real forces determining development in both parts of the advanced world. The problem was the same in both instances—a failure to understand the role of the state in capitalist competition, not only in indirectly supporting this competition but also directly acting as a state capitalist producer and competitor itself. The result of this failure has been a pre-disposition towards the market in both East and West that failed to appreciate the way in which expanded state action had emerged as a pragmatic response to past competitive pressures and structural constraints.

The consequence has been ideological programmes of rolling back the state which have floundered pragmatically wherever they have come up against the same constraints and pressures or new ones. This was the experience of Thatcherism and Reaganism in the 1980s and it is already evident that it will be the experience of eastern Europe in the 1990s. The fundamental reason is that, irrespective of the political party in power, so long as eastern Europe remains a weaker part of the world economy it will require a large state sector. It is possible to reduce its size, but it can only be abandoned at the expense of enormous de-industrialisation as state backed industries go under.

There is a second and more deeply rooted reason. This lies in the nature of the ideological structures that dominated Eastern Europe under Stalinism. Ideologies work in complex ways. At a casual glance, for example, Christianity, with its frequent positive comments on poverty, might be taken as an ideology of revolt. That indeed is how it began. But for the larger part of its history it has been an ideology of power, a means through which ruling classes have expressed their domination and articulated their interests and policies. The real content of Christianity was determined by the way that religious thinking developed as a total set of ideas with particular emphases and stress which marginalised and neutralised its origins. The relationship between class and ideology in

Eastern Europe has been the same. Although some phrases and concepts were retained from its origins in 1917 these were 'iconised'—workers were turned into what one Soviet writer has called 'poster heroes' while their real interests were trampled underfoot.

Behind this the inner content of socialist ideas that had been there in 1917 were emasculated, their core ripped out and replaced with a new core whose values were those more associated with the modernising conservatisms of the West. Many orthodox commentators, trapped in the concepts of the Cold War, were incapable of recognising this because they looked only to the outer shell, at the posters and icons, the set phrases and invocations. But without an understanding of the fundamentally conservative character of ideas in eastern Europe it is impossible to understand the past or the present ease with which it has been possible to sell the market idea.

The destruction of the revolution in the Soviet Union in the 1920s and 1930s also led to the death of the ideas that had informed early Bolshevik thinking.[47] But this did not simply leave an ideological vacuum or some confused and incoherent mix as some would have it. Instead a new and coherent ideology emerged which had two main components. At the most obvious and formal level Stalinism became a particular ideology of state capitalist development, of competitive modernisation stressing the need to remould society to meet the objectives of catching up and overtaking the West.[48] But at a deeper and more informal level this 'bourgeois' ideology was complimented by the proliferation of ideas and measures which expressed and reinforced the real class relations dominating the USSR and Eastern Europe. These attitudes affected every aspect of life, from an emphasis on the acquisition of material things (including money), to attitudes to women where, although they were expected to work to help the development effort, they were encouraged to adopt traditional feminine images, to attitudes to sex where a prudishness developed that would warm the heart of a good Catholic (and no doubt did comfort the future Pope in Poland), to a celebration of the virtues of the nuclear family and so on. The suspicion and repression of 'gays' as 'diseased' threats to the family and social values was just one of the better known extreme examples of the fundamental conservatism of the underlying social values. The extent to which this small minded thinking permeated the whole social ethos can be seen in any examination of the structures of thought about everyday life as expressed say in popular literature or simply a discussion with most Eastern Europeans.[49]

Its most important expression, however, was a genuine hostility towards the real working class which resembles nothing so much as the class prejudices that George Orwell describes as being instilled into the middle class English child in the early 20th century. The working classes were stupid, coarse, crude, violent, '... it is summed up in four frightful words which people nowadays are chary of uttering, but which were banded about quite freely in my childhood. The words were: *the lower classes smell*'.[50] Anyone familiar with the general attitudes of intellectuals and administrators in Eastern Europe to the working class will recognise the affinity of their views to those Orwell describes. It is a reaction that is often returned in kind by the workers. Consider again the resonance of the class prejudice in Kornai's comment about the need to avoid 'a complete demoralisation of the able-bodied and healthy unemployed'. Now listen to the Soviet reformer Nikolai Shmelev oozing the same attitudes and arguing that 'the threat of losing your job is an excellent medicine against idleness, drunkenness and irresponsibility'.[51] What we see here is not merely a reform programme based upon the abstract principles of the market but one built upon the gut principles of class—where the class at the top is a conservative force concerned to maintain its real power and privilege and to make someone else pay the price of reform.

Perhaps the most striking demonstration of the truth of this argument lies in the way that the mass Communist Party memberships in some eastern European countries have swung their electoral and political support to the new right wing parties. Unless we postulate an opportunism on an enormous scale the only explanation can be that once the need to pay homage to the old icons had disappeared these party members swung to their natural political homes. In the case of the former GDR, for example, it has been estimated that two thirds of the former SED membership—the old East German Communist Party—voted for the right wing Christian Democrats after the Berlin Wall fell.[52] No less tellingly in Yugoslavia and Romania we have the wholesale adoption of traditional nationalist programmes by wide sections of former and current 'communists'.

In these terms the appeal of the market is that it appears to allow people to get their 'just deserts' and coarse, feckless, alcoholic workers can be brought into line. The tragedy is that on the left those who have not shared these assumptions and had fought against such attitudes in the past have now compounded the problem by their own view that the only choice was between Stalinist planning and the market.

The result has been a process of transition which is not creating the basis for overcoming the legacy of backwardness with which Stalinism could not deal. Instead these economies are being restructured to fit in more closely with the world economy, thus allowing the ruling class to perform its 'great escape trick' while throwing the costs of the transition and crisis onto the working class. The people who were the real victims of the old order are now also the real victims of the new.

Bitter realities—the east German example

The former economy of East Germany has collapsed, it has experienced what one group of economists has called 'a depression... virtually without historic precedent'.[53] The reason for the collapse is simple. After unification the economy was opened to the full blast of competition from the most powerful economy in Europe. Unprotected by tariffs or an ability to manipulate the value of its currency, the usual weapons used by capitalist states, the economy was forced to sink or swim. It promptly sank.

The underlying reason was that east German productivity levels, although the highest in eastern Europe and high in world terms, were still low compared to the advanced economies that it now had to compete with. Here the logic of the market is clear. If you are less profitable, you go under. It does not matter whether you are 10 percent, 50 percent or 90 percent less efficient, your immediate competitors will still force you under. The alternative to this logic was a massive investment programme to renovate the old economies of East Germany and Eastern Europe and to bring them up to world standards. But the costs of such a programme would hardly make it attractive to Western capital. Nor could capital in the West be expected to look with favour upon the encouragement of a new group of direct competitors. Such a transition from Stalinism could only have been based upon a different kind of logic which contested the dynamics of the world economy. But to do this would mean to challenge the real social basis of power both East and West. Since that challenge has not been forthcoming it has been the logic of the world market that has set the form of the transition. What we have seen in east Germany has been a microcosm of the way in which this logic operates.

In fact subsequently published East German data have allowed economists to measure much more precisely the real costs of East German industry and its ability to compete at the exchange rate fixed for the mark. On this basis only 8 percent of the former East German industry was viable in direct competition with the West. The sectors with the lowest relative costs (though still excessive) were energy, metallurgy and glass—those with the highest costs were electronics, chemicals and food. Left to its own devices, therefore, the market would destroy large swathes of the more advanced industries of East Germany and integrate it into the German and world economies as a depressed, less advanced area rather than upgrading its production in the short or medium term to West German levels.

The same study also estimated that to make the leading 88 *least bad* industrial units viable (the Kombinate) would require an effective wage subsidy of 75 percent.[54] This scale of subsidy had not been anticipated. Helmut Kohl, the West German Chancellor, had promised a relatively painless transition. In the event subsidies had to be increased to stop an even more spectacular collapse occurring. By the spring of 1991 it was estimated that 50 percent of the GDP of the five new east German Lander were made up of transfers from the West but such transfers were being spent to directly hold up consumption, not to prop up the industrial core of the old economy.[55]

TABLE 8
SOME ELEMENTS OF THE CONTRACTION OF THE FORMER EAST GERMAN LABOUR FORCE[56]
percentage of current workforce in former East Germany experiencing

	Unemployment	*Short-Time*	*Job Schemes*	*Government Training*
1990				
Jun	*1.6*			
Jul	*3.1*	*7.5*		
Aug	*4.1*	*17.0*		
Sep	*5.0*	*19.4*	*0.05*	
Oct	*6.1*	*19.4*	*0.1*	
Nov	*6.7*	*19.4*	*0.2*	
Dec	*7.3*	*20.4*	*0.2*	
1991				
Jan	*8.6*	*20.9*	*0.4*	
Feb	*8.9*	*22.0*	*0.5*	
Mar	*9.2*	*22.6*	*0.7*	
Apr	*9.5*	*22.9*	*1.0*	*2.4*
May	*9.5*	*22.2*	*1.3*	*2.7*
Jun	*9.5*	*21.4*	*1.7*	*3.1*
Jul	*12.1*	*18.2*	*2.4*	*3.5*
Aug	*12.1*	*16.5*	*3.0*	*3.7*
Sep	*11.7*	*15.2*	*3.6*	*4.0*
Oct	*11.9*	*13.6*	*4.0*	

The result was that during 1991 the cumulative decline in industrial output reached 51 percent and it has continued to fall through 1991. Overall output fell by around a fifth in 1990. As this economic collapse took place the labour force suffered an equally dramatic contraction. The unemployment figures measured only a part of this as the workforce haemorrhaged. Table 8 gives some of the basic data that must be added together to gain a measure of the full impact of the collapse. To these must be added early retirers who were encouraged out of the labour force, women who also left the labour force and migrant workers from outside Europe forced home. A further 580,000 people, the majority of working age, migrated to west Germany between January 1989 and June 1990, the last date official figures were taken. After this migration was an 'internal' matter but estimates suggest it is still significant. In addition there are between 200,000 and 300,000 people commuting from east Germany to jobs in the West. Large numbers are also involved in various forms of state training. If we total each of these elements then it is obvious that somewhere between 40 and 50 percent of jobs in East Germany in 1989 have been lost.[57]

The decline in the standard of living for those eligible for benefits has been moderated because unification has involved the adoption of West German social security legislation. Workers in the rest of eastern Europe have been less fortunate inasmuch as their social security systems have been designed to relate to their existing levels of low pay. But even in the old East Germany the wider costs of such a dramatic collapse could not be moderated. One year after the Berlin Wall fell a notice was pinned to the door of the church in Leipzig which had been at the centre of opposition which simply read, 'With 2,000,000 unemployed we see little cause for celebrating'. A year on, such a notice might have spoken of twice as many.

Bitter realities—the eastern European case

TABLE 9
ACTUAL AND PROJECTED OUTPUT FALLS IN EASTERN EUROPE[58]

	Actual		*Projected*		
	1989	*1990*	*1991 (est)*	*1992*	*1993*
(a) OECD					
Bulgaria	*-0.4*	*-13.6*	*-20.0*	*-6.0*	*-2.0*
Czechoslovakia	*1.0*	*-1.1*	*-12.0*	*-5.0*	*1.0*
Hungary	*-0.2*	*-5.0*	*-7.0*	*1.0*	*2.0*
Poland	*0.5*	*-12.0*	*-8.0*	*-1.0*	*0.0*
Romania	*-7.9*	*-10.5*	*-9.0*	*-4.0*	*-1.0*
USSR	*2.4*	*-4.0*	*-12.5*	*n.a.*	*n.a.*
Total 6	*1.7*	*-4.9*	*-11.9*	*n.a.*	*n.a.*
(b) IMF					
eastern Europe & USSR	*1.9*	*-3.6*	*-10.6*	*-3.9*	*n.a.*
eastern Europe	*-0.7*	*-7.9*	*-12.0*	*2.1*	*n.a.*

The fall in output in the rest of eastern Europe is shown in Table 9. Unlike the East German case, the eastern European states still have control over their own policies. No economy, not even Poland, has been completely opened up to the world market as was East Germany. In this sense the crash elsewhere has not been as great. Nevertheless, during 1991 the optimism of Western agencies like the OECD and the IMF (both of which predicted smaller falls in output at the start of the year) was punctured by the real scale of the collapse. Their projections were sharply revised downwards. The reason is simply that the underlying logic of the collapse is exactly the same as in former East Germany.

Against this logic the theorists of transition have held out hope along the lines that the quicker the transition, the sooner the recovery will start. But the conditions for success are hardly likely to be met in the foreseeable future. Consider, for example, the argument of Lipton and Sachs:

> *In the case of eastern Europe...one can identify the primary engine of growth in the coming years: economic integration with Western Europe... To achieve the full fruits of trade liberalisation, existing trade barriers should be removed. The eastern European countries must negotiate a new association status with access to Western European markets...In the longer term, the European Community should be expanded to allow the actual membership of the East European countries.*[59]

In fact, even if they are right about the primary engine of growth, the most optimistic scenarios of the future development of the world economy hardly suggest that it is likely to experience a sufficiently powerful boom to fuel such an engine.[60] As a result, while there will be much rhetoric about integration and some concessions from the EC, 'the full fruits of liberalisation' in these terms are unlikely to emerge. Moreover the situation is so unstable in eastern Europe that even were such conditions met the chances of derailment would be high. Already the Gulf War and its embargo posed major problems in eastern Europe in the first half of 1991 through increased prices and trade losses. Hungary has been affected by an earthquake. Hanging over the whole of eastern Europe is the threat of conflict which even if it is contained militarily, still threatens to spill over in the form of fleeing refugees as in the Yugoslavian case.

But, of course, such optimistic scenarios are unlikely to need such 'unplanned' developments to disrupt them because they are based on a false logic which obscures the real potential of closer integration into the world market. We can see this if we look at the realities of the changing patterns of trade and flows of capital and labour.

Trade and the logic of comparative disadvantage

Before 1989 the pattern of trade in Eastern Europe reflected the attempt of the ruling classes to sponsor competitive processes of industrialisation. The trade pattern fell into three types. Because production was less developed than that in the advanced West, 'East-West' trade generally took the form of an exchange of raw materials and semi-manufactured goods for manufactured and high technology goods. Trade with the less developed part of the world had a different character. There the more advanced nature of the Eastern bloc did allow a higher export of manufactured goods but because these industrial exports were generally inferior to those available elsewhere in the world market it was necessary to boost this pattern by aid, subsidies, political leverage and a willingness to accept less competitive third world goods in return. The third area of trade, the largest, was within Eastern Europe itself. Here a more complex pattern developed reflecting the uneven levels of development within the bloc. But in general intra-bloc trade took the form of the Eastern European countries importing raw materials and energy from the USSR and exporting their manufactured goods to it. Unlike trade with the West, which was carried out in hard currencies at world market prices, this trade was carried out in eastern bloc currencies at prices which came closer to those of the world market over time but which all had a degree of deliberate insulation from it.

In particular because stronger trade barriers were put up against the world market to protect the process of competitive industrialisation, a double subsidy developed. The Soviet rulers sold their raw materials and oil to Eastern Europe at less than world market prices and accepted in return manufactured goods that were overpriced and poorer in quality than those available to it elsewhere. This trade pattern achieved two things. Economically it encouraged a higher level of industrialisation than would otherwise have occurred and so underpinned the attempt to compete with the West. Politically, the effective subsidy was part of the price the Soviet ruling class paid to hold the Eastern European bloc together in order to achieve its wider political and military objectives.[61]

Since 1989 this pattern has fallen apart. The result of opening up these economies to the world market and carrying out the larger part of trade at world market prices in hard currencies has been a major restructuring of trade which has effectively deindustrialised a significant part of the trade structure. It has also opened up a huge balance of trade deficits as these weak economies struggle to compete on equal terms.

To see how this is taking place it is necessary to look at the change in the total pattern of trade. Once the Soviet ruling class relinquished its hold on eastern Europe there was little incentive for either side to maintain the old trade pattern within the bloc and intra-bloc trade collapsed by 20-30 percent in 1990. This collapse continued through 1991. From January 1991 all intra-bloc trade is supposed to have been carried out in dollars at world market prices and the old Comecon structure through which trade had been organised was wound up. In particular eastern European and Soviet importers of eastern European manufactured goods stopped buying, either because they preferred to go elsewhere or they lacked the hard currencies to support their purchases as the Soviet Union began to charge dollars for exports of raw material and energy, especially oil.

At the same time trade with the less developed world also began to contract as hidden subsidies were removed and the eastern European countries looked for more hard currency payments. The only positive area was in terms of trade with the advanced West. In 1990 all the eastern European countries expanded their exports here with the exception of Romania whose exports fell by 30 percent. Hungary and Poland were especially successful, increasing their exports to the OECD area by 26 and 44 percent with the strongest growth in each case with the European Community.[62]

Western free market proponents have made much of this expansion of exports to the advanced West. Even the United Nations Economic Commission for Europe writes that 'it is tempting to draw attention to the perfect correlation between the progress of reforms in these countries and the strength of their export growth' and that the 'recent export performance suggests that there is room for cautious optimism about the...export prospects'.[63] But such comments obscure the total transformation that is occurring. Trade with the two areas characterised by a higher industrial content has contracted whilst trade with the area with a lower industrial content has expanded. The net effect of this has been three-fold. In the first place the overall level of trade whether measured in value or volume terms has fallen. This is a process that has been accurately characterised as one of trade 'destruction'. Secondly, the eastern European countries are being turned much more into exporters of agricultural goods, raw materials and semi or low level manufactures. Thirdly, the trade balance has sharply deteriorated as these countries must now pay for the larger part of their trade in hard currencies. During the 1980s, when only a part of the trade was in hard currency, it had been possible to more or less balance trade. Now huge annual current account deficits of 7 to 8 billion dollars are expected for the early 1990s which can only be dealt with by more austerity or borrowing.[64]

The prospects for changing this new pattern are far from good. There will no doubt be success stories in eastern Europe but they are unlikely to have much impact on the emerging trade pattern. These economies are being forced to compete by adjusting downwards into areas where there is both substantial world market competition already and considerable barriers to trade. For example 25-30 percent of the OECD exports of Hungary, Poland and Czechoslovakia and an even higher share of their European Community exports are in the areas of agriculture, textiles, iron and steel and chemicals.

> *These products are subject to significant non-tariff barriers—quotas, voluntary export restraints, price surveillance, anti-dumping measures and countervailing procedures—which are an important obstacle for central and eastern European countries in their effort to integrate into the multi-lateral trading system.*[65]

It is quite possible that some concessions will be made so that any discrimination is not too obvious. This is what has already begun to happen with the European Community. But it is highly unlikely that these barriers will be removed wholesale and especially not if growth becomes more difficult in the world economy. Already considerable furore has erupted over increased agricultural exports from eastern Europe to the West. Eastern Europe's agricultural exports have been worth some 7 billion dollars but only 2 billion dollars have gone to the European Community in the past. To expand these is an obvious possibility, especially as such imports make up only around 1 percent of EC output. Yet the agro-capitalist lobby has managed to forge a powerful alliance with many poorer farmers and peasants. Despite representing an area of diminishing importance to European capital this alliance has proved capable in the past of extracting enormous concessions and subsidies and resisting any major opening up to the world market.[66]

Capital—the missing boom

The hope that the eastern European economies would be able to adjust upwards rather than downwards was largely based upon the belief that foreign capital would flood in to the region bringing with it new techniques. On some accounts this is happening. In particular 1990 saw what has been called a 'joint-venture euphoria' in which private capital appeared to be seizing the initiative. The United Nations Economic Commission for Europe recorded the formation of nearly 14,000 joint ventures by the end of 1990 of which 11,500 had been formed in that year alone with a total 'commitment' of 7.3 billion dollars.[67] Journalists puffed up every private initiative. At the state level, heads of state and heads of international institutions like Jacques Attali of the newly formed European Bank for Reconstruction and Development (EBRD) encouraged the most optimistic interpretations. If a new Marshall Plan was not to be forthcoming there would nevertheless be Know How Funds, Enterprise Funds, economic aid, food aid that would help put eastern Europe on the right track.

All of this has been at best wishful thinking and at worst disingenuous manipulation of the record. To see this it is only necessary to put the real flows into perspective. After the Second World War the Marshall Plan involved the transfer of some 300 billion dollars (in today's prices). Currently some 50 billion dollars are being transferred from west Germany to east Germany with the credit to the Treuhand (responsible for keeping what is left of the east German economy afloat) running at almost 20 billion dollars. Estimates of the amounts needed to help keep eastern Europe afloat vary. If we exclude Yugoslavia and the former USSR, the World Bank has estimated that (on its optimistic scenario) some 20 billion dollars a year would be needed to maintain the economies at their existing levels. To refurbish them would require levels of aid similar to, or in excess of, that in the Marshall Aid programme. Include the old USSR and the figures leap again. As of December 1991 the most recent proposals suggest that the cluster of emerging states need a 20 billion dollar lifeline in 1992 for stability and this figure is sure to grow if the downward spiral is not halted.

Given the fact that huge sums have been committed once in the past at a time when the world economy was much less productive there is no question that a rationally organised system could provide what was necessary to help rebuild eastern Europe. But over the past decades similar possibilities have existed for helping the poorer countries of the world and they have been spurned. The same is now happening in the old eastern bloc. The real inflow of capital has been a trickle and, as in the Third World, it is in danger of being swamped by a massive outflow as these economies are forced to honour the debts of the old regime. For more realistic observers the immobility of Western states and capital in the face of the dimensions of the problem is a tragedy,

> *the politicians and officials who take refuge in the solecisms of self-help stand among the pygmies of this century—from the architects of German reparations to the proponents of appeasement—as being unable to grasp the seismic challenges before them, and to exercise just a little statesmanship.*[68]

Briefly such commentators hoped that the failed coup in the USSR in the summer of 1991 might lead to a significant revision of policy but it was soon back in its old tracks with only minor changes of commitment behind the rhetoric.

But the reason for this is not any failure of imagination—it lies in the real situation in the West. In the first place, the advanced West has problems enough of its own which restrain any willingness to bail out eastern Europe. In the second place, in 1945 the United States dominated the world economy and could therefore afford to encourage recovery safe in the knowledge that its own economy would benefit substantially. Today economic power is much more evenly distributed and the situation more competitive with no state prepared to give another a free ride. One reflection of this changing balance of power is the European Bank for Reconstruction and Development which is the first major world financial institution created since 1945 which is not effectively controlled by US capitalism. More centrally aid is now the responsibility of the Group of Seven (G7) leading industrial countries in which each state tries to push another to the front while telling everyone how committed they are to helping their 'eastern brothers'. In the third place, a realistic appraisal of eastern Europe's prospects suggests to any sensible investment analyst that too much good money has already been thrown after bad to warrant any further profligacy without cast-iron guarantees of reform and an eventual payoff in terms of interest paid or growth for aid.

As with the analysis of trade prospects it is important not to be misled by any selective presentation of parts of what is happening. To see the totality of the situation we must begin with debt. The debt burden for 1990 is set out in Table 10. With a total net debt of 123 billion dollars the outflow of interest payments in 1990 was 12 billion dollars which dwarfed any actual inflow into the area in that year. In other words these increasingly poverty stricken countries acted as capital exporters to the banks and states of the advanced West rather than vice versa. Even if more real aid is given rather than promised this problem is likely to remain.

TABLE 10
EASTERN EUROPEAN DEBT, DEBT RATIOS AND PAYMENTS IN 1990[69]

	1	*2*	*3*	*4*	*5*
	Net debt $ bill	*Net debt/ export ratio*	*Net Interest as percentage exports*	*Debt Service ratio*	*Net Interest Payments $ bill*
Bulgaria	*9.8*	*468*	*43*	*77*	*0.9*
Czecho-slovakia	*6.3*	*111*	*10*	*25*	*0.6*
Hungary	*20.3*	*343*	*35*	*65*	*2.1*
Poland	*41.8*	*418*	*41*	*71*	*4.1*
Romania	*1.3*	*38*	*1*	*10*	*0.03*
USSR	*43.4*	*139*	*14*	*29*	*4.4*
Total	*122.9*	*211*	*21*	*39*	*12.1*

Making Sense of Debt Measures

Net Debt	*total borrowing minus reserves in Western banks.*
Net Debt-Export Ratio	*described by the OECD as 'the best indicator of overall indebtedness'. Net debt as percent of annual exports. A figure of less than 100 shows low debt, 100-200 medium, 200+ high debt.*
Net Interest as percentage Exports	*shows the burden of annual interest payments in relation to export earnings.*
Debt Service Ratio	*shows burden of interest payments and debt repayment in relation to export earnings.*
Net Interest Payments	*shows the total capital transferred to the advanced West.*

What Table 10, columns 2 to 4, also shows is that the capacity to sustain this outflow is at a limit. These countries are on the verge of state bankruptcy or, in the more elegant but less blunt words of the OECD, 'virtually all the central and eastern European countries are highly vulnerable to a loss of market confidence'.[70]

Another aspect of this vulnerability is, of course, that reform has made these countries more unstable politically and there is now much less confidence that private loans will be repaid. The result is that Western banking capital has virtually suspended loan activity in the bloc. In 1990 private bank lending to eastern Europe fell by 65 percent and the resulting low level of lending will be maintained in the short to medium term.[71] The irony here, of course, is that Western banks were prepared to back the old regimes to the hilt because they believed that repression in the region was good for business. Economically the strong central control meant that it always appeared possible to manage things so that debt would be paid back. This indeed was what Ceausescu achieved in Romania for his own reasons in the late 1980s. Politically the repression meant both that there were few of the populist pressures evident in the Third World for debt defaulting and at the bottom the working class and peasant protest could be eliminated as a threat.

That is why the West shed crocodile tears whenever revolt broke out and continued to lend. 'It would be a good thing', said one banker in December 1981, of Poland, 'if Russia invaded, because then she would be obliged to honour Poland's debts'. Another was quoted the next day, in the midst of moves for martial law as saying, 'if a few people are shot in the cause of getting the (Polish) economy moving again, then it would be a small price to pay'.[72] Thus in the late 1980s, while Western banking capital was cutting back its lending elsewhere after having its fingers burned in the Third World, it continued to lend to the rulers of

Eastern Europe. In fact Eastern Europe not only recovered its credit rating after a fall in the early 1980s, it actually rose and 'international financial markets became increasingly bullish towards the region'. How different the situation is today! Take Poland, for example, 'no Western banker in his right financial mind would consider lending fresh money to Poland right now'.[73]

Thus inflows of capital are primarily taking the form of lending and aid by Western states and international institutions and direct private capital investment. So far as loans and aid are concerned the problem is the already high level of debt. Western policy has been to insist that debt is honoured partly as a weapon against the bloc itself and partly out of fear that too much generosity in eastern Europe will increase demands to do more than tinker with the debt structure in the rest of the world. The big exception to this has been Poland which in the spring of 1991 was granted what the OECD called 'unprecedented debt reduction' of 50 percent of its inter-state debt (which made up around two-thirds of its total debt). Just how unprecedented this was can be illustrated by the fact that the largest previous debt write off was only of one third for the poverty wrecked economies of Africa south of the Sahara.[74] But it was made clear that the reduction in the Polish case was a reward for good behaviour—unlike in Bulgaria which had been financially punished in 1990 for both getting the wrong election result and failing to honour its own debts with sufficient enthusiasm.[75]

Measuring the totality of flows to eastern Europe from international and state agencies is not easy. This is partly because of the sheer variety of initiatives but also because it is important to distinguish between rhetoric and reality. Much attention, for example, has been given to Jacques Attalai and the EBRD but within a short time of its creation it had become 'a by-word for corporate extravagance' with 'a resplendent City headquarters and a stratospheric expense bill for hotel and air fares'.[76] In reality the organisation has relatively few funds at its disposal compared to other agencies. Any assessment of Western aid must therefore take account of i) the real amount committed; ii) the amount actually disbursed i.e. given out each year; iii) the terms of the loans (for there are few gifts!); iv) the nature of the possible impact—for example, some EC funds are designed to deflect and dump eastern European agricultural exports onto the Soviet market creating another set of problems as one set appears to be solved.

If these issues are explored then the rhetoric is quickly deflated. Table 11 shows one example of this by looking at the total loans approved and disbursed by the main international bodies for eastern Europe (excluding the former Soviet Union). Readers should compare these figures with the minimum inflows noted earlier that were considered necessary for stability.

TABLE 11
VALUE OF IMF, WORLD BANK AND GROUP OF 24 LOANS TO EASTERN EUROPE JUNE 1989 TO SUMMER 1991 (BILLIONS OF DOLLARS)[77]

	Approved	*Disbursed*
Bulgaria	*1.9*	*0.2*
Czechoslovakia	*4.3*	*0.7*
Hungary	*9.0*	*1.4*
Poland	*13.3*	*1.7*
Romania	*2.5*	*0.9*
Total	*31.0*	*4.9*

What then of the much lauded private investment boom from Western business? The answer is that it hardly exists beyond a few sectors. High profile investment has certainly taken place in the services sector but there are three particular reasons for this. One is that eastern Europe is potentially a large market with an already existing level of pent-up demand backed by sufficient money to make investment worthwhile for producers and distributors of relatively low priced Western goods. The second is that at the world level in the retailing and consumer sector 'in the battle for markets, market shares and profits, the Western markets are very close to global consolidation'.[78] It is these two factors which account for the speed with which MacDonalds, Burger King, Pepsi, Marks and Spencer, Benetton and similar groups have moved into eastern Europe. The third is that Western banks, finance houses, accountants and consultants can make large profits not by bringing in investment but by telling eastern European governments how they can make their economies attractive—by selling their dubious expertise at inflated rates.

The rest of the story is quite different. In the heat of 1989 it was certainly true that some Western capital got carried away by the promise eastern Europe appeared to offer. Some 40 percent of early West German joint ventures, for example, were not preceded by any feasibility study.[79] Even now companies are prepared to speak with great enthusiasm about possibilities but their real strategy has been much more cautious. Commitments have been made on three bases. The first has been to snap up the eastern Europe 'jewels in the crown' as quickly and cheaply as possible. The second has been to grab the most attractive greenfield locations and the third has been to make strategic investments as pre-emptive moves against possible rivals. But in each instance the rule has generally been to make limited commitments. 'Given the risks...it may be best to try to obtain a strategic option in this region without investing too much', writes one leading investment consultant who goes on to urge that 'business decisions...should be even more cautious than usual' and that the best investment at the moment is of a minimal 'sleeping' kind.[80]

We can pull these arguments together by noting that the Group of Thirty Study on Financing Eastern Europe *on the most optimistic scenario* sees the total inflow of capital into eastern Europe rising from 13.5 billion dollars to 19.8 billion dollars (with private capital growing from around 12 to only 25 percent) in the years 1991-1995. And this optimistic scenario assumes rapid reform.[81] It is also only the inflow side against which must be set the outflow of interest payments, repayments of debt itself and the repatriation of profits.

But if much of the discussion of foreign investment and joint ventures has been hot air it has served a useful purpose of providing a distraction from the way that some of the acquisitions that have been made by Western multinationals have been on the basis of virtual give aways by eastern European states. The 'Skoda-Volkswagen Joint Venture', in reality Skoda's acquisition by Volkswagen, is a major case in point especially as it has been much lauded as a model agreement. The whole deal, however, has been subjected to a devastating analysis by a London based Czechoslovakian financial analyst who argues that the Czechoslovak government has allowed itself to be persuaded by its consultants—Price Waterhouse, Credit Suisse, First Boston and the Investment Bank Prague—that the only choice was between two inadequate deals offered by Renault and Volkswagen.

In the event Volkswagen acquired the most advanced car maker in eastern Europe with the best record in the West for a song. Whether the government acted out of stupidity, ignorance or naivety is not clear but if what the analyst claims are his conservative estimates are correct then Volkswagen has acquired Skoda for less than the price it would have fetched as a bankrupt concern in the West. In real terms Volkswagen appears to have paid no more than 200 million marks for assets worth possibly 3 billion marks—15 times as much. Such estimates are necessarily speculative but that is the point because virtually no information on costings has been published. 'The price of the factory was not determined by market forces, it was set arbitrarily by a small group of Czechoslovak officials and politicians'. And in its turn the reaction to the critique was telling—so strong was the ideological consensus in favour of such a deal that the new media refused the discussion publication. The issue was then taken up with the government by a Prague weekly which was advised against publication since 'Volkswagen could sue ... for damaging its reputation and the reputation of the new joint venture (sic) company'.[82]

Migration—'Keep them out'

We have already seen that one of the consequences of the pattern of state industrialisation was a tight control over the movement of labour across international frontiers and between East and West. Fully opening up eastern Europe will therefore give workers an opportunity to move freely but this, of course, is hardly an attribute of the market that proves attractive to the right. In fact already in the 1980s the gradual breakdown of the old system was allowing freer movement. Between 1981 and 1988, for example, emigration from Poland was equivalent to virtually the entire increase in the population of working age. The general pressure in eastern Europe increased in 1989. 'Ethnic Germans' moved to Germany from eastern Europe, 'Turkish Bulgarians' moved to Turkey. Between 1978 and 1988 185,000 left but in 1989-90 the figure was 310,000. Albanians fled to Greece and Italy, well over 100,000 Romanians left voluntarily and emigration from the Soviet Union rose steeply too.

To see the scale of the potential movement of labour and people it is helpful to follow a European study which divides potential migrants into three groups. The first consists of 'ethnic migrants' who might be tempted to migrate to what they consider their 'homelands' or stronger communities elsewhere in the world. There are still some 3 million 'ethnic Germans' who might move. The Soviet Jewish population is another example and a third would be the Armenian population living in Georgia and Azerbaijan who, left to their own devices, might prefer to migrate to join the American or French Armenian communities. A second group of potential migrants would be those affected by political migration due to persecution. There are some 1.6 to 2.5 million gypsies, for example, in eastern Europe who have a history of suffering oppression. In addition there are the unknown numbers who might become victims of the increases in national tension and violence in Yugoslavia. The third group is potentially the biggest of all—the economic migrants. The logic of the market is that people should move in search of better jobs and higher wages.[83] This is what freedom of labour means and for peoples denied that freedom for generations and facing worsening conditions in their own countries both the push of poverty and the pull of higher living standards in Western Europe will encourage them to move. Unless, that is, troops are set to control the borders and a new iron curtain is pulled down. And this is exactly what is happening.

It is important to understand what is at stake. Even if several tens of millions were to try to move there is little doubt that they could be accommodated. That has occurred in the past. Moreover internal population growth is stagnating in western Europe as the birth rate has fallen to below or near replacement levels. But for those in power this is not the point. Unlike in the 1950s and 1960s Western capital is not looking for a massive increase in unskilled labour flows. It already has access to large existing pools of such labour within Europe and from legal and illegal flows from its existing periphery. Thus while nationalistic and racist arguments about 'cultured central Europeans' might lead capital to prefer Hungarians to Turkish workers, in the immediate future western European capital is more interested in particular flows than large scale movements from either area. A spokesman for Citroen in France has made this point well,

> *we no longer hire—as we did in the past—a large number of immigrant workers who only speak their native language and are often illiterate. We're not worried about finding enough workers in the future, it's finding enough qualified workers that concerns us.*[84]

In other words while industries like building might find eastern European migrant labour attractive, in general big capital's interests will be in a much more selective 'middle' and 'top' level 'brain drain'. As one Soviet journalist has put it,

> *if you're the creme de la creme they will welcome you with open arms. Otherwise they are keen to prevent floods of Soviet emigrants pouring over their borders...Soviet people categorised as 'especially useful' have no problems...apart from the independently wealthy these may include defectors from the KGB or Soviet military intelligence, sports stars, outstanding scientists, artists, musicians etc. There are also good chances for Soviet people under 30...if they are well-educated...a 26 year old computer programmer with a good knowledge of English or an electrical engineer of similar age...*[85]

Such needs dovetail well with the political pressures on governments from the right and short-sighted sections of the labour movement. They also fit well with governments' own desires to use an internal European 'race' card to their political advantage. By the autumn of 1991 this card had begun to be played in every country as the flames of racist violence and immigration scares were being fanned.[86]

The unequal crisis—the escape of the ruling class

The consequence of this analysis of what is happening in terms of integration with the world economy is to suggest that eastern Europe is unlikely to experience vigorous growth. But this does not mean that the costs of transition will be shared equally. It is precisely because that burden will be unequal that those at the top have been engaged in supporting change.

We have already argued before 1989 there was a ruling class in control which was determined to hang on to its power and that it was already making significant moves to accommodate itself to the 'winds of change' blowing in the bloc. It is now time to analyse how this ruling class has shifted its base in order to retain its grip on power.

Analysing the contours of a modern ruling class requires a sensitivity to the real distribution of power in both East and West. Marxists have frequently shown themselves to be hamfisted in both areas. In the case of eastern Europe this hamfistedness had three common expressions. One was the simple identification of class with legal property ownership rather than effective control of the means of production. A second was a woeful ignorance of the real scale of the inequalities that arose as a consequence of the real distribution of control. A third, which flowed from the first two, was a tendency to focus only on the narrow party political-administrative elite at the top rather than see this group as a component of a wider ruling class. The real power of this wider class in eastern Europe was expressed through its effective control of the economic, social and political assets of society and it is this that it has sought to hang on to through the transition while certain of the party and security groups within it have been beheaded. Even amongst these groups, however, what is often striking is their resilience and the jails have hardly been bulging with those responsible for the old order.

Commentators on eastern Europe have made much of the fact that in Warsaw the old Communist Party headquarters has been turned into the Stock Exchange. But the real irony of the joke runs rather deeper than they have allowed because what this better illustrates is a fundamental continuity of power. This is not so much because the communist bureaucrats have all become stockbrokers, though some certainly have. Rather what we see here is an expression of the basic continuity in class relations of exploitation.[87] It is not possible in the space available to trace this across the whole of the ruling class so here our attention will focus on those holding the economic levers of power.[88]

Before 1989 the Eastern European economies were state run in the sense that legally most property was nationalised and economic activity was administered from the centre through the central planning network. In reality the 'plans' expressed the central planners' attempts to direct the enterprise within the economy along lines determined by the competitive international networks in which these economies were imprisoned.

The top planners in the various central planning offices and the factory managers formed part of the ruling class alongside those controlling the state machine, the media, party and so on. Their effective control of the means of production was expressed in similar ways to those found in the West amongst managerial and bureaucratic sections of the ruling class. That is, not only did they control society and act as the agent of accumulation but they also benefited personally in terms of high incomes, wealth accumulated on the side and an ability to pass on their general class position to their children and wider families. Indeed the more that is revealed about the contours of power and the way that these societies structurally reproduced it over time the more obvious it becomes that the class rates of social mobility, income and wealth distributions were little different from those in the West. It was the Hungarian sociologist Hankiss who again painted one of the clearest pictures of this concentration of power in an analysis of Hungary. Here he wrote, those at the top,

> *created their fiefs, pacified and protected their subjects, developed their patron-client networks, siphoned off more and more resources out of society, built their castles, socialised at hunting parties, enjoyed the comfort of their luxurious holiday centres, sent their children abroad, poured huge resources into wasteful mega-projects, financed their power by huge loans from abroad, and hid their claws in velvet gloves or behind the smiles of paternalistic benevolence.*[89]

If we focus particularly on the economic core of this ruling class then in its heyday in the old society greater power lay with those in the central institutions rather than the enterprises. In the last decades, however, there is evidence that the balance was changing as managers became more professional and, under the impact of partial reform and crisis, there took place what has been called 'the shrinkage of central planning'. Those who half saw the way in which change was going took opportunities to move sideways from the party, state or planning structures to the business and commercial ones. In Hungary the shift was so obvious that it was given the name 'parachuting'. In the transition this shift in power to the enterprise bosses and the financial system has become even clearer as the old central structures have been partly dismantled.

The dismantling has been partial because, of course, although central planning is disappearing the state continues to play an important role. As a result many of the old personnel continue to be needed. At the same time the old personnel have been ideally placed to make the sideways step to the more market based structures. Thanks to the investigations of an Hungarian journalist we can see clearly how this has worked in the Hungarian Finance Ministry. Consider first the case of Mihaly Kupa, the Finance Minister. Under the old regime Kupa was Head of the Fiscal Policy Unit in the Ministry of Finance. He left the state in May 1990 to organise the Hungarian office of an American-Japanese firm only to return in the early summer as the new Finance Minister of the Antall government. Kupa's case is by no means untypical of what has occurred, 'those who held middle level positions in the economic administration shifted to managerial posts at Hungary's big companies, and one time government experts can be found in the management or board of directors of almost every Hungarian bank'.

In the Finance Ministry, with the new government, all five deputy ministers and nine out of 11 section heads resigned. The former Finance Minister and Deputy Prime Minister went to work for the Hungarian branch of the French banking group Paribas. One deputy finance minister went to work for London firm James Capel; another became Chief Executive of Reviconsult, a Hungarian Accounting Company co-operating with James Capel; a third deputy minister became President of the Hungarian Industrial Bank; a fourth, President of the Agrobank. The President of the National Bank of Hungary became a manager of the Vienna based Indosuez investment group, the chief economic adviser to the former government became head of Central European Economic Research and Counselling Ltd, a company working for Hungarian banks and Western investors in which a former justice minister was also a partner. The Kadar regime's banker, Janos Fekete, who had appeared regularly in the West and helped to build up Hungary's debt, went to work for the Israeli Bank Leumi in Hungary and so on.[90]

These sideways movements or circulation within the existing ruling class are taking place not simply at the visible level of the ministries but below them at the level of enterprise management. In the first place we should note that large chunks of industry will continue to remain in state hands with little or no change in the nature of their management groups. Privatisation schemes have everywhere ground to a halt and state privatisation agencies have become seen by critics as state procrastination agencies. But the basis of their procrastination is real.

The proposed privatisation schemes were unrealistic on any scenario. A Polish minister put it this way, 'the task is colossal. The totality of privatisation made in the world in France, Great Britain, Argentina, Mexico...only represents 11 percent of the privatisation to be carried out in Poland'.[91] When attempts were made to begin this process a cluster of technical issues arose—ownership squabbles, legislative problems, accounting difficulties, lack of personnel, inexperience and so on. But the more fundamental problem is simply that few enterprises could survive on their own. 'A change in ownership of deeply troubled enterprises will not make much difference: what is needed is capital—that's the critical issue', is how Jan Vanous of the American PlanEcon consultants has put it. But this argument has found little favour with other Western consultants and even less with those like Sachs who see the solution as dumping whole sections of industry, 'the idea is to privatise and then to solve the problems of enterprises, not the other way round. British style privatisation is an illusion. It's an expensive and slow way whose sole virtue is solving the unemployment problem in the City of London'.[92] Given that Western privatisation advisers are charging up to 20 percent of the value of the flotation it is not difficult to sympathise with this last point. But neither offloading chunks of industry or giving away shares to the population will work if enterprises cannot survive. Share markets throughout the world depend upon institutional investors to support them and few institutional investors will be attracted to privatised eastern European companies in any form in the immediate future.[93]

Smaller scale privatisations have taken place but these have usually involved effective 'management buy-outs' or they are examples of what has been called 'nomenklatura privatisation' after the nomenklatura lists of the old regime which indicated people acceptable for the top positions.

Much the same applies to the development of new companies in the private sector. As with other aspects of the transition much nonsense has been talked about the emergence of new entrepreneurs. Crisis and austerity has certainly led to the proliferation of Third World style informal sectors but this is no more relevant to future economic development than the proliferation of car boot sales in Britain in the last decade. Beyond this there has certainly been a dramatic rise in small scale business activity. In 1990 and early 1991 516,000 new enterprises were created in Poland, 300,000 in Czechoslovakia and 250,000 in Hungary but the vast majority of these were examples of self-employment.[94] Undoubtedly there will be examples of rags to riches stories from this sector but these will be no more a guide to the real process of class reproduction than the rise of the occasional Alan Sugar is to the dynamics of class in the West. What is important here is to take out the significant new companies—the larger ones, and these are defined by the way that their owners have been able to establish themselves through access to education, knowledge, capital and contacts i.e. through using their existing position in the system, their class position. This is most obvious in terms of 'nomenklatura privatisation' which also takes the form of the sponsoring of new companies alongside the state ones, but let the President of the Warsaw Economic Association explain how it works,

> *The state and party apparat are interested in founding as many companies as possible. They see chances for themselves to sit on various company councils and even to hold stocks...The apparat is only whetting its appetite for profits that companies can provide them with, and so not only is it not trying to hamper the growth of entrepreneurs but it is even making life easier for companies by opening up a protective umbrella over them...The first companies have already been founded at the initiative of the apparat, and even of people representing medium-level Party authorities, and some of those new companies are chaired by people from the top echelons of power in Poland.*[95]

But it is not just formal nomenklatura privatisation that is important here. What matters is also the way in which those at the top have the capacity to reproduce themselves as a whole both in the state and the private sectors. One Hungarian study, for example, has shown that the entrepreneurial, intellectual and managerial groups in that country have all been recruited from 'people of more or less the same origin'. In the case of new entrepreneurs in the private sector,

> *only one fourth or fifth of the total number of those participating in enterprises come from the lower social groups. All this indicates that this group of self-employed entrepreneurs has successfully taken advantage of the parents' socio-economic position making use of the opportunities provided by the 1980s.*[96]

One reason for this is that it is only these people who were able to accumulate money and convert it into and out of foreign currencies to maintain and increase its value. Andrea Gallai, for example, an Hungarian businesswoman running a chain of artshops and identified by *Business Week* as one of the new generation of entrepreneurs 'poured $80,000 of private savings into her first venture..."Everyone has stashed away some wealth", says Gallai'.[97] But not the equivalent of $80,000 in either Hungarian or even less hard currency. To get this you had either to be a member of the existing ruling class or serving it through the black market.

And finally when Western companies move in they are interested in building on existing unequal social relationships. At the top they hand out jobs 'for the boys' as we saw in the case of the Hungarian Finance Ministry but below this level they draw on the existing managerial groups and especially the younger managers serving their 'apprenticeships'. These people are then retrained in house or in the country concerned on Western style programmes or, for a select few, they are taken abroad for training. Even in the former East Germany this has been true. Western capital has not been interested in re-equipping the old productive assets of eastern Europe but it has put itself behind the re-equipping and reskilling of the management stratum of the ruling class. This is how Axel Osenberg of the leading German financial conglomerate Deutsche Bank puts it,

> *We are training the staff we took over from the East. In the first six months they took part in more than 6,000 seminars. More than 1,000 people attended training courses in the West. We now have more than 700 apprentices, 130 of whom we took over from Staatsbank. Our East German staff are highly motivated...they clearly identify themselves with the objectives of our bank.*[98]

What all of this evidence points to therefore is a process involving a recomposition of the ruling class as a whole with some groups experiencing downward mobility and new groups being co-opted. The power of the class as a whole is surviving and so is that of many of its individual members. This process of co-option provides a safety valve through which those with an understanding of what is happening can be integrated into the new. Ironically this has included Elemer Hankiss who has moved from being the sharp-eyed observer to a fully integrated new Head of Hungarian television!

This recomposition is not a chance happening. It is a reflection of deeper social processes which have created the opportunities for movement. These social processes are rooted in the structural characteristics of the eastern European societies. It is precisely because both sides of the transition show the same structural features that individual opportunism on the scale we have analysed has been possible. We are not merely looking at class societies, but class societies rooted in a common mode of production where what has been changing has been the form rather than the essence. Unless this is understood it becomes impossible to understand how, beneath the turnover at the top, the same people, the same families, the same social networks are still toasting their good fortune in the 1990s as they had toasted it in the 1980s. It is true that as they chatter and socialise they might on occasion spare a thought for some of their absent friends but they will not lose sight of the greater whole—that they are still on top despite the transition. Beneath them is the same working class, still carrying the burden of their wealth, privilege and their incompetence as it has done in the past.

The unequal crisis—making the workers pay

If we turn to the other side of this process we can now trace how the working class and (to a lesser extent) the peasants of eastern Europe are being made to pay for the crisis through increased unemployment, a falling standard of living and increased exploitation.

Identifying the full rise in unemployment is difficult because the statistics are only just beginning to be created and they do not measure the real rise. Right wing critics have argued that official figures overstate real levels because people are being encouraged to register for benefits. This argument has already led to a tightening of regulations especially in Poland. In this sense one level of controversy about real levels of unemployment is exactly the same as that in the West where similar accusations of 'scrounging'and 'moonlighting' are made. But the problem is compounded in eastern Europe by the way that the labour markets in these societies worked before 1989.[99]

Contrary to what their supporters often claimed these regimes did have real unemployment, but it is true that in the past the drive to compete created a general labour shortage which led to high participation rates especially amongst women. The crisis is therefore acting not only to restructure production but also to restructure the labour force and this means squeezing women and the old either out of the labour force altogether or into part-time work. The official figures in Table 12 therefore do not really capture the true extent of the change. Nevertheless they still paint a telling picture of who is experiencing the burden of transition.

TABLE 12
MONTHLY PERCENTAGE UNEMPLOYED IN EASTERN EUROPE ACCORDING TO THE OFFICIAL STATISTICS[100]

	Poland	*Czecho-Slovakia*	*Czech Republic*	*Slovak Republic*	*Hungary*
1990					
Jan	*0.3*	*0.1*	*0.1*	*0.1*	*n.a.*
1991					
Jan	*6.5*	*1.5*	*1.1*	*2.4*	*2.1*
Feb	*6.8*	*1.9*	*1.4*	*3.0*	*2.7*
Mar	*7.1*	*2.3*	*1.7*	*3.7*	*3.1*
Apr	*7.3*	*2.8*	*2.0*	*4.6*	*3.5*
May	*7.7*	*3.2*	*2.2*	*5.4*	*3.4*
Jun	*8.4*	*3.8*	*2.6*	*6.3*	*3.9*
Jul	*9.4*	*4.5*	*3.1*	*7.8*	*n.a.*
Aug	*9.8*	*5.1*	*3.4*	*8.7*	*5.2*
Sep	*10.4*			*9.5*	*6.1*

Problems also arise with the measurement of the fall in the standard of living. It is the case that the old official figures overstated the standard of living (though by how much is less clear). Simple comparisons of pre- and post-1989 can therefore overstate the fall but the evidence of a real decline in the standard of living is so clear that no amount of revision can disguise its nature.[101] The most extreme case is that of Poland where the average standard of living was cut by around a third when the shock programme was introduced. This decline was probably the greatest sudden reduction in a peacetime standard of living through 'normal' economic processes anywhere in recent world economic history. It was much greater, for example, than in the crisis of the 1930s and comparable only to the collapse in the standard of living of the Soviet worker that was brought about by the introduction of the first five year plan between 1928 and 1932. The comparison is an important one for it shows the way in which both the birth and death of regimes built around state directed competitive industrialisation were undertaken at the expense of the working class.

A third element in the pressure on the working class has been the attempt to tighten work discipline in order to improve profitability which has meant a cut in absenteeism, improvements in productivity and so on. This process is being quite consciously manipulated with the approval of Western agencies and advisers. Lipton and Sachs (advisers to Solidarity remember) boast that 'with workers afraid of job losses, sick leave has dropped sharply according to unpublished government surveys...wages pressures have abated' and they quote one commentator describing how, 'in industry, sick leave decreased by 80 percent. I discovered that it became nearly impossible to lure even my most devoted friends out for a chat during their office hours: with the threat of unemployment looming, skipping work became too risky'.[102] Which is fine, save that these workers will no more be the direct beneficiaries of this productivity drive than they were under the old regime. Rather we can taste here the logic of General Jaruzelski who said in May 1990, in an interview with a Western journalist, 'we tried economic reforms time and again. But it always met with public resistance and explosions. It is very different now. Now with a government that enjoys public confidence, it has become possible to demand sacrifices'.[103]

The disorientation of the Left

All of this raises the question of where the left is in eastern Europe? An active left concerned to fight both against the old system and the new one for a real alternative that reflected the real potential of 1989—the power of the workers who struck and demonstrated on the streets, the optimism and the hope that affected the crowds of protesters could now be making a substantial difference. The success of the transition, the escape of the ruling class, demands the complicity of workers. To take but one example, 'privatisation will not be possible if employees resist: who will buy a company where the employees are on strike?'[104]

Unfortunately the left is encouraging this complicity at the moment. Throughout eastern Europe the left has also drawn the conclusion that socialism equals state and the market equals salvation. Nowhere has there been an attempt to confront the real nature of the old regime. The result is that the arguments on the left have been moralistic rather than political. The result is what Havel has called in Czechoslovakia 'a coalition of sacrifice'. But it is the right which has set the agenda to such an extent that many on the left fear to discuss socialism and prefer instead to identify themselves as 'Western', hoping to indirectly defend a less harsh transition through an argument for 'successful Western social democratic models'.

This disorientation is general but its impact is clearest at the level of trade union organisation. Here a precondition of any attempt to defend workers' interests is independent organisation. But there has been a real failure to build alternative union structures that really represent workers and can displace the old Stalinist structures that in the past were simple transmission belts for the policies of the regimes themselves. In most countries these old 'company unions', for that is what they were, still have significant followings.

This is even true in Poland where Solidarity has failed to re-emerge on its earlier scale and today has only around one fifth of its peak membership. There, although its working class membership appears to be less than that of Solidarity, the old official National Trade Union Alliance (OPZZ) has managed to remain a force and, untied to the government, has found it easy to sound radical. This reflects the second aspect of the problem which is that the leaders of the new union structures often see their task as defending what is emerging on the grounds that there are only two alternatives. This is clearest in the case of Solidarity where the new government sprang from the organisation and where, despite more recent changes and separations, the Solidarity Trade Union organisation still has to carry what its Chairman called, at its 3rd Congress in February 1991, 'the burden of coresponsibility of reform'.

Such views make it hard to develop a resolute defence of workers against the impact of the transition. But this is not to say that the material is not there. In eastern Europe today small disputes proliferate and occasionally break out into larger ones. In the autumn of 1990, for example, the whole of Budapest was brought to a halt by a taxi drivers' strike. Despite the unpromising nature of the group taking action the strike briefly became the focus of more general resentments about the government that found no echo through the more conventional organisations.

But there has been no real leadership from those whose arguments might have had some resonance because of the positions they had established in the opposition in the past. In Poland, for example, leaders like Adam Michnik and Jacek Kuron have not only made themselves responsible for defending the transition, they have even fought shy of vigorously taking up issues like the power of the Catholic Church for fear of weakening their own positions.

The result has been an astonishing wilting of popular interest in formal politics especially in Poland and Hungary. In the case of Poland it had been Solidarity's striking electoral victory in 1989 that had forced the hand of the old government and led to its replacement by a new Solidarity government. By 1990, however, in the two rounds of the presidential election in the autumn, Solidarity's voting strength had fallen. Partly this was a result of the drift to other candidates like the maverick Tyminski and, partly, because of a simple refusal to vote at all which led to a dramatic decline in electoral turn out. This was continued into the autumn of 1991 as parties proliferated and in the first major free elections in Poland the main winner was apathy. But Poland is in no sense alone. In Hungary in the first round of the parliamentary elections on 25 March 1990 65 percent voted, in the second round in April the figure was down to 45 percent. A year later, in April 1991, two by-elections had to go to the second round because of poor turn out. In one, a Budapest seat, there was a 3 percent increase in turn out the second time to take the number of voters over 25 percent, enough for it to count. In the second case, a rural seat, the elections were abandoned after an 11 percent turn out. But studies of voting patterns in Hungary, notwithstanding the latter by-election, show that it is manual workers who are less likely to vote, not because of apathy but because they do not see that the existing choice has any meaning for them.[105]

If the economic collapse has been one of the most spectacular in history, this collapse into indifference is its political parallel. A huge vacuum has opened up in the political system.

But the fact that such a vacuum exists confirms in a distorted way the thrust of our analysis: that what has been at stake has been a change in the form of class society and not a shift to a class society. Those who argued that what existed in Eastern Europe before 1989 was some form of socialism, however degenerate, were never able to fully confront the scale of exploitation and alienation under the old regimes and their difficulties were compounded with the rise of Solidarity which organised the majority of the working class against one such regime.

The subsequent events of 1989 and after have intensified these problems, for workers have shown no interest in defending the old forms. This still emerges strongly today despite the evidence of growing crisis in a material sense.

The evidence clearly points to the belief that it is better to be poorer but freer than better off in an unfree society. And this is a view that deserves every support from socialists for in that freedom lies the ability to organise and fight for new ideas and real change. But it is also clear that no real commitment exists to the societies that are emerging the other side of the transition. Rather what is happening is that those on the left who have been seduced by the new order are not building a consensus of legitimacy, they are sowing confusion when they should be building resistance from below. To say this is not to argue that simple sloganeering is sufficient—it clearly is not. The effect of the association of the old regimes with the name of 'socialism' has been enormous. 'In my country', said Haval in late 1989,

> *for ages now, socialism has been no more than an incantation that should be avoided if one does not want to appear suspect...socialism...was transformed long ago into just an ordinary truncheon used by certain cynical, parvenu bureaucrats to bludgeon their liberal minded fellow citizens from morning till night, labelling them 'enemies of socialism' and 'anti-socialist forces'.*[106]

To overcome this heritage of distrust the starting point must be different, it must be the practical question of the nature of class power that we have posed here. The urgency of this question is simple. Vacuums do not exist indefinitely. As the crisis intensifies then people will look for answers and it is already clear that the existing rulers will try to supply them in increasingly nationalistic and divisive forms in order to divert blame from themselves.

Nationalism and the political vacuum

The extent of the lurch towards nationalism has been another aspect of the eastern European situation that has shocked many people. It should not have. The problem is not, as some have suggested, that there has been a simple return to the petty nationalisms of the inter-war years. There is no transcendent logic of nationalism in eastern Europe any more than there is in the rest of the world. Rather nationalism has become such a potent force because it was carried and reproduced by the old 'communist' regimes. This was so in the negative sense, that these regimes failed to confront the structural conditions that gave rise to nationalism and, in the positive sense, that their policies were informed by nationalism and they were prepared to use it and some of its equally unpleasant relations, like anti-semitism, for their own ends.

The most fundamental aspect of this was the way in which the ideology of development—'socialism in one country'—was national in its objectives, an expression of the interests of a national ruling class. At the same time the competitive drives which determined development also limited the real effort that could be directed towards eliminating regional and 'national' differences within countries. In this way policies of 'regional' development experienced the same difficulties faced by their counterparts in the West. It was possible to moderate but never eliminate national and regional inequality because such uneven development was built into the logic of the competitive world economy where resources have to be allocated to ends and areas that yield the greatest returns.

So long as the Eastern European regimes boomed nationalism could stay in the background though, whenever difficulties emerged, those at the top often had easy recourse to it. In some countries it went beyond this. In Poland, for example, 'instrumental anti-semitism' was often used against the opposition. In Romania Ceausescu similarly extolled his vision of the Romanian past and present (including making a hero of Vlad the Impaler) against 'internal enemies' in the form of gypsies and the Hungarian minority. But nationalism also came from below in that, given the unequal development and the absence of a clearly articulated alternative explanation, people looking for answers sometimes found them in the existing ideas.

Since nationalism was always there in some form, nurtured and reproduced by the old order, it is easier to understand why it should have become such a strong force for the larger part of the political spectrum in eastern Europe today, often expressed most intensely by former Communist Party members. This nationalism is occupying the vacuum and pushing country against country and pulling them towards 'national models' in the West that the leaderships admire. More disturbingly it is fracturing internal politics wherever there are significant national minorities. In Czechoslovakia, for example, (which many imagined to be one of the most stable countries) the uneven impact of crisis is forcing home the lesson of the uneven development of the Czech and Slovak lands and playing into the hands of politicians using nationalism to build their constituency. It is in the continuity of the inequality of exploitation and oppression in Czechoslovakia, and eastern Europe more generally, that we find the answer to Vaclav Havel's plaintive question posed as the second year of the transition began, 'why is our political climate systematically poisoned by demagogy, by political, ethnic and racial intolerance?'[107]

The contradictory power of religion is to be explained in the same way. The fact that the old regimes were rooted in class society meant that they could never eliminate the forces which pushed people towards the church as a source of hope and salvation. Instead, after a period of trying to suppress religious observance, the regimes moved to a tacit 'concordat' with the various national churches as useful allies helping them to keep stability. Ever the opportunists, the official churches seized their chances to negotiate an area of limited freedom. But this also made them centres which the opposition could use. The pattern is a familiar one and by no means restricted to Eastern Europe. It can be found in Latin America and South Africa. In the Eastern bloc it was most obvious in Poland where the Catholic Church maintained an uneasy stand-off between the regime and Solidarity with 'a finger in both pies'. Now, as the the late Jan-Josef Lipski, a long time social democratic oppositionist, put it shortly before his death, 'the Church is presenting its bill for the support of Solidarity'.[108]

The bill is not one over which there is agreement. In Poland the Church has also suffered a loss of support since the heady days of 1989. But it is still insisting on payment in terms of religion being taught in schools, an end to abortion and a general commitment to traditional, conservative, national values. Moreover, even in decline, the Polish church remains a powerful national symbol commanding a significant and vocal minority support. For Walesa it is part of his natural constituency of support. And on the left his opponents are reluctant to challenge the Catholic church openly for fear of losing support. Yet such a calculated 'electoralism', for that is what it is, usually ends up producing what it most fears. By ducking the debate, refusing to challenge, the initiative is left with those pushing the 'centre ground' ever more to the right.

In this way the mixtures of nationalism and religion feed off real difficulties. But their targets are at a tangent to the real causes of the problems and their solutions non-solutions. This is most obvious in the widening development of anti-semitism.

It should hardly need saying that anti-semitism does not depend on Jews for its success. In inter-war Germany less than 1 percent of the population was Jewish. It is not Jews that define the problem but the problem that defines Jews. This was well expressed by Karl Luegar, a leading, late 19th century, anti-semitic Mayor of Vienna who attacked the 'corrosive influence' of Jews. When asked for the definition of a Jew, Luegar's response was simply to say that he would define who was a Jew and who was not. This was the view taken by Hitler.

Today in eastern Europe we find similar processes at work. In Poland, for example, Lech Walesa has found the hint of anti-semitism part of the natural vocabulary of his populist nationalism. He, at least, is '100 percent Pole going back generations'. As Marek Edelman (a veteran of the Warsaw Uprising and Solidarity) has put it, 'Walesa is not an anti-semite, he's a populist. But he doesn't tell people to stop this shouting'.[109] One of the less attractive reasons for the defeat of the Mazowiecki government (over which, for other reasons, few tears should be shed) was the widespread impression that Mazowiecki (a Catholic) himself was a Jew and surrounded by 'leftist Jews'. In fact Hitler had already seen to it that there were few Jews left in Poland—some 4,000 compared to a pre-war community of 3 or 4 million. But this did not matter and nor does it matter in Romania where only 18,000 of the pre-war Jewish community of 800,000 are left. Nevertheless for Cornelieu Vadim Tudor, once a leading Ceausescu supporter and now responsible for a virulent nationalist and anti-semitic political programme, 'in parliament and in the government, it rains Jews by the bucket'.[110]

Yet there are grounds for optimism. For all the way that nationalism and its relations feed off crisis they still need to be kicked into full gear and this can be resisted. This is the ironic lesson of Yugoslavia where in 1991 they took such an apparently firm grip. There is a real sense in which the previous decade reflected a race between growing opposition from below, expressed in a dramatic rise in industrial conflict, and attempts at the top to divert discontent into nationalistic channels. It took a long time to achieve this and the power of those at the top was frequently under challenge. It should be recalled that the Yugoslavia which erupted into bloodshed in the middle of 1991 was that same Yugoslavia where, earlier in the year, there had been huge strikes, demonstrations and even an invasion of parliament protesting against the policies that were to produce the conflict. The problem was that no political organisation of the left had been created of sufficient size and with sufficient clarity in its politics that could allow it to expose the old regime for what it was—exploitative and oppressive—and challenge the non-solutions being offered. In eastern Europe there is the opportunity and necessity of avoiding that mistake.

Big tasks and small beginnings

No one should be under any illusion about the scale of the economic and political crisis in eastern Europe and the problems this poses for building a real alternative. The dissident movement that existed before 1989 was always brave but weak in numerical terms. Its isolation drove it together for mutual support and suppressed the full articulation of political differences. At the same time it was easy for those in the West to have influence as it looked anywhere for sustenance. Now that open organisation is possible, in part because of the brave efforts of these people, the movement has fractured completely while some of its members have been absorbed into the new regimes and others remain as marginalised today as they were yesterday, displaced by those who had tacitly supported the old and now are seizing their opportunities to do well in the new.

In these terms the real socialist tradition in eastern Europe is having to be built again from the bottom up by people who are arguing on the ground in ones and twos, in the same way that socialists began their movement in the 19th century. It is easy in this context to look for short cuts. There are none that do not lead to dead ends. The old regimes subordinated their populations to the needs of their rulers, they forced the pace of accumulation at the expense of the working class in order to be better able to compete with the rest of the world. Today the forms are changing but that same logic prevails. The difference is that people now have an opportunity to have these arguments and to organise openly in however small a fashion without the fear of arrest.

This has been the great advance of 1989, the opening that has been created. In that opening there is now the possibility of building an alternative based upon a defence of workers' interests against the old and new forms. On the success of these small beginnings depends not only the future of real socialism in eastern Europe but also how long that democratic opening remains. As in the West a vigorous and independent left wing working class movement, based in the workplace, with strong trade union roots and a political party to represent it, is the only basis for an effective fight to defend workers' interests in the present and to keep the democratic opening open in the face of a ruling class prepared to consider alternative solutions. Indeed it is on the basis of such a defence that movements are built that offer the real prospect of change East and West.

Notes

1 This comment was made in Washington, 18 November 1989. See *The Failure of Communism: The Western Response. An International Conference Sponsored by Radio Free Europe, Radio Liberty Fund* (Munich, 1989), pp49-50.

2 Quoted in *Guardian*, 14 December 1990.

3 On the pre-1914 situation see N Crafts, 'Gross national product in Europe 1870-1910: some new estimates', *Explorations in Economic History*, vol. 20, 1983, pp387-401. On the inter-war years see P Bairoch, 'Europe's Gross National Product: 1800-1975', *Journal of European Economic History*, vol. 5 (1976). For detailed discussion of pre-1939 growth rates in Eastern Europe see M Kaser and E Radice eds, *The Economic History of Eastern Europe, 1919-1975, vol. 1 Economic Structure and Performance between the Wars* (Oxford, 1986), *vol 2 Interwar Policy, the War and Reconstruction* (Oxford, 1987).

4 Quoted in D Aldcroft, 'Eastern Europe in an age of turbulence, 1919-1950', *Economic History Review*, vol. xli no. 4, Nov. 1988, p593-596.

5 See PN Rosenstein-Rodan, 'Problems of industrialisation of Eastern and South Eastern Europe', *Economic Journal*, vol. LII, June-Sept 1943. To break out of a situation where 25 percent of the population were either totally or partially

unemployed Rosenstein-Rodan advocated a broad state directed development push, 'if the industrialisation of international depressed areas were to rely entirely on the normal incentive of private entrepreneurs, the process would not only be very much slower, the rate of investment smaller and (consequently) the national income lower...the whole economic structure of the region would be different'. p206-7.

6 See Y Gluckstein, *Stalin's Satellites in Europe* (London, 1952).

7 These growth rates are based on the standard Western calculations and recalculations for eastern Europe. See W Baumol, 'Productivity growth, convergence and welfare', *American Economic Review*, vol. 76 no. 5, December 1986.

8 One measure of this was the weak development of intra-industry trade—one of the major growth areas in the West as the underlying integration of the world economy increased. In the mid-1980s, for example, only 17 percent of Anglo-Soviet trade was on an intra-industry basis compared to 64 percent of Anglo-French and 62 percent of Anglo-German trade. M Kaser, 'The East European Economies in transition', *European Management Journal*, vol. 8 no. 3, September 1990, p295.

9 Data for West and East Germany from A Yakolev, 'Monopolizm v ekonomike SSSR i faktorui ego obuslovlivaoushschie', *Vestnik Statistiki*, no.1, 1991, p4. Data for Poland and Western sample from D Lipton and J Sachs, 'Creating a market economy in eastern Europe: the case of Poland', *Brookings Papers on Economic Activity*, no. 1, 1990, p84.

10 Yakolev, op cit, pp3-4. See also IMF et al, *A Study of the Soviet Economy*, 1991, vol. 2 chap. IV. 2, pp36-40.

11 In an economy like South Korea there is only limited internal competition for similar reasons. See the data quoted in '"Poor Man's Burden": A survey of the Third World', *Economist*, 23-29 September 1989, pp38-39.

12 Quoted in Lipton and Sachs, op cit,(footnote 9), p76

13 OECD, *Financial Market Trends*, Feb 1991, no. 48, p20.

14 Lipton and Sachs, op cit, pp104-105.

15 *Financial Times*, 12 March 1990.

16 Hankiss has used this example in a number of places. For a short statement see his 'Reforms and the conversion of power' in P R Weilemann, G Brunner and R Tokes eds, *Upheaval against the Plan: eastern Europe on the Eve of the Storm* (1991). For his fuller analysis see his *East European Alternatives* (Oxford,1990).

17 A Aganbegyan, *The Challenge, The Economics of Perestroika* (London, 1988).

18 I Pozsgay, 'Hungary for change', *Marxism Today*, May 1989, p27.

19 Elemer Hankiss, *Vilag*, 23 November 1989 quoted in A Gresh, 'Les sentiers escarpes du passage a la democratie', *Le Monde Diplomatique*, Feb 1990, p5.

20 A Maddison, 'Origins and Impact of the Welfare State, 1883-1983', *Banca Nazionale del Lavoro Quarterly Review*, March 1984; A Maddison, *The World Economy in the Twentieth Century*, 1989, (p71) for later data.

21 The precise balance between these two tendencies has been subject to ongoing debate in this journal and elsewhere. See C Harman, 'The state and capitalism today', *International Socialism*, 2.51, (1991) and the references given there.

22 V Tanzio, 'Eastern Europe: the state's role in mobilizing savings', *IMF Survey*, 27 May 1991, p166.

23 S Shahid Husain, 'Reviving growth in Latin America', *Finance and Development*, June 1989, p2. See also the *Economist* survey 'Poor man's Burden' op cit on state action in the Third World.

24 Husain, op cit.

25 *The Rise of World Poverty*, Socialist Economic Briefing, 1990

26 M Pastor Jnr, 'The effects of IMF programmes in the Third World: Debate and evidence from Latin America', *World Development*, vol. 15 no. 2, 1987, p250.
27 For the critical debate on the impact of such policies see Pastor, op cit; MD Ramirez, 'The impact of austerity on Latin America, 1983-1989: A critical assessment', *Comparative Economic Studies*, vol. xxxiii no1, Spring 1991.
28 For the defensive discussion of the IMF and World Bank on the costs of their programmes see G. Pfeffermann, 'Economic crisis and the poor in some Latin American countries', *Finance and Development*, June, 1987; C Humpheys and W Jaeger, 'Africa's adjustment and growth', *Finance and Development*, June, 1989; J Greene, 'The debt problem of Sub-Saharan Africa', *Finance and Development*, June, 1989.
29 J Weiner, 'Capitalist shock therapy: the Sachs Plan in Poland' in his *Professors, Politics and Pop* (London, 1991).
30 This discussion draws heavily on 'Bolivia: the poverty of progress', *Report on the Americas*, vol. xxv no. 1, July 1991.
31 See J Newsinger, 'The Bolivian Revolution', *International Socialism*, 2.18, (1983).
32 Quoted in 'Bolivia: the poverty of progress', op cit, pp28-29.
33 *Guardian*, 2 July 1991.
34 See the report of Sachs' contribution to the 1991 World Bank Annual Conference, *IMF Survey*, 27 May 1991.
35 Quoted in 'Bolivia: the poverty of progress', op cit, p12.
36 Quoted in Pastor Jnr, op cit, p259.
37 Lipton and Sachs, op cit, p75.
38 See K. Bossanyi, 'An interview with Janos Kornai', *Acta Oeconomica*, vol. 42 no. 3-4, 1990, pp315-328.
39 J Kornai, *The Economics of Shortage, Growth, Shortage and Efficiency: A Macrodynamic Model of the Socialist Economy* 1980.
40 A Nove, 'Reforming the Soviet economy', *Dissent*, Winter 1991, p11; J Kornai 'The Hungarian Reform Process: visions, hopes and reality', *Journal of Economic Literature*, December, 1986 also expresses his disillusion with reform and the possibility of coping with bureaucracy; J Kornai, *The Road to a Free Economy, Shifting from a Socialist System: The Example of Hungary* (London, 1990).
41 Kornai, *The Road*, op cit.
42 D Lipton and J Sachs, op cit, pp77, 138 (their paper is followed by Kornai's comments).
43 Kornai, *The Road*, op cit.
44 Bosanyi, op cit, p327.
45 See, for example, the publicity and campaigns of *Labour Focus on Eastern Europe* as well as the individual campaigns of groups all over the world to the left of the communist parties.
46 See Bush's speech to the IMF-World Bank Annual Meeting, 25 September 1990.
47 Two older studies of this process are still useful. See Barrington Moore Jnr, 'Some readjustments in communist theory', *Journal of the History of Ideas*, vol. 6, 1945, pp468-482; RV Daniels, 'The State and Revolution: a case study in the genesis and transformation of communist ideology', *American Slavic and East European Review*, vol. 12, 1953, pp22-43.
48 There is much of interest on this ideological shift in B Chavance, *Le capital socialiste, histoire critique de l'economie politique du socialisme, 1917-1954* (Paris, 1980) although it operates with a different conception of state capitalism to that discussed in this journal.
49 The conservative role and conservative content of Soviet ideas and their links to Western conservatism were noted by Nigel Harris many years ago. See his *Beliefs in Society* (London, 1971). There is a fascinating study of how this conservative

mentality, the development of 'bourgeois values', came to be reflected in popular literature in Vera Dunham, *In Stalin's Time. Middle Class Values in Soviet Fiction* (London, 1976).

50 B Crick, *George Orwell, A life* (London, 1980), pp52-53.

51 N Shmelev, 'Avansy i dolgi', *Novy Mir*, no. 6, 1987, p147.

52 *Financial Times*, 29 October 1990.

53 G Akerloff et al, 'East Germany in from the cold: the economic aftermath of currency union', *Brookings Papers in Economic Activity*, no. 1, 1991, p1.

54 Ibid.

55 *Observer*, 31 March 1991, estimate quoted from German source.

56 The extent of labour force contraction in the former East Germany is examined in M Haynes, 'Labour Force Contraction in the former GDR', Working Paper, School of European Studies, Wolverhampton Polytechnic, 1992.

57 Based on data in the monthly bulletin of the (West) German Labour Office.

58 OECD, *Economic Outlook*, no. 49, July 1991, p36; IMF, *World Economic Outlook*, p2 October 1991; OECD, *Economic Outlook*, no.50, December 1991, p55.

59 Lipton and Sachs, op cit, pp101-102.

60 The IMF (see footnote 58) predicts an optimistic 2 percent growth for eastern Europe, excluding the USSR, for 1992—if this was sustained it would still take 10 to 15 years to recover pre-1989 levels of output. Whilst this recovery took place the rest of the world would have moved on and divergence increased since both the advanced and 'developing world' are predicted to grow at faster rates.

61 There have been a number of attempts to calculate the scale of these effective subsidies. By way of illustration it is estimated that in the period 1970-1984 each Soviet citizen subsidised East German industry—the most advanced in the bloc—by 270 dollars a year through purchases of lower quality, overpriced manufactured goods, *Financial Times*, 12 March 1990.

62 OECD *Economic Outlook*, no. 49 July 1991, p37.

63 United Nations Economic Commission for Europe, *Economic Survey of Europe in 1990-1991*, (New York, 1991), pp90-91.

64 OECD, *Economic Outlook*, no. 49, July 1991, p39.

65 Ibid.

66 A major expansion of agricultural trade is a significant part of the Group of Thirty's proposals for Eastern Europe. *Financing Eastern Europe: A Study Group Report*, 1991. (There is a brief summary of its main conclusions in *IMF Survey*, July 29 1991. Agriculture now produces only around 5 percent of West European output using some 8 percent of the labour force. But agricultural subsidies which go disproportionally to big farmers and the big food processing companies make up some 60 percent of the European Community's budget. Weekly food subsidy costs are estimated to be the equivalent of £14 per family.

67 OECD, *Economic Outlook*, no. 49, July 1991, p37.

68 Will Hutton in the *Guardian*, 10 July 1991.

69 OECD, *Financial Market Trends*, no. 48, February 1991, pp20-26.

70 Ibid, p.29.

71 Ibid, pp30-31.

72 *Sunday Times*, 13 December 1981. The second banker was quoted on the BBC radio on 14 December 1981. See M Haynes, 'Russia, eastern Europe and the world economy', paper given to the Critique Conference, London, 15 January 1982.

73 OECD, *Financial Market Trends*, op cit, p16; D Fairlamb, 'Eastern Europe Opportunities for Bankers', *Banking World*, April,1990, p22.

74 OECD, *Economic Outlook*, no. 49, July 1991, p40. The contrast between the treatment of Poland and the poorer countries of the world has not been lost there.

In the Philippines, for example, there has been enormous pressure not to default, '"But then", observed one human rights lawyer, "the Philippines hadn't just overthrown communism (sic); we had merely chucked out Reagan's chum Marcos". Perhaps, some are saying cynically, the way to get debt forgiven is to go communist and then overthrow the government'. J Seabrook, 'Bad Debts', *New Statesman*, 21 June 1991.

75 See M.Glenny, *The Rebirth of History: eastern Europe in the Age of Democracy*, (London, 1990), p185.

76 *Economist*, 10 August 1991, *Guardian*, 27 August 1991. In its pinstriped junketing 'while the poor starve' the EBRD is following a well established pattern in the IMF and World Bank. See the critique 'Pinstripes and Poverty: Inside the World Bank', *New Internationalist*, December 1990 which should be compared with the *Economist*'s survey celebrating their activities, 'IMF and World Bank Survey', 12 October 1991.

77 *Economist*, op cit, p49.

78 Boston Consulting Group, 'Eastern Europe—the free market makes its debut', *Director*, November 1990, p122.

79 R Hunerberg, 'Risk and opportunities in eastern Europe', *European Management Journal*, vol. 8 no. 4, December 1990, p518.

80 Ibid. For similar caution see A Hermann and M Hermann, 'Eastern and Central Europe: opportunities and problems', *European Management Journal*, vol. 8 no. 3, September 1990; I.Zloch-Christy, 'Political risk assessment in lending to Eastern Europe', idem., vol. 8 no. 4, December 1990; Boston Consulting Group (footnote 78). Private consultancy advice is even more cautious. One such report, seen by the author, advises Asian business to treat Poland as an 'upfront expense needed to gain a greater share of the market later on' rather than a source of immediate profit. But investing companies should give the appearance of substantial long term commitment so as to 'potentially win more favourable terms for investing in Poland. Such terms might include longer tax holidays, lower taxes thereafter, more favourable initial valuation etc'. Countries like Poland and Hungary are already moving to create the most favourable legal climates in the world for attracting foreign investment.

81 'Business in eastern Europe Survey', *Economist*, 21 September 1991, p25.

82 'The Skoda-Volkswagen Merger: Salvation or Steal?', *East European Reporter*, Spring-Summer, 1991, pp56-58.

83 'Is freedom of movement a threat for Europe?', *Forum Council of Europe*, February 1991, pp39-41. Interestingly Akerloff et al (see footnote 53), otherwise apostles of the market, try desperately to disprove that migration in eastern Germany is determined by wage differentials in order to support lower wages in the former East Germany.

84 Quoted in 'Paying guests', *International Management*, February 1991, pp39-41.

85 I Baranshas, 'West erects its own Iron Curtain', *Guardian*, 12 July 1991.

86 In the spring of 1991 the author attended a meeting at which a Polish speaker began by announcing that Poland had just removed its visa restrictions for outward travel and how proud he therefore was that it had rejoined the 'civilised world'. Unfortunately the British government still insists that all Poles should have a British visa! This is despite some offence to its own right wing. John Major justified the restrictions to Lord Bethell, the right wing commentator on eastern Europe:

> *we have reluctantly concluded, that with the best will in the world, we cannot overlook the impact on employment which immigration from Poland on the scale we expect would cause. In 1990, nearly 60,000 Poles came here. On top of that there were over 2,000 visa refusals and 20,000 Poles withdrew their*

visa applications in the expectation they would be refused. So the potential numbers are large.
Mail on Sunday 8, September 1991.

87 In fact the KGB and other such organisations have been well placed to make this particular shift and have been argued to be prominent in setting up the Soviet stock exchange.
88 This discussion summarises a wider analysis of 'Class Recomposition in Eastern Europe' available from the author.
89 Hankiss, 'Reforms ...' op cit, p 31 (see footnote 16).
90 G Tamas Koranyi, 'Where have all the experts gone?', *The Hungarian Observer*, no. 3, 1991, p16.
91 Quoted in I Rammonet, 'Pologne—annee zero', *Le Monde Diplomatique*, December 1990, p8.
92 *IMF Survey*, 27 May 1991.
93 The level of individual share ownership varies but in all major countries it is less than institutional share ownership and declining in importance. Between 1980-1988 private share ownership fell from 28.2 to 21.3 percent of all shares in the UK; 50 to 42 percent in the USA and 29 to 23 percent in Japan. See C Breheny, 'Wider share ownership in danger', *Investors Chronicle*, 15 March 1991, pp14-15.
94 *Business Week,* 15 April 1991.
95 Quoted in M.Levinson, 'Reforming the economies of eastern Europe', *Dissent*, Winter 1991, p129.
96 T Kuzci and A Vajda, 'The social composition of small entrepreneurs', *Acta Economica*, vol. 42 no. 3-4, 1990, p322.
97 *Business Week,* 15 April 1991, p21.
98 A Osenberg, 'Deutsche Bank moves East', *Banking World*, June, 1991, p27.
99 This discussion of unemployment summarises a longer paper M.Haynes and M.Perry, 'The measurement of unemployment in eastern Europe and the USSR', Second European Research Conference, Nottingham, April 1991.
100 Polish, Hungarian and Czechoslovakian figures are now published regularly in their respective monthly statistical bulletins. Other figures are announced regularly and are drawn from the BBC *Survey of World Broadcasts*.
101 Lipton and Sachs, op cit, argue that before 1989 Poles had to queue to get little or nothing. Now they know they can afford little or nothing so they do not queue. Thus the real standard of living has improved in this area and therefore the overall fall exaggerated. I have yet to find an eastern European who I could persuade of the merits of this argument.
102 Ibid, p121.
103 *Guardian,* 7 May 1990.
104 J Seddon, 'Privatisation in eastern Europe', *European Management Journal*, vol. 8 no. 4, December 1990, p508. (The author is head of the privatisation unit at Barclays de Zoete Wedd who offer advice to eastern European governments).
105 See the discussion in Radio Free Europe bulletins *passim*.
106 *Guardian,* 30 December 1990.
107 *Guardian,* 19 November 1990.
108 Quoted in I. Ramonet, op cit, p9.
109 *Guardian,*19 November 1990.
110 *Guardian,* 15 August 1991.

A miracle without end? Japanese capitalism and the world economy

COSTAS KOSSIS

Introduction

Japanese capitalism is shrouded with mystery in the West. The questions about it abound. Why was economic development so fast after the Second World War? Is Japan impervious to economic instability and crisis? Will Japanese imperialism re-emerge as a serious threat to US imperialism? Such questions are not only expressions of innocent curiosity. Virulent anti-Japanese prejudice, particularly in the USA, has become rife. A stream of largely worthless books have been written on the various threats from Japan.[1] Fervent American patriots and highly trained economists have been trying to devise a strategy to defeat the new 'yellow peril'.[2]

American capitalism feels vulnerable in its decline and so the anti-Japan poison is particularly virulent. To be sure, European capitalism is not far behind. In her frequent racist outbursts French prime minister Edith Cresson has railed against the Japanese and even likened them to ants. She has joined forces with the anti-Japanese hardliner Jacques Calvet, president of the car company Peugeot, who has been calling for tough trade measures against Japan.[3]

This article is an attempt to answer some of the questions about Japan. Evidently the complexity of a great country's development cannot be captured in a few pages. The aim of the article is to sketch the broad trends characteristic of the staggering growth of Japanese capital. The nature of these trends and the remarkable ability of Japanese capital to restructure itself explain its present dynamism. In the light of the fundamental trends I will also discuss possible developments for the 1990s. The central argument of this article, contrary to the exceptionalism favoured by many when analysing Japan, is that Japanese capitalism is very much a part of the world economy and follows the rhythms of the latter. It is simply not true that Japan has escaped the crisis ridden logic of capitalism and can continue to expand while Western capitalism declines. At the same time there is no denying the fact that Japan has done better than its capitalist rivals and to understand this we have to look at the peculiarities of the Japanese economy.

Characteristic features of the Japanese economy

For ten years after the Second World War Japan was primarily engaged in reconstruction. The return to peacetime activities provided a domestic market for Japanese capital. Demand was boosted by 'special procurement' for the US forces in the Korean War. This was a period of poverty and uncertain beginnings. Then from the mid-1950s to the mid-1970s the 'Rapid Growth Period' took place. Annual growth rates averaged 10 percent, the working class expanded enormously and Japan emerged as an economic superpower. The crisis of 1973-1975 signified the end of this period. Since the mid-1970s annual growth rates have averaged less than 5 percent, Japanese capital has become increasingly global and Japan has been established as the second largest economy in the world.

Two propositions are fundamental in order to analyse this historical pattern. The first proposition is that the pressures of the world economy are acutely felt in Japan. The long post-war boom of the world economy roughly coincided with the Rapid Growth Period. Japanese capital took advantage of the opportunities of a rapidly growing world market and of the easy transfer of technology. The international crisis of 1973-1974 signalled the end of the Rapid Growth Period in Japan. Similarly the slowdown of the world economy since the mid-1970s has also been reflected in Japan.

The second proposition is that the peculiar characteristics of the Japanese economy shaped its post-war path. Marxists appreciate that no two national capitalisms are alike. The specific features of Japanese capital allowed it to grow faster and to restructure itself more efficiently than its competitors in the world market. In this article I will first analyse some of these features and then I will consider the role of the world economy and the mechanics of capital accumulation.

The role of the state in the economy

Two aspects of the Japanese state in the post-war period need elaboration. First, throughout this period, the Japanese state has been smaller than Western states as far as claims on national resources are concerned.[4] This is explained by the extremely low level of military spending and the low (but rising) level of welfare expenditure.[5] Since the war Japanese capitalism has lived without a severe arms burden and under the shadow of the US military presence in the Pacific. During this period large parts of the costs of the reproduction and restoration of labour-power were pushed onto the family and the large pool of the peasantry.

The second key aspect of the Japanese state has been its heavy intervention in the economy. The US occupation of 1945-1952 purged the state of the most compromised collaborators of the statist military regime. Hundreds were condemned to death as war criminals. Despite this, the outlook of the post-war economic apparatuses of state was heavily influenced by the wartime experience of directing a militarised economy.[6] The Ministry of International Trade and Industry, MITI, the Ministry of Finance, MoF, and the Economic Planning Agency, EPA, acted as the masterminds of Japan's effort to catch up economically with the West.

There has been debate in the pages of this journal on the relationship between state and capital.[7] Recent arguments have centred on whether the integration of national capitals into the world economy is reducing the nation state to a marginal economic role. With respect to Japan it would be wrong to assume either that there is complete fusion of state and capital or that relentless ascendancy by capital is reducing the state to economic impotence. The Japanese state is certainly not a mere 'nightwatchman' securing the terrain for the competition of private capitals. On the contrary, it has played a leading role in forming Japanese capital and supporting its drive in the world market. The relationship of state and capital remains critical for capitalist accumulation. The point to remember here is that although the state and capital depend on each other, their interests do not coincide and their relationship is riven with conflict, divisions and clashes of interest.

Since the mid-1970s, as Japanese capital started to become increasingly global, the relationship of state and capital has changed significantly. The ability of the state to foster growth and to stabilise national markets has suffered. However the state has not at all ceded its privilege, indeed its right, to influence economic activity. On the contrary, it has carved out a critical role for itself in managing the violent crises of the last two decades and defending its national capital in the world market. Japanese capital is not trying to rid itself of the embrace of its national state. Instead, globally-minded capital looks to the state for overall strategy, defence from trade attacks, provision of a skilled labour force, and leadership in times of restructuring. Three types of relations are important in order to understand the active economic role of the Japanese state.

Plans: Governments have employed a series of economic plans since 1955. Japanese plans were not Soviet-type plans, organising the transfer and utilisation of resources in order to achieve economic targets. They were, rather, indicative plans setting targets for growth, investment, consumption and so on. By and large, targets were missed as the plans were typically too conservative during the Rapid Growth Period. Yet their role was important in encouraging businesses to borrow and to reinvest profits. They provided a propitious climate for the headlong rushes to invest, characteristic of Japanese accumulation. The state was seen to be there, supervising the process through MITI and ready to shore it up through MoF and the central bank. The state has continued to play the role of confidence booster and insurer of the economic choices of the capitalist class to this day.

State measures: The Rapid Growth Period was underpinned by a battery of state measures promoting the accumulation of private capital. A heavily regulated credit system kept rates of interest low and directed cheap funds toward investment. Import controls were operated. Tax breaks were given for exports and for depreciation of capital equipment. Technology transfer from the West was organised with a state-operated system of licences. Land reclamation created much of the narrow strip of land on the Pacific coast on which Japanese industry is concentrated. The state bureaucracy, furthermore, actively discouraged direct investment into Japan by foreign capital, aiming to keep the domestic market as the exclusive preserve of Japanese firms. [8]

The increasing integration of Japanese capital into the world economy has reduced the ability of the state to promote such measures. Japanese import controls became unacceptable to American and European capitalists in the early 1960s. Throughout the 1970s and 1980s technology transfer became increasingly difficult and blatant export promotion impracticable. In recent years the rate of interest has also been left to find its market level. It is probably wrong to speak of state control of any sector of the economy since the mid-1970s.

Growth-fostering measures became untenable but the state's fiscal and monetary policies have remained very important. The relaxation of tax policy, for instance, was one of the reasons for the expansion of domestic demand in the late 1980s. Large borrowing needs by the state in the mid-1970s were instrumental in creating the money markets of contemporary Japan. Monetary policy is vital for the determination of the rate of interest in those markets. The international flows of loanable capital rely on state policy as a reference point for their movements. Thus a strong yen allowed loose monetary policy and low interest rates in the second half of the 1980s. Low interest rates fed an investment and credit boom. By the same token, tight monetary policy since the end of 1989 was instrumental in deflating the credit bubble. Processes such as these are contradictory and crisis-ridden but there is no denying the fundamental role of the state in them.

Administrative guidance: A host of national organisations of capital, characteristic of the Japanese economy, maintain a continuous relationship with the state. These include the national organisation of employers, the *Keidanren*, as well as various employers' associations for sectors of the economy such as the Shipbuilders Association. Large units of productive and commercial capital as well as banks also have regular links with the state. The top echelons of the state bureaucracy (MITI, MoF, Foreign Ministry and so on) are graduates of a handful of universities, especially Tokyo University. They are very likely to have known the leaders of industry since university days. The links of state and capital are further strengthened by the practice of *amakudari*—'the descent from heaven'. Retired high ranking state bureaucrats are parachuted into the boards of large companies where they provide crucial personal connections with the state machine.

Regular meetings of industry and state bodies and a constant mingling of personnel allow the Japanese state to promote the interests of capital as a whole versus individual and sectoral interests. Generally speaking, the state offers leadership to capital with specific policies, suggestions and mechanisms for resolving disputes between capitalists. The state has been key to agreements between capitals on how to divide the domestic market. It has been concerned to expand the share of Japanese capital in the world market. It has also consistently tried to increase the concentration of capital in important sectors of the economy such as steel, cars and so on.

The crucial role of the state in giving leadership to private capital is sometimes called 'administrative guidance'. In the past this role led Western observers to think that all changes in the Japanese economy originated with the state. [9] At its crudest this is expressed as the misconception 'Japan Inc'. In reality the relationship of private capital and the state is complex and ridden with conflict. Policies which private capital deeply desires are often made to appear as state-induced policies. Shipbuilding firms, for instance, were instrumental in passing legislation in 1978 which fostered the restructuring of the industry in the face of world crisis.[10] Most of the time the interests of capital as a whole are sufficiently overwhelming to force concessions from individual capitals. If its essential interests are jeopardised, however, private capital will fight the leadership of the state. This was true during the Rapid Growth Period and it is true now. Two celebrated cases will suffice to demonstrate the point.

In 1962 MITI attempted to pass the Designated Industries Temporary Measures Act. The bill proposed mergers, rationalisation, standardisation of production and so on in order to restructure key industries such as automobiles and petrochemicals. MITI's aim was the strengthening of Japanese capital as a whole in the world market. Funds to promote the restructuring would have come from the banks. MITI would have emerged as the true overlord of the economy, controlling the allocation of resources. Furious conflict with private capital was the result. The banks in co-operation with the affected sectors defeated the bill.

Again, throughout the second half of the 1960s, MITI attempted to promote mergers in the car industry with a view to reducing 'excessive competition'. The aim was to concentrate production in two mass producers, Toyota and Nissan, which would have been able to compete in the world market. Other car makers, namely Honda, Mitsubishi and Toyo Kogyo (Mazda), strongly resisted MITI's pressure and averted the mergers. Some of these independent producers, such as Honda, have been successful competitors internationally.

Such profound conflicts of interest between capital as a whole and individual or sectoral capitals lead to divisions within the ruling class. They then translate into divisions within the state machine as capitals mobilise support from areas of the state apparatus with which they have close relations. Far from a monolithic state machine overlapping with and leading an equally monolithic private capital, the true picture is one of constant bargaining accompanied by antagonisms and conflict.

The end of the Rapid Growth Period has wrought significant changes to the relationship of the state and capital. The slowdown of growth has necessitated the restructuring of several industries such as textiles and shipbuilding. The state has played a key role in organising recession cartels which manage the reductions in capacity. It has also provided finance necessary for restructuring. More importantly, the increase in trade friction with the USA has given a new role to the state. The Japanese state now undertakes the promotion of imports into Japan and the negotiation and management of Voluntary Export Restraint.

The structure of Japanese industry

It is characteristic of Japanese capital to form industrial groups which wield enormous economic, political and social influence. Before the Second World War these groups were the cartel-like *zaibatsu,* formed around a bank and possessing a trust company and a general trading company. The occupation authorities dismantled the *zaibatsu,* reduced industrial concentration and established the anti-monopoly Fair Trading Commission, FTC. Soon, however, the centralisation of capital reasserted itself and the large *zaibatsu,* such as Mitsui and Sumitomo, reappeared. *Zaibatsu* groups are held together through credit provided by the bank, through the regular transfer of directors between companies and through mutual shareholding. Member companies retain a significant degree of independence in pricing, sourcing of supplies and so on. Central, cartel-like control is not nearly as tight as it was before the war. Price-fixing, a key feature of cartels, is not crucial to holding together the various companies of a Japanese industrial group.

Since the war other industrial groups, often called *keiretsu,* have evolved around the major banks, like Dai Ichi Kangin and Sanwa banks. The main connecting link for these groups is bank finance. *Keiretsu* are not instances of Hilferding's finance capital, that is fusions of industrial and banking capital with the latter in the dominant role. Rather such groups are more developed cases of the 'the main bank' relationship which is characteristic of Japanese industry. Japanese firms typically borrow from a variety of banks but one or two of those are recognised as 'main banks'. The latter maintain a close watch on the creditworthiness and general performance of the firm. They also have a director placed in the executive board of the borrowing firm. Links are strengthened by a degree of interlocking shareholding between banks and industrial companies. Banks do not dictate the strategy of industrial capital, however, and it is possible for firms to change their main bank within a relatively short period of time. [11]

The significance of the 'main bank' relationship emerges clearly in a crisis. If the borrowing firm is in serious difficulties the 'main bank' will normally provide loans in order to avoid collapse. Firms which belong to the *keiretsu* of major banks have a strong guarantee of the availability of bank finance when they face a crisis.

Finally there are industrial groups which emerged after the Second World War around major industrial companies such as Hitachi and Toyota. These groups are held together through production and trade links with the core company. Around the core company there is a web of subsidiaries, affiliates and subcontractors which rely on each other for the supply of inputs, the sale of output, trade credit and so on.

Beneath the large units of capital there is a great mass of small and medium firms. The latter are particularly numerous in some areas of the economy such as agriculture, distribution, textiles. The division of the Japanese economy into giant firms which tend to form groups and, on the other hand, a huge mass of small firms has been termed 'the dual structure'. Several points are important in this connection.

First a web of subcontracting relationships connects small and medium firms with each other and with the large firms. The connections are long term and involve co-operation over quality of output, product specifications, delivery times and other aspects of production and exchange. Second a clear hierarchy, based on size, exists among the units of capital. For a firm, the higher up the ladder it is the better the terms it can secure from its suppliers. Indeed the subcontracting relationship usually involves a leading and a led firm. Third firms higher up the hierarchy normally have better working conditions, wages, stability of the workforce and workers' productivity. Thus, they attract better qualified workers and so sustain their productivity advantages. Fourth in times of economic difficulty large firms pass some of the pressure onto small firms. Typically, workers are seconded from the large to the small firm, profit margins are tightened and credit terms are worsened. Small and medium firms play the role of 'shock absorbers' in times of crisis.

Large firms in the same industry engage in cartel-like behaviour and attempt to limit competition.[12] Despite the anti-monopoly legacy of the occupation and the existence of the Fair Trading Commission, collusive behaviour among firms is favoured by MITI. The Japanese state has persistently tried to limit 'excessive competition' by discouraging new entrants into industries and by fostering mergers.

It is important to realise, though, that a fierce competitive struggle also takes place in Japanese markets. Severe competitive pressures arise from the orientation of the largest companies toward the world market. International competitive pressure has forced ship, car, electrical and electronic goods and other manufacturers to innovate, reduce costs and improve quality. Moreover, in the domestic market, firms are constantly trying to climb the ladder of hierarchy in order to secure the advantages of the larger units. The system of life-time employment, which I will discuss below, also forces firms constantly to expand their market share in order to accommodate the regular, annual inflow of workers and the promotion expectations of existing workers. Competition comes, finally, from the great mass of small firms, which Rosa Luxemburg has called the 'pioneers of technical progress ... the vital pulse of the capitalist economy'. [13] The upshot of these competitive forces has been continuous innovation and increases in efficiency, particularly for capitals directed to the world market.

The working class and the labour process

There has been a lot of theoretical and practical interest in Japanese work practices recently. Many writers have asserted the inherent superiority of life time employment, flexibility of job definition, team work, training within the firm and single union agreements. [14] Others have argued that labour relations in Britain will become increasingly 'Japanised'.[15]

At the heart of the Japanese system is life time employment. Male, skilled workers of large companies join those companies straight after school or university and have more or less secure employment throughout their working life. Companies have an annual intake of recruits who fill the lower reaches of the rigid labour hierarchy as other workers are promoted over time. The regular intake of fresh labour power itself acts as a powerful incentive to increase market share in order to accommodate these workers. It is important to realise that life-time employment only holds for roughly 40 percent of the workforce. For women workers and temporary workers employed by large firms there is no life-time employment guarantee. For the workers of the hundreds of thousands of small firms again there is no guarantee of secure employment. During economic crises women, temporary and small firm workers bear the brunt of unemployment. By no stretch of the imagination, however, are skilled male workers of large firms free from the fear of unemployment. As we shall see later, in the most serious crisis of the post-war period, 1973-75, hundreds of thousands of such jobs disappeared.

Before the war Japanese industry did not really practice life-time employment. Turnover of workers in companies was as high as in the US.[16] A series of bitterly contested victories for the capitalist class from the end of the war to the early 1960s shaped post war capital-labour relations. The occupation authorities opened the prisons of the militarists and released thousands of communists, socialists and liberals. The Americans also legalised trade union activity and turned a blind eye to socialist agitation. Trade union membership literally rocketed, exceeding 40 percent of the workforce by 1948. In the conditions of post-war destruction the Communist Party went from strength to strength, reaching a peak of 10 percent of the vote in 1949. This was the year of the victorious Chinese Revolution. The possibilities for working class power in Japan were very real indeed.

The Cold War and Stalinist politics changed all that. The high point of the first post-war workers' mobilisation came in February 1947 with a proposed general strike led by Communist and Socialist unions. The Americans, already hardening in their Cold War attitudes, banned the strike. The Communists offered practically no resistance. Defeat led to a limitation of the right to strike in 1948. In 1949, as the Cold War intensified, the Americans launched a 'Red Purge'. Tens of thousands of communist workers were dismissed from government, education and industry. Enterprise unionism began to take a hold as the politicised, industry-wide unions were purged and union membership declined. The Korean War solidified this transformation. In a mad ultra-leftist lurch the Communist Party went 'underground' in the early 1950s, threatened to undertake terrorism and lost the bulk of its support.

Yet in the impoverished conditions of the 1950s social stability was not possible. The Peace Treaty of San Francisco of 1951, which confirmed American hegemony over Japan, acted as a focus for mass struggle against US imperialism. Subsequent opposition to the emergent Liberal-Democratic Party stronghold on power took very sharp and violent class forms. Peasants, workers and students regularly clashed with police, often over issues associated with the US military presence in Japan. In the struggle against the Police Duties Bill of 1958 millions of workers were brought to the streets by the General Council of Trade Unions.

The high point of this tumultuous period came in 1960 with the renegotiation of the San Francisco Treaty. The Japanese ruling class was keen to remain under the protective umbrella of the US superpower and to take advantage of US markets for its exports, particularly textiles. A huge mass movement erupted, led by workers' unions and by students. When the Japanese Diet ratified the new treaty there were mass demonstrations throughout Japan and riots in Tokyo. The government decided to ask Eisenhower to postpone his proposed visit to Japan. A few days later the government fell. Yet despite the struggle, the new treaty was ratified and established the framework for US-Japan relations for the 1960s and 1970s.

Meanwhile, sharp industrial action also took place in 1960 with railway strikes, and, above all, miners' strikes. The Japanese ruling class planned to take advantage of cheap oil imports in order to facilitate industrial expansion. The massive coal-mining industry was to be ruthlessly scaled down. Resistance by miners was fierce and the struggle was brutal. In the event, however, the restructuring went through and Japan does not possess any significant coal-mining capability today. Yet the general tumult of the 1950s and the costs involved in achieving those victories for the ruling class were instrumental to the system of labour relations which is now recognised as 'typically Japanese'. Given the combativity of the working class and the general scarcity of skilled labour, confrontation was a very costly strategy for the ruling class. Life-time employment was part of a systematic effort at class collaboration which became the hallmark of the period after 1960.

Supplementing 'life time employment' is the seniority wage system. Upon entering a large company a young worker can expect to earn a relatively low wage. Earnings will rise rapidly as the years of service increase and the promotion ladder is climbed. Moreover large companies supplement wages with a range of paternalistic benefits: cheap housing, education allowance, commuting and heating allowance and so on. The system is a conscious attempt to instigate class collaboration at all levels. Company unionism of the most compromised kind constantly negotiates the flare ups between capital and labour. A climate of 'the company as family' is encouraged. This is particularly admired by those who marvel at Japanese productivity and only see one side of things. The other side is the tremendous fragmentation of the working class fostered by the system. Constantly and perniciously, men and women, permanent and temporary, large and small company, old and young workers are divided from each other. An intensely hierarchical, almost militarised, regime prevails in the labour process.

Class collaboration together with the fragmentation of the working class has allowed the ruling class to enforce inhuman patterns of exploitation. There is a lack of clear job demarcation and workers are constantly shifted within the company, geographically and in terms of departments. Management assumes an 'egalitarian' demeanour, constantly rubs shoulders with workers and creates the illusion that workers make a significant input in the improvement of production technique. The result is that Japanese workers work longer hours than American, German and British workers. They are forced to do endless unpaid and hidden overtime. They face constant speed ups and the cruelties of constant quality control. The social cost of this extensive and intensive exploitation, simply in terms of endemic death from overwork and ruined family lives, is enormous. 'Serious' studies of the Japanese labour process never talk about the brutality of exploitation. The most vivid accounts of the grim realities of life on the shopfloor are given by journalists.[17]

The importance of regular economic growth since the mid-1950s for sustaining the arrangements of the labour market cannot be overstressed. Growth has allowed a steady rise in wages and the achievement of low rates of unemployment. The gradual rise of living standards prevented a repetition of the massive struggles of the early years. The proponents of 'Japanised' industrial relations in the West normally forget this side of the equation. They imagine that the US and British ruling classes can simply intensify exploitation without providing to workers any of the benefits of the Japanese system.

Japan is not a country of low-paid, patriotic helots. It possesses a highly literate and skilled working class with a tradition of struggle. For decades after the war the working class has been enormously exploited but has also improved its living standards. To maintain the present equilibrium the Japanese ruling class must ensure regular growth and wage increases. In this respect, Japan's rulers are under much more pressure than Americans or Germans. The very rigidity of 'life time employment' implies brittleness if growth is not achieved and some benefits earned by workers. Indications of how precariously the system is balanced were provided during the crisis of 1973-1975.

The Rapid Growth Period and the crisis of 1973-75

Rapid Growth Period, mid-1950s to mid-1970s: With the specific features of the Japanese economy in mind we can analyse the place of Japan in the world economy and the mechanics of capital accumulation in the post-war period. Here I will engage in unavoidable generalisations. The conditions for rapid growth were set by the long post-war boom in the world economy—underpinned by arms expenditure—and the spectacular growth of world trade during the same period. Japanese capital was able to compete particularly successfully because of its peculiarities and because it was free of arms expenditure

Protectionism operated by the state allowed room for infant industries to grow. Japanese capital, however, did not aim at autarchy. With state encouragement, shipbuilding, steel, chemicals, automobiles and electrical appliances aimed at the world market. Under state auspices, technology was furiously imported from abroad, industries were restructured, enterprises fused in order to create mass production and exports were promoted. By the mid-1960s Japan possessed the biggest shipyards and some of the biggest steel mills in the world.

The single most important aspect of post-war Japanese accumulation was the tremendous rate of investment. Gross investment as percentage of GNP averaged more than 35 percent annually in the period 1960-1974. [18] This was roughly twice the proportion for the USA. Firms were encouraged by the state to renew and enlarge their capital equipment, and counted on the state's safety net if their plans failed. Credit was cheaply provided through the state-controlled credit system. Never was accumulation for accumulation's sake more blatant. Orientation to the world market and competition between Japanese capitals ensured the efficient use of such investment. Given the rates of investment, the importation of technology and the intensity of exploitation, productivity increased steeply. Average annual productivity growth in 1960-1973 was 11.0 percent in Japan compared with 2.9 percent in the USA and 5.9 percent in West Germany. [19]

Rapid growth was by no means unstoppable or smooth. On the contrary, it was characterised by balance of payments instability, a token of Japan's susceptibility to world market fluctuations. Japan had its own stop-go cycle: recessions with balance of payments deficits were followed by booms. However the recessions were very shallow and the booms very fast. Manic investment sprees would accelerate growth while the world market permitted, only to come up against the barrier of a balance of payments deficit. A spell of mild recession and the elimination of the deficit would follow accompanied by intense gloom and uncertainty. After restructuring the economy would enter another 'go' period. In this manic, haphazard and unstable way the world's second economic superpower emerged.

Although a broad-based national economy was created, rapid growth was anything but evenly balanced across all sectors of manufacturing. Japanese manufacturing has developed as an integral part of the world manufacturing industry. Exceptional strength exists in some areas, like automobiles and semiconductors, but certainly not across the whole range of manufacturing activities. The Japanese ruling class concentrated its efforts on a shifting range of activities in which the world market allowed rapid growth. Initially it was steel and shipbuilding, later it was electronics, cars, machine tools and so on. By world standards, key sectors of industry are weak or non-existent in Japan, for instance, aerospace, aluminum, pharmaceuticals and petrochemicals. Furthermore, agriculture and commodity distribution are not internationally competitive and have inefficient structures.

The social costs of the transformation into a superpower have been enormous. Japanese peasantry was brutally destroyed: in the late 1940s, more than 50 percent of the population lived on the land compared to less than 10 percent at present. Large tracts of the countryside have been depopulated and enormous, ugly, urban sprawls have appeared. The streets of Tokyo have a permanent traffic jam. Housing has been notoriously poor, inadequate and expensive. Industry has concentrated on a narrow corridor along the Pacific rim, probably the most productive area in the world. Virulent industrial pollution caused much illness throughout the Rapid Growth Period, for instance, Minamoto disease and Yokkaichi asthma. Blindly, brutally and haphazardly post-war capitalist accumulation transformed the lives of the vast majority of the Japanese people.

The crisis of 1973-1975: The international crisis of the mid-1970s which signified the end of the long boom was particularly acute in Japan. The collapse of the Bretton Woods international monetary arrangement in 1971 brought a severe revaluation of the yen and hit the competitiveness of Japanese capital. The massive rise in oil prices after the oil embargo of 1973 was another severe blow as roughly 90 percent of Japan's energy needs were met with imports. The outlines of the crisis were pretty familiar. Company profitability collapsed, inflation rose to 24.5 percent in 1974 (only Britain did worse), mining and manufacturing output fell almost 20 percent in 1974, equipment investment declined and unemployment rose. For a period there was panic in the shops and it seemed as if the Japanese miracle was over.

The immediate response to crisis by the ruling class was to hit working people hard. National union organisations accepted 'wage restraint'—wage increases which did not match the rate of inflation. Unemployment increased among women, temporary workers and workers in small firms. Large firms passed the pressure on to the 'shock absorbers' but such was the severity of the crisis that the limits of 'life time employment' became clear. Intense pressure on the life time employment system across industry was revealed through widespread reductions of working hours. This was the main way in which the labour input into production was reduced. In addition hundreds of thousands of skilled manufacturing jobs disappeared and the numbers of laid off workers increased.[20]

The state and capital together co-ordinated industrial restructuring through recession cartels in the worst affected industries. Firms reduced inventories and investment in 'Operation Scale-Down'. Capacity reductions were agreed by several industries—shipbuilding, steel, aluminum and so on. To reduce inflation monetary policy was tightened and the rate of interest rose. Finally the export drive was redoubled in order to provide some stimulus to production. The key point here, however, is that the total response of the Japanese ruling class was much more profound than simple austerity measures.

The choices were stark. Japan had emerged as a major economic power but the period of rapid growth had culminated in a serious crisis. The parlous state of the world economy and the slump in the Japanese economy showed that this was no mere 'stop'. Rather, the crisis indicated that future growth on the basis of heavy and chemical industrialisation was untenable. The role of the state in changing the strategic direction of Japanese capitalism was fundamental. Administrative guidance by MITI began to nudge Japanese capital in the direction of electronics, automobiles, capital equipment and semiconductors. A slower, 'sustainable' rate of growth was proclaimed desirable. Companies began to increase expenditure on research and development in order to raise the technical sophistication of production. In the period since 1973 Japan has enormously increased its output of technology patents and its cadre of trained engineers. [21] In a fumbling way Japanese capital left the Rapid Growth Period and began to restructure itself for the post-crisis period. The collaboration of state and capital, the control of major industries which large companies exert and the acquiescence of union leadership to restructuring pressures allowed the transformation to go through without dramatic class conflict.

Fundamental trends in the Japanese economy since the crisis of 1973-1975

The period since the crisis of 1973-1975 has its own distinctive features. Outwardly it is characterised by slower growth, the spread of consumerism, highly sophisticated manufacturing and enormous power in world trade. The restructuring of the Japanese economy has been so successful that the world recession of 1980-1982 left Japan relatively unscathed. Yet in the 1980s new sources of economic instability have appeared. Heightened trade friction and financial instability now bedevil Japanese capitalism. To understand these processes we have to look at two fundamental trends in the transformed Japanese economy:

i) the globalisation of Japanese productive and loanable capital and ii) the liberalisation of the financial system. Below I will first consider the performance of the Japanese economy compared to the US and German economies in the 1980s.

Economic performance in the 1980s: A look at the comparative economic performance of the US, Japan and West Germany in the period 1980-1989 reveals that Japan did better than the main rival capitalist economies. The average growth rate for the Japanese GNP was 4.2 percent, well above 2.7 percent for the US and 1.9 percent for Germany (and 2.3 percent for Britain). Japan is now firmly the second biggest economy in the world, with roughly 60 percent of the US GNP and more than twice that of Germany. Moreover inflation and unemployment over the period averaged 2.4 percent and 2.5 percent respectively, clearly better than the US and Germany.[22] At an immediate level, two factors are important in order to explain this performance. First the Reagan boom in the US provided Japan with the stimulus of a huge export market. Japan's current account surplus climbed from 35 billion dollars in 1984 to 87 billion dollars in 1987. Secondly the 1985 Plaza Accord among the major capitalist countries led to a rise in the value of the yen. From roughly 270 yen to the dollar in 1985 the yen rose to 130 yen to the dollar in 1987. The export stimulus gradually lost its potency but lending money abroad, particularly to the US, became easier. Judging by net assets abroad Japan lent the world 240 billion dollars in 1987 while the US borrowed 370 billion dollars.

In the middle of the 1980s the economy slowed down as the yen rose. In an attempt to avoid stagnation by strengthening domestic demand the state began to relax its fiscal and monetary policy. The tax system was overhauled in order to boost private consumption. The official discount rate went down to 2.5 percent in 1987, stayed at that level for two years and severely reduced the market cost of borrowing money.

The impact of these forces on the restructured Japanese economy was pronounced. The very low rate of interest allowed companies to maintain an enormous investment drive. Gross fixed capital formation (a measure of investment) as part of the GNP averaged 29.4 percent in 1980-1989, compared with 17.6 percent for the US and 20.4 percent for West Germany. The figure went well above 30 percent in 1988-1989. Manufacturing equipment investment in 1980-1988 grew at almost 9 percent annually compared to just over 4 percent for the US.[23]

Since the end of the Second World War the characteristic drive of Japanese capital to invest has resulted in much higher per capita investment for the whole of the population than in the US and the European Community. A quick glance at the table will bear out the point.

TABLE 1: GROSS DOMESTIC INVESTMENT PER CAPITA (constant 1980 US dollars)

	Japan	US	EC
1967	1599	1657	1759
1977	2698	2030	2193
1987	3801	2373	2432

Source: IBRD World Tables 1988-89

The investment drive, the shift to higher technology since the mid-1970s and intensive labour exploitation help to explain average annual productivity increases in manufacturing of 3.1 percent, compared to 3.6 percent for the US and 2.8 percent for West Germany. These productivity increases were accompanied by a rise in manufacturing employment while that of the US and West Germany declined. Industrial production as a whole increased by 4 percent annually compared to 2.9 percent for the US and 1.4 percent for West Germany.[24]

On the whole the 1980s were Japan's decade in three important ways. First, the country surpassed its main industrial rivals in growth rates and firmly established itself as the second biggest economy in the world. Second, Japanese industry systematically increased output, investment and productivity. In this respect, it is probably better placed to compete with US and European capital than at the beginning of the 1980s. Finally Japan emerged as a major commercial power with the ability to lend and invest enormous sums abroad.

We have to be careful here. It is easy to imagine that Japanese capitalism is an unstoppable juggernaut, inexorably overtaking its competitors. Throughout this article I have argued that Japan is susceptible to the rhythms of the world market. This was again demonstrated in 1990 and 1991. As US and British economies moved into recession, growth in Japan slowed down to 3.5 percent. Banks reported a dramatic fall in profitability in 1990.[25] Large companies have also begun to feel the impact of world recession on their profitability. Nissan, for instance, has reported a collapse in profits for 1990.[26] The car industry as a whole is now facing problems of profitability and competitiveness. Meanwhile higher rates of interest in 1990, which I will explain below, have practically ended the investment spree.

These elements of crisis are products of the transformation of Japanese capitalism which was intensified during the boom of the 1980s. Two trends are particularly important in this respect—first, the globalisation of Japanese productive and loanable capital, second, the liberalisation of the financial system. Japanese capitalism became decisively more integrated into the world economy in the 1980s. This integration has resulted in types of economic instability which will be characteristic of the 1990s.

The position of Japanese capitalism in the early 1990s is profoundly contradictory. On the one hand, it took advantage of the openings in the world market in the 1980s and did better than its rivals. It will probably be able to compete even more powerfully in the 1990s. On the other hand, the same forces which fed the boom of the 1980s have produced economic disruption. Financial instability is already present and can be expected to continue in the 1990s. Trade friction with the US and the EC is potentially even more destabilising. The accumulation of Japanese capital in the 1990s will be deeply contradictory and not a harmonious and smooth process.

Globalisation of Japanese capital: The first fundamental trend of the 1980s was the increasing integration of Japanese capital into the world economy. Japanese commodity capital has been international since the beginning of the Rapid Growth Period. Vestiges of pre-war international, financial and other activities of the *zaibatsu* have also been in evidence throughout the post-war period. However, after 1973-1975 a qualitative change took place. Japanese productive and loanable capital have become immeasurably more global in their operations and outlook. For productive capital a large wave of internationalisation took place in the aftermath of 1973-1975. In a drive to secure supplies of energy and raw materials, for instance, the trading giants established Japanese-controlled production of oil, iron ore, bauxite and other raw materials across the world. Smaller firms began to establish textile, clothing and other production in Korea, Taiwan and other South East Asian countries.

This, though, was only a taste of what was to come in the late 1980s. The strength of the yen during the period made exports expensive and foreign acquisitions cheap. A desire to avoid trade friction also increased the attractiveness of production abroad for capitalists. This was further strengthened by low labour costs and the availability of subsidies in the EC and the US. A large wave of foreign direct investment materialised in the late 1980s, led by large manufacturers, cars, electronics and so on. Annual investment increased by more than five times from 12.2 billion dollars in 1985 to 67.5 billion dollars in 1989.[27]

The most important factor which contributed to this wave is also the most difficult to quantify. The continuous expansion of the world market since the early 1950s meant that as Japanese capital matured only global participation in the world economy would make sense. Capital concentrations such as Toyota and Hitachi (not to mention more adventurous ones such as Sony and Honda) realised that in order to continue to penetrate the US, European and other markets they needed to produce locally in those markets. Connections with the local state power and improved knowledge of local market conditions, both of which would come with localised production, were vital factors behind direct investment abroad. Japanese capital reached this point later than US and British capital.

TABLE 2: JAPAN'S FOREIGN DIRECT INVESTMENT
(31st March 1990, US billion dollars cumulative basis)

	Manufacturing	*Non-manufacturing*	*Total*
Europe	*7.9*	*37.0*	*44.9*
N. America	*33.5*	*75.5*	*109.0*
L. America	*5.6*	*31.2*	*24.9*
Asia	*15.6*	*4.9*	*40.5*
Oceania	*1.9*	*12.0*	*13.9*
M. East	*1.3*	*2.1*	*3.4*
Africa	*0.2*	*5.0*	*5.2*
Total	*66.1*	*187.8*	*253.9*

Source: Japanese Ministry of Finance

Several important conclusions follow from Table 2. By far the leading area in which Japanese capital has established direct production abroad is North America, mainly the US. Cumulative investment in North America over the years was almost half the total. The second most important area overall is Europe but for manufacturing it is Asia, the traditional destination of investment by small and medium firms. Most of the manufacturing investment in Europe, incidentally, was made toward the end of the 1980s in the UK with a view to beating the 'single market' of 1992 and the spectre of Fortress Europe. Significant investment in extractive and other industries has been made in both Latin America and Oceania. Decaying Africa, Eastern Europe and the Middle East have been of very little interest to Japanese capital.

Thus Japanese direct investment has been aimed overwhelmingly at other advanced industrialised countries and at the Asian developing countries. The evidence shows that the integration of the heartlands of world manufacturing continued in the 1980s. The three leading receivers of Japanese direct investment in 1989 were the US with 54.5 percent of the total, the UK with 7.2 percent and Thailand with 4.8 percent. Japanese productive capital is connected, first and foremost, with the territory and the productive structure of US capital. In the 1980s the productive base of Japanese manufacturing became increasingly globalised. The car industry is a case in point. Nissan, Toyota and Honda have invested the very large sum of £1.7 billion in UK production. Nissan UK already produces 120,000 vehicle units annually and aims to produce another 100,000 units by 1993. This will be roughly 15 percent of total British-based output. Toyota is also building a massive 100,000 unit plant at Burnaston, Derbyshire, and Honda has taken a 20 percent stake in Rover. There is even talk that within five years or so one third of all cars made in Britain will be Japanese makes.

Equally significant has been the globalisation of the flows of Japanese loanable capital. Capitalist activities such as borrowing and lending of money are naturally more international than production. Loanable capital appropriates part of the surplus generated in production without actively involving itself in the latter. The geographical location of production, and even its social character, are not of fundamental significance to loanable capital. Loanable capital has been international in its outlook for a very long time. Lenin thought that the global spread of banking capital was one of the trends which underpinned imperialism at the turn of the century.[28]

In the 1980s Japanese loanable capital became noticeably more international in sourcing, customers, lending techniques, location and so on. Japan fully participated in the global trend toward integration of the financial system. The balance of long term capital movements in and out of the country swung violently from an inflow of 2.3 billion dollars in 1980 to an outflow of 49.7 billion dollars in 1984 and a peak outflow of 136.5 billion dollars in 1987.[29] Japanese banks now dominate the top ranks of international banks and do sizeable business in London and New York. Tokyo, previously a financial backwater, was propelled into the front rank of world financial centres together with New York and London.

The globalisation of Japanese productive and loanable capital has brought a change in the role of the state, which I have analysed earlier. The trend toward increasing integration into the world economy has made the adoption of growth-promoting measures redundant, indeed counterproductive, for Japanese capital. State control of the credit system has become much less direct and more complex. Administrative guidance by the state has to contend with much more powerful units of capital with the ability to shift production internationally. This, for instance, will make it much more difficult to restructure the Japanese car industry which is currently overpopulated with medium-sized firms beset with problems. The most advanced sections of Japanese capital, on the other hand, rely on the state to tackle the trade and other frictions which they increasingly encounter worldwide.

Globalization of capital will reproduce capitalist rivalries and economic instability at a higher level. Take, for instance, trade friction, a typically contradictory phenomenon in late capitalism. The capitalist class is putting obstacles in the very path of trade on which it depends. Much Japanese investment—particularly into the EC—has aimed at combating trade friction by producing 'locally'. Connections are established with the local state, Japanese capital enters the local fraternity of 'hostile brothers', the 'local content' of the product is meticulously policed and so, hopefully, the spectre of protectionism is banished. There is no doubt that direct production does indeed make a crude reversal to protectionism very difficult. This is the chief reason why the world market is unlikely to collapse into trade blocs in the near future.

But has 'local production' resolved the contradiction of protectionism? Not at all. It has simply made that contradiction more complex. Thus protectionists and chauvinists in the EC and the US confront Japanese-owned plants as a Japanese fifth column. French car manufacturers—the boss of Peugeot mentioned above—openly see such plants as a Trojan horse brought into Europe. The call for protectionism becomes more virulent and protectionist measures more complicated. As, for example, the EC comes to reconsider the percentage of its car market allowed to Japanese imports, a balance has to be struck between Japanese imports and Japanese production of cars locally. The British ruling class, within whose territory a lot of Japanese car production takes place, is immediately at loggerheads with the French ruling class. In these circumstances conflicts of interest between sections of the US and European capitalist classes and sudden lurches toward extreme measures become much more likely. Uncertainty, economic instability and the potential for crisis are increased.

The liberalisation of finance: The second crucial trend of the 1980s was the liberalisation of the Japanese financial system. Throughout the rapid growth period the Japanese financial system was heavily regulated. The regulatory framework aimed at directing cheap funds to industry for investment. The internationalisation of loanable capital and the emergence of deep and fluid credit markets in Japan have changed the financial system beyond recognition. The recession of 1973-1975 generated significant borrowing needs for the Japanese state which have remained sizeable ever since. Those needs provided crucial impetus to the emergence of markets in long term bonds and short term instruments. The commercial banks demanded a less regulated environment in order to participate in those markets. Gradually deregulation became a condition for more integration in the world financial flows and for further growth of the credit markets.

There are three key aspects to the liberalisation trend. First, controls on interest rates have by and large been lifted. Market rates prevail for long term deposits with banks, and increasingly for short term deposits too. Second, the functions of financial institutions have started to overlap. Commercial banks have begun to provide a much larger range of financial services than in the past, moving into the territory of other banking institutions. Third, 'securitisation' of company debt in large and diversifying credit markets has become a reality. New markets are constantly created in, for instance, financial futures, options and Bankers' Acceptances. Banks have shifted their lending toward medium and small firms in the 1980s. The share of the latter in the total lending of the leading commercial banks reached 70 percent in 1990. [30]

Liberalisation of finance was the hallmark of the 1980s globally. It was hailed as a development improving welfare and economic efficiency. The reality is different. The more the credit system reverts to a globally competitive state the more it will create credit crises. Japan's experience demonstrates this. We can see clearly the trend toward increased financial instability for the 1990s, a major source of economic instability for contemporary Japanese capitalism. In the 1980s competition among banks intensified as a result of liberalisation. As large firms turned to the credit markets banks had fewer lending opportunities. Looser state monetary policy in the second half of the 1980s compounded the situation by increasing the availability of funds to the credit system. Banks lent cheaply for Stock Exchange and real estate speculation. A tremendous credit bubble resulted as stock and real estate prices rocketed.

In classic fashion, the bubble grew as long as prices continued to rise. Speculators realised their profits, banks were paid interest and their loans, backed by rising land prices, seemed secure. A whole culture was created of small private investors regularly placing their savings in the Stock Exchange in expectation of capital gains through rising prices. When, in line with international trends, the state began to tighten its monetary policy and raise interest rates in late 1989, the bubble burst.

The completion of the first business cycle under a liberalised financial regime finds Japanese banks in an extremely precarious position. Their profitability has collapsed as deregulated interest rates on bank deposits rose. Even worse, international guidelines issued by the Bank of International Settlement—BIS, the bank of central bankers—have obliged them to keep 8 percent of their total assets as own-capital in order to strengthen their balance sheet. The credit boom was good to Japanese banks since they counted their fictitious Stock Exchange capital gains as a large part of their own-capital. They still do to the tune of 45 percent of their paper gains. But the massive fall of the Stock Exchange since early 1990, as the credit boom fizzled out, destroyed those paper gains. Thus to meet the 8 percent target banks have reduced their domestic and international lending.

Every time the Stock Exchange falls a bit more, the 8 percent target becomes more difficult to meet and banks are obliged to restrict their lending further. The repercussions are felt on firms and already the investment boom of the 1980s is practically over. If the Stock Exchange continues to fall and if land prices are brought down from their absurd heights, particularly in Tokyo, things could get much worse. Banks could then find themselves with even more bad debt in their books and even face insolvency. A financial mess of this size and complexity is new for Japanese capitalism and the direct result of liberalisation. It is also an indication of things to come in the 1990s and beyond. The integration of world credit markets, the reliance of firms on the credit markets and the continuing heavy borrowing needs of the state indicate that the trend of liberalisation will continue. Financial instability will become more intense and complex.

In this context the Japanese state will play a significant role. The Bank of Japan and the Ministry of Finance will instigate interest rate cuts and use other technical ways of preventing the Stock Exchange from falling disastrously. Furthermore, the Ministry of Finance has already promoted bank mergers as a way of restructuring the banking system out of crisis. Two major mergers have already taken place, Mitsui-Taiyo Kobe and Saitama-Kyowa banks. More mergers are likely between large and small commercial banks. The emerging giants will be more competitive worldwide and ready for a repetition of the boom-slump cycle on a higher level.

Trade friction and relations with the US: Trade friction will be another major source of economic instability for Japanese capital in the 1990s. Trade friction is also indicative of the turmoil in the broader US-Japan relations and I will consider these below. The first issue here is whether Japan is more protectionist than the US and the EC. Judging by tariff barriers the answer is a clear no. Japan's tariff for manufactured goods is below that of the US and the EC. Present day protectionism, however, comes in the form of 'Non-Tariff Barriers' such as Voluntary Export Restraint (VER), quotas on imports, Orderly Market Agreements (OMA) and so on. These are very difficult to quantify and compare from country to country. Even here, though, economic studies show that Japan has fewer non-tariff barriers than the US and the EC. [31]

Japanese behaviour is less protectionist than that of the US and the EC, if one judges by conventional economic criteria. Precisely because of this, anti-Japanese protectionists are using the astounding argument that the very structure of Japanese economy and society is a barrier to trade. Presumably industrial groups, the archaic structure of the distribution system, government procurement methods, not to mention Confucian mentality, the education system and even the Japanese language (!) are barriers to imports from the West. The current Structural Impediments Initiative (SII) of the US government is aimed at forcing the Japanese to reform their economy and society in ways more compatible with US ideals.

US pressure reflects haughty imperialist arrogance but it also has its ridiculous aspect. The US state, presiding over enormous budget and trade deficits in the midst of a deep recession and a massive borrower abroad, is giving economic advice to the Japanese! A society riven with racism, poverty, a collapsing education system and resurgent militarism is telling Japan to follow suit. There is a real issue here, however. Does Japan import abnormally little, particularly in manufactures? Studies which also take into account Japan's paucity of raw materials (hence the need to import them) conclude that imports of manufactures are not abnormally low.[32] Moreover, since trade friction intensified in the 1980s and MITI began to drive Japanese capital toward increasing its imports, Japan has almost doubled its manufacturing imports as percentage of GNP.[33]

Japan is not more protectionist, just more successful. And so the vitriolic racist attacks intensify. For the historian there is nothing new here. The first capitalist power to decline, Britain, produced its own crop of racists spewing out invective against the rising Germans and Americans.[34] That alarmist nonsense was worthless from a scientific point of view but it played an insidious role in fomenting chauvinism before the First World War.

So what can we expect with regard to trade friction for the 1990s? The pattern of development of world trade is subject to two contradictory trends. The first trend is toward an increase in protectionist pressure. The recessions and the instability which have marked the period since the end of the long boom have led states to increase protection for their capitals in the world market. Trade disputes have proliferated. Managed trade is the order of the day. In a recent one-sided deal, called by the *Financial Times* 'an important milestone on the journey toward managed trade', [35] the Japanese state undertook to provide 20 percent of the Japanese domestic semiconductor market to US firms. It seems that import, as well as export, management has arrived in earnest.

The second trend is toward more integration of the world economy. We have already seen the productive and loanable capital aspects of this trend. It is equally apparent for commodity capital. The US, chief market for Japanese exports, absorbed 26 percent of total Japanese exports in 1978 going up to 34 percent in 1988. Similarly the share of US exports going to Japan—the US's second most important export market—were 9 percent in 1978 and 12 percent in 1988. [36] This, furthermore, was in a context of steadily increasing world trade throughout the 1980s. The largest component of US exports to Japan was manufacturing products. Mutual dependence of the two economies actually increased in the 1980s and the picture would not at all change if we also considered the EC.

The world market is not simply and inexorably fragmenting into trading blocs. In fact the rise of managed trade and the emergence of free-trade areas such as the EC and North America are taking place within the confines of the General Agreement on Tariffs and Trade,

GATT, which has overseen the liberalisation of world trade since the Second World War. The underlying globalisation of production—accelerated with the emergence of Japanese multinationals—will prevent a simple break up of the world market into trading blocs. Despite threats and alarms the GATT rounds have not collapsed and, far from fragmenting, the world market actually became more integrated in the 1980s.

For Japan, especially, its natural trading bloc is exceedingly difficult to form. Economic links with China and Korea are not, at present, vital for Japanese capital. Japanese exports to Korea and China were, respectively, 6 percent and 3 percent of the total in 1978. In 1988 this had barely changed to 6 percent and 4 percent respectively.[37] There is simply no comparison with the significance of US trade for Japan. Furthermore, Foreign Direct Investment by Japan in the whole of Asia is just over a third of that in North America as we saw in Table 2. For the large concentrations of Japanese capital, Toyota, Mitsubishi, Sony etc, the American market is easily the most important area in the world. Glib talk about the emergence of a Japan Bloc in Asia is misleading. Asian countries, moreover, are positively hostile to anything that smacks of renewed Japanese domination.

In the 1990s both trends are likely to continue alongside each other. This will lead to ever more complicated and profound trade conflicts which require state intervention to be resolved. The car industry again provides an example of those contradictory trends. All the US giants have technological, production and trading tie ups with Japanese firms: General Motors with Isuzu, Ford with Mazda, Chrysler with Mitsubishi. Ford cars are often sold under the Mazda brand. Thus, a degree of dependence of the US car industry on the Japanese one has been created. Despite these links, the US giants are pushing for more protectionism and they are repeatedly using the law in order to attack Japanese imports into the US. It was mainly the car giants who were behind the belligerence of the recent bullying Bush visit to Japan. In much the same way, the major capitalist powers will be trying to escape from each other's ever-tightening embrace throughout the 1990s. Constant flare-ups, uncertainty and distortions of trade can be expected for the foreseeable future.

Trade friction between the US and Japan is only one—although major—aspect of the relationship between the two capitalist powers. Since the war Japan has assumed a subordinate role in its relations with US imperialism. Its submissive posture in the trade disputes is indicative of the post-war outlook of the Japanese ruling class. In the remainder of this article I want to deal with the broader dimension of US-Japan relations in the 1990s.

It should be said at the outset that the Japanese ruling class has done very well out of the US-imposed post-war settlement. US imperialism kept the old enemy Russia—which continues to occupy Japanese territory—at bay. It also removed the need to spend on arms. Japan was left free to concentrate on the world market. For this reason there is pronounced reluctance in Japan to change the post-war arrangement. Moreover, despite increasing economic integration, it is still the case that Japan needs the US more than the US needs Japan. This explains the aggessive bluster of the recent Bush visit and the fact that Japan had to petition humbly for the visit. It is true that flows of Japanese loanable capital have been significant for the financing of the US budget deficit. Yet Britain and Germany together were more important lenders to the US. The present tight conditions in the Japanese financial markets have reduced the outflow of long-term capital to just 17 billion dollars in 1990. It is also true that US industry will feel the pinch if Japanese exports of machine tools and other investment goods are restricted. This, however, does not alter the basic fact that the US can hurt Japan much more than Japan can hurt the US. In 1978 Japanese exports to the US were over 3 percent of Japan's GNP. By contrast US exports to Japan were around 0.6 percent of the US GNP. In 1988 the disparity was equally pronounced. Japanese exports to the US had almost reached 4 percent of Japan's GNP while US exports were still hovering around 0.7 percent of US GNP.[38]

A third factor explaining the current submissiveness of Japanese capitalism is that the bogeyman of the US is convenient for purposes of Japanese domestic politics. As we have seen, the Japanese ruling class has embarked upon a process of integration with the world economy. There has been a measure of domestic opposition to this from sections of society which stand to suffer from this move, such as farmers. Blaming the foreigners is a convenient strategy for the ruling class, much in the manner of 'the gnomes of Zurich' taking the blame for Labour's austerity measures in Britain in the 1970s.

In the 1990s, however, the Japanese ruling class is likely to become more assertive. There are two reasons for this. First, the US superpower has continued to decline relative to Japan, as the comparison of economic performance in the 1980s has shown. The Japanese ruling class is only too keenly aware of this crucial fact. It costs the US ruling class 40-50 billion dollars annually to maintain its Pacific military presence and it simply cannot afford it. [39] Thus the US has been trying to give Japan a greater role in the Pacific military system, especially in the navy and air commands. US rulers would ideally like to maintain overall military command as well as make the Japanese pay for military hardware. The Japanese ruling class will have to be fools to accept such an arrangement without some very substantial political gains. The potential for strife and political friction in the Pacific appears enormous.

The second, and equally significant, reason is the proceeding economic and political collapse of the USSR. Soviet military pressure on Japan from the North remains substantial but its underpinnings have been eroded. Japanese capital is already beginning to confront the USSR much more confidently, witness Gorbachev's failed visit to Tokyo last year. As economic collapse continues in the former USSR we can expect Japanese imperialism to begin to emerge more assertively and demand its 'rights' in the region.

It should be stressed here that huge obstacles exist on the path to a more assertive global role for Japanese capital and I have already mentioned the attitude of Asian countries toward Japanese aggrandisement. Not least is the strong anti-militarist current among the Japanese people which prevented any adventures during the Gulf War. Japan, though, has already begun to acquire the trappings of a world imperialist power. Its military budget is, in absolute terms, the third biggest in the world. Since 1990 Japan is the chief foreign aid donor in the world to the tune of roughly 10 billion dollars annually. It has recently begun to use this aid more aggressively, demanding checks on the recipient's policies. It is probable that its hesitant failure to intervene during the Gulf War will make the Japanese ruling class prepare more decisively for the conflagrations of the future. As its assertiveness grows so will friction with the US superpower and political instability in the Pacific.

Conclusion

In 1945 Japanese capitalism lay in ruins, decisively crushed by American imperialism. Its subsequent rise from the ashes was staggering but not miraculous. As I have argued here, Japan took advantage of the exceptional circumstances of the long post-war boom and its own low military expenditure. Manic investment, import of technology and furious exploitation of workers resulted in high growth. It is undoubtedly true that Japanese capitalism has responded remarkably flexibly to new challenges. When the long boom finished a massive restructuring, aimed at the world market, took place in Japan. It goes without saying that workers paid the price of that restructuring.

I have argued that present day Japanese capitalism is in a contradictory position. On the one hand it has coped with the post-1973 slowdown in the world economy much better than its rivals. On the other hand financial and trade instability have emerged to haunt it. Friction and intensified capitalist rivalries in the 1990s will be the result. The collapse of Stalinism and the economic malaise of Western capitalism will make the years to come tumultuous for Japanese capitalism and for the peoples of the Pacific.

Notes

Thanks are due to S Cockerill, M Haynes, C Harman and P Green for comments on the manuscript.

1 The latest offering is G Friedman and M Lebard, *The Coming War with Japan*, (St Martin's Press, 1991). The title is self-explanatory.
2 R Dornbusch has been leading the chorus. See 'Give Japan a Target and Say "Import!"', *New York Times*, 24 September 1989.
3 *Financial Times*, France Survey, 17 June 1991.
4 T Nakamura, *The Post-War Japanese Economy* (Univ of Tokyo Press 1981), p138.
5 R Minami, *The Economic Development of Japan* (MacMillan, 1986), p342.
6 Johnson Chalmers, *MITI and the Japanese Miracle* (Stanford Ohio Press, 1982), ch 5.
7 C Harman, 'The State and Capitalism Today', *International Socialism* 51, Summer 1991.
8 Some free market believers have argued that the role of the state was insignificant and the dynamism of private capital explains the 'miracle'. For a typical example of that see D Friedman, *The Misunderstood Miracle*,(Cornell Univ Press, 1988). D Okimoto *Between the MITI and the Market* (Academic Press, 1989), tries to have it both ways. This is clearly incorrect. Even market-oriented economists have had to admit that the state significantly lowered costs for Japanese capital and gave it an advantage in the world market. See, T Toshimasa, 'The Rapid Growth Era', in *Industrial Policy of Japan* R Komiya, M Okuno, K Suzumura, (eds), (Academic Press, 1988).
9 'The Risen Sun', *Economist*, 27 May-2 June 1967.
10 M Young, 'Structural adjustment of mature industries in Japan', paper presented to Conference on Government-Industry Relations, Brasenose College, Oxford. To be published.
11 R Clark, *The Japanese Company*' (Yale Univ Press, 1979), p79.
12 R Caves & M Uekusa, *Industrial Organisation in Japan*, (Washington, 1976), ch 3.
13 R Luxemburg, *Reform or Revolution* (Pathfinder, 1970), p20.
14 M Aoki, *Information, Incentives and Bargaining in the Japanese Economy*, (Cambridge Univ Press, 1988).
15 See the article by the former industrial editor of the *Daily Mirror* G Goodman, 'How Japan Prepares Britain for the Global Market', *Anglo-Japanese Journal*, January-March 1991, Vol 4, No 4.
16 J Mincer & Y Higuchi, 'Wage Structures and Labour Turnover in the US and Japan', *Journal of the Japanese and International Economies*, June 1988.
17 See S Kamata, *Japan in the Passing Lane* (Allen and Unwin, 1983).
18 K Sato 'Saving and Investment', in K Yamamura & Y Yasukichi (eds),*The Political Economy of Japan* Vol 1 1987.
19 Bank of Japan, International Comparative Statistics, 1985, quoted in D Okimoto & G Saxonhouse, 'Technology and the Future of the Economy', in *The Political Economy of Japan*, ibid.
20 R Dore, *Flexible Rigidities* 1986, Athlone, op cit, pp91-92.
21 D Okimoto & G Saxonhouse, 'Technology and the Future of the Economy' op cit.
22 Bank of Japan, Comparative Economic and Financial Statistics, 1990.
23 Ibid.
24 Ibid.
25 *Financial Times*, 28 May 1991.
26 *Financial Times*, 31 May 1991.

27 Source: Ministry of Finance.
28 V Lenin, 'Imperialism, the Highest Stage of Capitalism', in *Collected Works*, Vol 22 (Lawrence & Wishart, 1964) pp240-245.
29 Bank of Japan, Balance of Payments Monthly, August 1990.
30 Bank of Japan, Economic Statistics Monthly, May 1990.
31 JJ Nogues, A Olechowski, LA Winters, 'The Extent of Non-tariff Barriers to Industrial Countries' Imports', *World Bank Economic Review*, Vol 1, 1986.
32 J Bhagwati, *The World Trading System at Risk* (Harvester, Wheatsheaf, 1991), pp35-36.
33 Ibid., pp41-43.
34 The most notorious was E E Williams, *Made in Germany* (London, 1896).
35 *Financial Times*, editorial, 10 June 1991.
36 IMF, Direction of Trade, *Yearbook 1989*.
37 Ibid.
38 IBRD, World Tables, 1988-1989, and Bank of Japan, *Economic Statistics Monthly*, March 1991.
39 T Kataoka & R Myers, *Defending an Economic Superpower*, (Westview Press, 1989) p100.

Capitalism and the state system: A reply to Nigel Harris

ALEX CALLINICOS

The international system of states underwent in 1989-91 its third great shock of the present century. Nineteen eighty-nine to 1991 can only be understood in the light of the two earlier episodes of transformation at the end of the world wars. The East European Revolutions of 1989 undid the work of 1945, ending the superpower partition of Europe and thereby making possible the unification of Germany. The failure of the conservative coup in Moscow of August 1991 rendered inevitable the disintegration of the Russian Empire forged by the Tsars and reconstituted by Stalin: the work of 1918-19, the unravelling of the multinational states which had dominated Eastern Europe, was thus completed.

We find ourselves travelling in uncharted waters. To what extent will our existing theories help us map them? Nigel Harris argues that they are of little use. His response both to my review of his book *National Liberation* and to Chris Harman's analysis of the contemporary capitalist state affirms explicitly much that was only implied by his previous writings.[1]

Nigel's reasons for doing so have to do chiefly with trends—above all that towards the global integration of capital—which long antedate the political convulsions of 1989-91. But the validity of his arguments must be assessed in the light not only of the development of the world economy but also of these transformations in the state system.

Nigel defends two main propositions. One is a theoretical assertion, namely, that the capitalist system is composed of 'two parallel systems', 'a world economy' consisting of 'competing companies (whether public, private or other) which make, distribute and exchange the world's output of goods and services', and 'a world political order' consisting of 'competing states' which 'administer clearly defined territories'. Although the two systems continually interact, they are 'driven by different imperatives'.[2] Nigel's second main proposition is a historical claim about the changing form of their interaction. Between the 1870s and the 1960s an 'alliance' existed between the two systems, 'which was the foundation for a state capitalist period, one where the state sustained monopolies whether in its own or private hands'. In the past generation, however, 'a radical change' has occurred, leading to 'the emergence of a global capitalist system' increasingly dissociated from the state system.[3]

I don't wish in this reply to add too much to what is already a rather lengthy debate.[4] A few observations seem, however, in order. In the first place, Nigel's theoretical claim seems admirably stark and clear, whatever one thinks of its truth or falsehood. In delineating a distinct order of states and in insisting that 'historically, the primary function of the state has been external, in continuing struggles with other states for territory and power' he adopts a stance reminiscent, as I suggested in my review, of that of neo-Weberian sociologists like Tony Giddens and Michael Mann.[5]

Nevertheless, when we turn to the detail of Nigel's argument he seems guilty of precisely the kind of equivocation of which he accuses Chris Harman. He says, for example, that 'the role of the state is being changed . . . from representing a national society and capital to the world . . . to enforcing on the domestic economy and society the imperatives of a global economy; from promoting the interests of domestic capital to seeking to capture and seek a share of global capital', and so on.[6] This hardly sounds like a 'world political order' governed by a different 'imperative' from that of capital. Rather, we seem to be confronted with a shift from one form of subordination of the state to capital to another—from 'representing national . . . capital' to 'enforcing . . . the imperatives of a global economy'.

This ambiguity is important because how it is resolved has political implications. If the state system is governed by the imperatives of capital, whether national or global, then Nigel's insistence that the two 'systems' together 'constitute world capitalism' and that therefore 'a struggle against the police' for example is 'a struggle against the capitalist system' is soundly based.[7] If, however, state system and capitalist world economy really are autonomous (and autonomy is nothing else but being governed by one's own laws or 'imperatives'), then in principle one could be abolished without the other. It is on these grounds that Giddens argues, entirely logically, that combating the threat of war represented by the 'global military order' requires a different kind of movement from one directed against the excesses of capitalism.[8] Perhaps Nigel's equivocation about the relationship of the state to capital reflects a justified reluctance to draw the political consequences of his theoretical claim.

There are, in any case, good reasons for rejecting this claim. Nigel's argument is that the fact that the state is 'a component of a state system' invalidates traditional Marxist analysis, where the state is 'primarily defined relative to a domestic class structure'.[9] Three comments are in order here. The first is that the importance of competition between states is hardly news. Within our tradition Colin Barker as long ago as 1978 criticised the 'capital logic' school for treating 'the state as if it existed only in the singular' and argued that 'the very multiplicity of capitalist states is of great importance to the theory of the capitalist state-form'.[10]

Secondly, the fact that inter-state competition precedes the domination of the capitalist mode of production in no way invalidates Marx's insistence on seeing the state as fundamentally a form of class domination, since of the two external driving forces behind the great flurry of European state building in the early modern era one was the struggle of the feudal lords to increase their income by seizing each other's land and peasants;[11] the other was the formation of a capitalist world market, domination of which gave particular Great Powers the edge in their European rivalries—first Spain, then the United Provinces, and finally England after it had finally triumphed in its long struggle with France. But these external pressures cannot be separated from the gradual evolution of networks of trade and production on particular patches of European soil which both made possible and necessitated the formation of relatively coherent territorial political units. Nigel's dismissal of this process, so carefully analysed by Chris, is astonishingly cavalier. It helps to explain what I called Nigel's 'overpolitical' analysis of the formation of nation-states. By contrast, Benedict Anderson, for example, has stressed the importance of 'print-capitalism' in Reformation Europe—the relatively large scale commercial production of books in the vernacular—in 'creat[ing] unified fields of exchange and communications' each of which formed 'the embryo of the nationally imagined community'.[12]

The modern state system was the largely unintended consequence of *both* the politico-military rivalries among the European ruling classes, *and* the gradual formation of a capitalist world market whose nodal points could develop into nation-states.

Thirdly, there is the main evidence that Nigel cites to support the idea of two 'parallel systems', namely that states wage wars for reasons which differ from those motivating private capital. This only counts against the crudest form of instrumentalism, in which the state is treated as a tool directly controlled by the bourgeoisie. The relationship between state and capital theorised by Chris Harman is a very different one, that of '*structural interdependence*', in which the state bureaucracy's pursuit of its own interests is constrained by the fact that its revenues depend on 'successful capitalist exploitation and accumulation' and therefore, 'whether it likes it or not, it is compelled to act as an agent of capital accumulation and to identify its own interests as national capitalist interests in opposition both to the interests of foreign capital and the working class'.[13] This analysis in no sense requires that the state bureaucracy's interests be the same as those of capital, only that their interdependence sets limits to their variation.

Now Nigel's response to this argument is very odd.[14] He concedes the point, but asserts: 'The prodigious surpluses generated in the system mean that, unlike in earlier periods, there is no "final analysis".' On the face of it this seems to suggest that the position of capital, which presumably controls these 'prodigious surpluses', has been strengthened, and that therefore what is true 'in the final analysis'—namely that the state must promote capital accumulation—operates also in the short run. Nigel doesn't elaborate on this apparently contradictory sentence, but instead goes on to assert a palpable falsehood about an 'earlier period': 'Capital swallowed the Second World War, the Korean War and the Vietnam War without a bleep.' Really? So historians are mistaken to claim that central to the Roosevelt administration's war aims was the construction of a global order in which US capital and commodities could flow freely. And the Korean War played no part in the development of the permanent arms economy. And, most absurd of all, the inflation generated by the Vietnam War had nothing to do with the financial disorders which helped precipitate a small recession in 1970-71 and then the slump of 1974-75.

Nigel believes that reasoning of this kind establishes 'the general indifference of private capital to what I have identified as the primary function of the state', ie waging war. But, to take the most recent case, had the second Gulf War developed into a long drawn out conflict then US capital would have been far from indifferent to the likely consequences—disruption to oil supplies, higher US military spending probably financed by inflationary means, increased tension between Washington and its non-belligerent allies in Tokyo and Bonn, popular challenges to pro-Western Arab regimes.

Nigel's problem is, in part, that he confuses motives and outcomes. That is, he tends to argue that because the immediate motives behind a particular state policy or measure have nothing directly to do with demands from capital therefore capital has no interest in the outcome of implementing that policy or measure. Thus he responds to my argument that immigration controls are in the interest of capital because they mean that labour power is provided on terms that keep the working class divided by saying: 'we can indeed invent reasons as to why capital favours immigration control, but are these the reasons immigration controls exist?'[15] But my argument wasn't about why immigration controls were introduced—in Western Europe at any rate the lobbies which have made the running in forcing the imposition of progressively more restrictive immigration controls haven't been big capital but right wing conservative and openly fascist political forces—but about who benefits from them. Capital may not have initiated immigration controls, but it is perfectly happy with a state of affairs that divides the working class split between 'natives' open to the appeal of racism and immigrants vulnerable because often illegal. Nigel says: 'Private capital has an interest in dividing the working class only when it is united and threatening'.[16] But how can the working class be prevented from becoming 'united and threatening' except through various mechanisms which keep it divided?

Nigel further claims that 'it is a bad methodology to infer the interests of capital from the behaviour of the state, without any independent evidence to support it.'[17] Indeed it is, but no such inference is required by the idea that the state and capital are structurally interdependent. The interests of the state bureaucracy and those of capital may often diverge and sometimes directly clash. The state may do things that are, from the point of view of capital, irrational, or even plain stupid. Anyone who followed the *Financial Times*'s consistently acerbic commentary on the poll tax knows this well enough. But denying that the state and capital are identical is not the same thing as seeing them as separate 'systems'.

The structural dependence of the state on capital means that *persisting* in a policy which conflicts with the interests of capital will have negative consequences for the state, certainly in the long term, sometimes sooner. Capital flight is one of the most obvious mechanisms which keep states in line with capital. But there are other less drastic ways. If capitalists don't like a policy, they lobby against it. The informal networks linking them with the state bureaucracy, as well as the latter's economic dependence on capital, mean that more often than not they win out. The fact that West European big business has acquiesced over the past couple of decades in a marked tightening of immigration controls is itself 'independent evidence' that these controls don't work against the interests of capital.

Of course, matters are far from being as simple as this. One major problem in concrete analysis concerns who 'capital' is in any given situation—the international class of capitalists which operates across borders as well as being organised in national segments, one of these national segments, or perhaps an individual firm? Nigel thinks that, on the whole, we should concentrate on the international class, abstracting from its national embodiments. It is on these grounds, presumably, that he criticises Chris for 'mixing the accidental detail of the moment with . . . long-term trends'.[18] But precisely one of the points at issue is whether the involvement of capitals with individual nation-states is an 'accidental detail of the moment' or a constitutive feature of modern capitalism. Chris thinks the latter, and rightly so, I believe.

The issue isn't whether there has been over the past generation a qualitative shift in the direction of the internationalisation of capital. The existence of this trend is undisputed. Nigel's claim that Chris equivocates between 'agreeing that there has been a fundamental change' and treating the signs of greater global integration as 'no more than a change of ideological fashion' doesn't stand up to serious examination.[19] In fact, having documented in detail 'the massive internationalisation of finance, trade and production', Chris goes on to distinguish this transformation from its 'reflection in a tendency for bourgeois economists to talk as if the system did not need states'.[20] Far from ignoring the greater global integration of capital, both Chris and I make it central to our explanations of the collapse of Stalinism.[21] The real issue is whether this tendency implies a break in the typically strong connections which exist between individual capitals—particularly large firms—and particular nation-states. Nigel provides no real argument to counter Chris's careful demonstration of the continued importance of these connections, merely asserting that 'these are contingent factors', not 'necessary linkages'.[22] What this amounts to is an insistence on exaggerating and extrapolating one particular trend and refusing to acknowledge that the contemporary world economy confronts us with a real *contradiction*—between capitals' global operations and their dependence on the nation-state—which isn't going to go away.

This refusal to recognise a complex reality leads Nigel seriously astray when he comes to discuss particular developments. Thus he asserts that 'in economic terms, the decline of nationalism is everywhere apparent', citing as examples the emergence of regional blocs such as the European Community and the development of forms of international co-ordination such as the Group of Seven meetings.[23] Undoubtedly trends of this sort are, in very general terms, responses to a rapidly changing, globalised economy. But to suppose that they imply a decisive weakening of the nation-state is to indulge in the merest wishful thinking. Thus the moves towards European union—of which the treaty approved at Maastricht last December is merely a staging post—reflect, if anything, an intensification of national antagonisms between the major EC states. Bonn and Paris in particular see European union as a means of respectively legitimising and harnessing German economic power.[24] The tensions within the EC were highlighted in the weeks after Maastricht. Germany flexed its muscles by increasing the Lombard rate, leading to a ripple of interest rate rises across Europe, and insisting that the EC, against the better judgement of both the French and the British, recognise Croatia and Slovenia. Meanwhile, the French government announced plans to create a huge state conglomerate combining nuclear energy, semi-conductors and consumer electronics; predictions that the new firm would be a 'French Siemens' gave an indication of the target of this move.

As for the G7, undoubtedly it has developed into an institutionalised form of co-operation between the major Western powers, involving significant initiatives ranging from the February 1987 Louvre agreement on currency stability to recent attempts to stave off the economic collapse of the ex-USSR. Nevertheless, the G7's higher profile is a reflection less of the decline of the nation-state in general than that of one particular nation-state, namely the United States. The *Financial Times* pointed out: 'Financially weakened through its massive budget deficit, the US has tried to exert power through the G7'. But Washington's dependence on the EC and Japan to mount major economic interventions can sometimes make for greater divisions among the Western powers. Thus the *Financial Times* described the G7 meeting in Bangkok last October as 'acrimonious': 'some European officials criticised the US strategy as one of solving the world's problems in line with its own interests, using other people's money. "The troops rebelled", a monetary official said.' The biggest point of dispute concerned Germany's successful opposition to a US proposal to defer repayment of capital on what was still then the Soviet Union's foreign debt. But there were disagreements on other issues as well—Germany, Britain, and Italy all refused to contribute towards George Bush's Enterprise for the Americas initiative—a fund to promote private capital in Latin America.[25] Both rows were indicative of significant conflicts of interest arising from US and German capital's greater involvement in, respectively, Latin America and the former USSR.

The political transformations of 1989-91 seem likely to highlight the continued importance of the nation-state—not simply in the shape of the emergence of 15 new ones on the ruins of the USSR and several more where once there was Yugoslavia—but because for the capitalist classes of the advanced economies the politico-military power of their states represents an essential hedge against the anarchy now lapping at the borders of the cosy OECD world. Nineteen ninety one began with a dramatic demonstration of the armed might of the US state; it ended with the US, now genuinely the 'lone superpower' thanks to the collapse of the USSR, confronting a world its military establishment is even more essential to control. As for Europe, the historian J G A Pocock recently observed that it 'is once again an empire in the sense of a civilised and stabilised zone which must decide whether to extend or refuse its political power over violent and unstable cultures along its borders but yet within its system . . . These are not decisions to be taken by the market, but decisions of the state'.[26] The state on which these decisions mainly devolve is, of course, Germany, which has now resumed its historical role as the frontier power between the advanced West and the backward East. According to the *Independent*, 'as almost everything Soviet melts away from Central Europe Germany—German money, German trade, even the German language—is surging ahead of other Western countries to take its place'.[27] Behind Bonn's strong commitment to transforming the EC into a federal union is its recognition of the need for a state with the authority and the resources (including the formidable military establishments still fielded by Britain and France) to contain the vast zone of instability that now begins on the Elbe and ends at the Pacific.

All this, however, might as well not exist for the attention Nigel pays it. Instead he wanders into cloud cuckoo land, favourably quoting the idea that 'the result of an integrating world economy is to push the level both upwards (between global corporations) and downwards, between regions (as in Europe *des regions*) and cities, but away from the level of the existing states', and therefore envisaging a scenario in which 'nationalism faded into much weaker (in military terms) local loyalties'.[28] It is amazing to find Nigel, normally so splendidly hard headed when confronted with self indulgent fantasy, giving credence to the sort of guff about the displacement of power from the nation-state to the region in a united Europe that Eurobores have been serving up for as long as I can remember.

'Regionalist' movements become of political importance when they threaten to break up an existing state by raising the demand for their own separate state. That this involves, not a 'fading' of nationalism into a celebration of regional 'tradition' or whatnot, but the potential for ferocious inter-communal fighting is illustrated by the civil war in Yugoslavia and the as yet low intensity wars that have broken out in parts of the former Soviet Union. Nor is this just a matter of the backwash from the shipwreck of Stalinism. The upsurge of right wing Anglo-Canadian nationalism in response to the quite mild concessions made to Quebecois self determination in the abortive Meech Lake Agreement shows the kind of forces which may be unleashed when a state's integrity seems under threat.

Nigel is encouraged into confusing his hopes with the reality of the world system because he treats nationalism as an orientation towards the nation-state, conceived as essentially a political phenomenon disjoined from the capitalist mode of production. Thus 'national liberation is a response, not to the world of private capital, but to the state system'.[29] The era of state capitalism breathed some economic life into nationalism, since then the nation-state could promote capital accumulation, but as the epoch of global capitalism dawns, nationalism 'fades'. So Nigel criticises my claim that 'nationalist movements are . . . the expression of, if not an actual, then an *aspirant* capitalist class' on the grounds that this is like Isaac Deutscher saying the Chinese Communist Party was proletarian because 'it *aspired* to create a proletariat'.[30]

The point is, of course, that bourgeoisie and proletariat are different kinds of classes: workers can only take power themselves, whereas precisely because the nation-state can act as an engine of capital accumulation, it is quite possible for aspirant capitalists to turn themselves into real ones once they have taken political power, and the world is littered with examples of them—the 'political capitalists' Chris analyses so well. Failing to see the material involvement of the state in the capitalist economy leads, for example, to a failure to appreciate that one entirely rational response of sections of the *nomenklatura*, faced with the unravelling of the bureaucratic command economy in the USSR, is not to dissolve themselves into some abstract 'global capital', but rather to convert local political apparatuses into new states controlling resources which will give their rulers bargaining power in the world market. Today, as in the past, the nation-state is an economic as well as a political phenomenon.

Finally, how depressed should we be by the picture I have painted of the vitality of nationalism? A lot, Nigel thinks, although he believes 'the giant roadlock of nationalism . . . can be weakened within the contradictory evolution of global capitalism'.[31] This is, I think, to overestimate how great a 'roadblock' to class politics nationalism is even at its strongest. Nigel forgets a point stressed in the more historical sections of *National Liberation*, namely how fluid national identifications often are. Let me illustrate with the case of the last time a multinational empire disintegrated in Central and Eastern Europe—Austria-Hungary in 1918. This is usually depicted as the triumph of nationalism over both the dynastic Habsburg state and the Bolsheviks' revolutionary socialism. Thus Lewis Namier dismisses 'the fear of social revolution in Europe in 1917' as based on 'an intellectual illusion', the underestimation of popular nationalism.[32] Eric Hobsbawm, however, reports a study by Peter Hanák of correspondence between Austro-Hungarian soldiers and their families during the First World

War. As the war progressed, 'the fundamental theme' became 'war as a disruption and destruction of the *order of life and labour*'. The letters, especially those of workers and peasants, expressed 'an overwhelming wish for social transformation'; 'nationality appears most often as an aspect of the conflict between rich and poor'. The immediate impact of the Russian Revolution was to strengthen 'the wish for peace and social revolution'. 'But even when in the course of 1918 the national theme finally became dominant in popular consciousness, it was not separate from or opposed to the social theme. For most poor people the two went together, as the monarchy crashed.' The final outcome—'national independence without social revolution' for the new states of Poland, Czechoslovakia, Austria, Hungary and Yugoslavia—was 'a feasible fall-back position for those who had dreamed of both.'[33]

The moral of this tale is, in a sense, the ABC of Marxism. Nationalist movements are, for the exploited as well as would be exploiters, typically the expression of socio-economic impulses. It follows that those who attach themselves to a national banner because it seems to offer a solution to the problems of their material life may abandon it when that promise is not fulfilled. Nationalism is both weak and strong—strong because of the social forces which may invest it, weak because these forces may as easily desert it, provided a plausible alternative is available. We can afford to look nationalism in the face, and not to despair at its influence—so long, of course, as we busy ourselves trying to make sure the right sort of alternative is around to challenge it.

Notes

1 N Harris, 'A Comment on *National Liberation*', *International Socialism*, 2:53 (1991), replying to A Callinicos, 'The End of Nationalism?', and C Harman 'The State and Capitalism Today', both in *International Socialism*, 2:51 (1991).
2 N Harris, op cit, pp83-84.
3 Ibid, p81.
4 The main landmarks in this debate are N Harris, *Of Bread and Guns* (Harmondsworth, 1983), P Green, 'Nation-States and the World Economy', *International Socialism*, 2:19 (1983), N Harris, *The End of the Third World* (London, 1986), and A Callinicos, 'Imperialism, Capitalism and the State Today', *International Socialism*, 2:35 (1987).
5 N Harris, 'Comment', p82. See A Callinicos, 'End', p61, and, for example, A Giddens, *A Contemporary Critique of Historical Materialism* (London, 1981), and M Mann, *The Sources of Social Power*, I (Cambridge, 1986).
6 N Harris, 'Comment', op cit, p80.
7 Ibid, p84.
8 A Giddens, *The Consequences of Modernity* (Cambridge, 1990).
9 N Harris, 'Comment', pp82-83.

10 C Barker, 'A Note on the Theory of Capitalist States', *Capital and Class*, 4 (1978), p118. See also A Callinicos, *Is There a Future for Marxism?* (London, 1982), ch 8.
11 A Callinicos, *Making History* (Cambridge, 1987), pp157-172.
12 B Anderson, *Imagined Communities* (London, 1983), p47.
13 C Harman, 'State and Capitalism', op cit, pp13, 18.
14 All quotations in this paragraph and the next are from N Harris, 'Comment', op cit, p83.
15 Ibid, p87. See A Callinicos, 'End', op cit, pp63-64.
16 N Harris, 'Comment', op cit, p87.
17 Ibid, pp87-88.
18 Ibid, p86.
19 Ibid, pp79-80.
20 C Harman, 'State and Capitalism', op cit, p32; see also ibid, pp26-32.
21 C Harman, 'The Storm Breaks', *International Socialism*, 2:46 (1990), and A Callinicos, *The Revenge of History* (Cambridge, 1991), ch 2.
22 N Harris, 'Comment', op cit, p85.
23 Ibid, p88.
24 See my discussion of European union in *Socialist Review*, January 1992.
25 *Financial Times*, 19 October 1991.
26 J G A Pocock, 'Deconstructing Europe', *London Review of Books*, 19 December 1991, p10.
27 *Independent*, 31 December 1991. On Germany's historical role see, above all, A J P Taylor, *The Course of German History* (London, 1961).
28 N Harris, 'Comment', op cit, p88.
29 Ibid, p85.
30 See A Callinicos, 'End', op cit, p61.
31 N Harris, 'Comment', op cit, p88.
32 L Namier, *Vanished Supremacies* (Harmondsworth, 1962), p159.
33 E J Hobsbawm, *Nations and Nationalism since 1780* (Cambridge, 1990), pp126-130. Despite its reaching rather similar conclusions to Nigel's, this book is an excellent critical survey of recent historical research.

Do animals have rights?

STEVEN ROSE

I am a biologist, not a philosopher, and I experiment with animals in the laboratory. I study the mechanisms of memory, and my research is funded by the Medical Research Council, Science Research Council and various foundations and charities in Britain.

The animal rights movement is a coalition of forces which runs back for at least a century, but in its present form has developed particularly over the course of the last 20 years. It runs from older established organisations such as the British Union for the Abolition of Vivisection, through to groups such as the Animal Liberation Front and Advocates for Animals, which are more activist and concerned with the *liberation*, as they call it, of animals in laboratories.

I wish to begin by looking historically at why the animal rights movement has emerged in the way that it has. Then I want to look at their arguments and the implications of those arguments, and explain why I think they are false. I do so both as a Marxist and as a working scientist, and I wish to concentrate on the animal rights activists view of experimentation, rather than their view of factory farming or other sorts of uses of animals.

In order to understand the origins of the animal rights movement you have to understand something historically about the relationship of humans (people and social organisations) to non-human animals—philosophically, politically and economically. There is a lot of romantic nonsense talked about how in pre-capitalist societies there were different sorts of relationships of humans to animals—much more harmonious—than exist in capitalist or even feudal society. Yet what is abundantly clear is that from the beginning of the Judaeo-Christian tradition (as shown in the Bible, in the history of agriculture, and in the history of the domestication of animals) there is a very strong belief that humans should have domination over nature. This idea and practice of domination runs right the way through the development of civilisation from its earliest possible times. But it was encapsulated very strongly with the birth of modern—that is Western—science which began contemporaneously with the birth of modern capitalism, back in the middle 17th century. The commitment of the scientific method was unequivocally to the domination of nature. It was humanity's right, according to the ideologues of both modern science and capitalism, to extract from nature, whether animate or inanimate, all the wealth, all the riches and all the extractable products that nature could provide. This ethic of the domination of nature thus goes right to the heart of the growth of the scientific method from the 17th century onwards.

It is important to understand the growth of this tradition within science and within capitalism in order to understand what the animal rights movement is objecting to, and to set up the critique of science in order that you can see the strength of the animal rights position before looking at its weaknesses.

Modern science however shifted the philosophical base of the problem of the relationship between humanity and other animals, between biology and human life. If humans were biological organisms, and they were subject to the same laws of biology as all other animals, what happened to the soul, to human consciousness and to those things that the Christian religion was committed to believe were uniquely human? The answer given by Descartes, one of the founders of modern science, was that humans were biological organisms just like any other organisms, but differed from other biological organisms because as well as being biological they had a *soul* which was locked somewhere in the brain. This meant they had the breath of God within them, which gave them certain sorts of divine rights and divine responsibilities. The point of Descartes saying this was to deny that non-human animals had any sort of soul at all. For Descartes the cry of pain of an animal was the squeak of a rusty cog in a machine.

The Cartesian split symbolised the birth of a type of reductionism within science which made it possible to treat animals and the rest of nature as mere objects, a view compatible with the growth of modern capitalism. Cartesian thinking enabled the scientist and the capitalist to exploit animals and the rest of nature perfectly contentedly six days a week, and then remember their soul on Sunday morning. But this convenient compatibility with Catholicism didn't last beyond the industrial revolution at the beginning of the 19th century, and was given its death-blow with the emergence of Darwinian ideas in biology in the middle of the 19th century.

The work of the early physiologists seemed to accept Descartes' view of animal pain as the squeak of a rusty cog. Despite the importance of much of this work for medicine, it was not for nothing that physiology became known as 'the science of pain'. In order to explore animals, particularly in the days before anaesthetics, the whole range of activities which the British Union for the Abolition of Vivisection calls vivisection began to be developed. Undoubtedly the sort of experiments that were conducted, although they revealed a great deal of scientific information, also caused a substantial amount of pain. They could even be termed brutal (although perhaps relatively no more brutal than the way hospitals treated their patients at that time, nor the way most workers were treated in the factories of the industrial revolution).

But the main point is this: the whole background and tradition of science in the Western world has emphasised this idea of the domination of nature by science (ie humanity). This idea was accepted rather uncritically by Marx, who speaks strongly about the right of humans to dominate nature, and the role of a communist society in liberating the full productive powers of science. Later Marxists were no less enthusiastic—certainly if you read Trotsky on the rights of animals and humans you will find he also supports this exploitative and dominating tradition. There is an alternative tradition which can be read into the writings of the early Marx and even more strongly in Engels—a tradition which writers like Ted Benton have tried to rescue—but there is no doubt that the ideology of domination has been central to the view of human-animal relations as much in 'actually existing socialism' until its collapse in the last few years, as in the capitalist societies.

Since the 1939-45 war, and increasingly in the last decades, a deeper and more critical view of science has begun to develop, both amongst radical movements and the left. This criticism sees science, far from being beneficial and progressive, as arcane, mysterious, damaging to global ecology, damaging to humans and as intervening oppressively in human and non-human life. Thus the whole thesis of the domination of nature, which had hitherto gone unquestioned amongst bourgeois or socialist critics, began to come under very sharp criticism from a variety of movements—the peace movement, CND, the ecology movement and, of course, the animal rights movement. These oppositions to the activity and products of science appear to have a sort of coherence. However, I believe that far from having coherence they are very divergent, and the argument put against science as being sexist and racist and concerned with the propagation of a class structure of society has to be very sharply separated from those arguments that the animal rights movement uses against scientific work and experimentation.

My criticism of the animal rights movement should not be seen as a blanket defence of all that science does. More than 95 percent of all the funding of science in capitalist societies goes on research directed towards the military or to profit or both. It is inevitable, therefore, that a lot of the experimentation on animals is serving either or both of these two purposes. Thus any criticisms that we make of science must also be criticisms of the sort of society we live in—a capitalist, racist, sexist and imperialist society.

I therefore don't wish to defend factory farming, which I see as an abuse which comes out of a determination to extract maximum profit from the ways in which animals are handled. I don't defend either a substantial proportion of the research that is done on drugs and the development of new products, which are often concerned primarily with innovation to increase extractable value or to circumvent patent laws rather than responding to genuine human needs—insofar as such needs can ever be distinguished from those of the social order that promotes them. What I do believe, however, is if you want new drugs and new products you have to research their safety.

Let me now turn to the two key arguments of the animal rights movement, in the context particularly of animal experimentation. One of these arguments is plainly false, the other hypocritical. On the one hand the ideologues of the movement—writers like Tom Regan or Peter Singer and their many followers—say that animal experimentation can tell one nothing at all that is useful about human diseases or the human condition. They argue that the disjunction between humans and other animals is so great that it is not possible to learn anything from animal experiments. This is the false argument. On the other hand they say that because non-human animals, like humans, are sentient and they are creatures that have brains and are organised in a particular way, they therefore have rights. The demand for animal rights, it follows, is exactly the same as the demand for black people's rights, for women's rights, disabled rights and so on. That is the hypocritical argument.

It is abundantly clear that, firstly, animals and humans form a biological continuum. The same sort of biochemicals which constitute the biological and physiological processes of our human bodies, constitute those of animal bodies as well. The major difference between human animals and non-human animals is that humans have larger and better developed brains. We have the capacity of speech, to make and manipulate tools, and because of this we can create social organisations. Therefore humans have a *history* whereas non-human animals on the whole only have a *past*. This technological and social history is primarily what divides human from non-human animals, not anything unique about our biology or theirs.

It is precisely because of this similarity that one can learn things about the human condition and human diseases by the study of animals.

Many of the drugs and medical treatments which can now be used to treat human diseases exist because of animal experimentation. Treatment for diseases like diabetes, the knowledge of immunology and of immunisation which lie at the basis of transplants and much preventative medicine, and the development of most surgical procedures and drugs, have been contingent on doing animal experiments. There was no alternative in the past, and there is still no alternative now, to the use of animals in this context. It is particularly true in the case of the area in which I work—the brain sciences. The animal rights movement sometimes argues there are alternatives to animal experimentation, such as using tissue culture or bacteria. But for the study of the conditions which are the major causes of distress, disease and death in contemporary industrial society—schizophrenia, depression, anxiety, neurological diseases, strokes and so on—you have to study animals which have brains.

Although there are deep biological continuities between humans and non-humans, some processes certainly work differently in human biology compared to other non-human animal biology, as the thalidomide case proves, where the drug turned out not to have the birth defect producing effects on the animals on which it was tested, though it would have done on other species. But all this example shows is that if you want a drug like thalidomide you need more animal experimentation, on different species, and not less in order to be sure the drug is safe before it is used on humans. And those of you who go to the Body Shop and see all their products labelled 'not tested on animals' (at least until they were stopped from doing so) need to ask the question: do you really want them to be tested on humans? Most of the Body Shop products have in fact been tested on animals—by contractors, or by other manufacturers, or in the past. The argument should be about whether you want the product and not about whether you want the testing. Some also argue that some sorts of animal experimentation are acceptable but that they are against the testing of new cosmetics. It is worth pointing out that less than 1 percent of all the animal experimentation done in this country is cosmetics testing. But, nevertheless, my response is simple. If you want new cosmetics then I would rather they were tested on animals than humans.

The alternative of course is precisely that—to work on humans—and that is the point the animal rights people want to make. They say that the rights of a non-human animal are identical with the rights of a human, therefore there is no difference between working on animals and working on humans, so why not experiment on humans? To take a position which is opposed to this they call 'speciesism' and they use the term in the same way that racism and sexism is used. I wish to say that I am, unashamedly, a speciesist. That is I have an unqualified loyalty to the human species and I think it is perfectly possible to draw a dividing line between human and non-human animals which makes sense to everyone but the most perverse.

The argument about rights as advanced by people such as Peter Singer in Australia, Tom Regan in the States, Richard Ryder in Britain is to say that animals are sentient beings and do have particular sorts of rights. The problem, however, is that they use this word rights and animals in an extremely broad way. Where do you stop? For example does a gorilla have the same right as an ant? Does a mouse have the same right as a cat? Does a wasp have the same right as a shark? Where is the dividing line in the biological continuum? I think if you ask the animal rights people what they believe, they will say that animals with large nervous systems and which are closest in appearance to humans—ie large furry mammals or primates—should have more rights than wasps or mosquitoes. The deputy editor of the *New Statesman* wrote, in response to my article there, that he had no compunction in killing a prawn, I guess because he likes eating them in his cocktails, paella and so on, but he is very hostile to me killing chickens. Yet this is biological ignorance on his part because a prawn has in many ways as complex a nervous system as a chicken.

The moment you put the argument in that way it becomes clear that there are a number of paradoxes. Firstly, no animal, other than the human animal, worries about the rights of others—a cat doesn't worry about the rights of a mouse before killing it. This makes the whole concept of rights a very puzzling one because it is not the animals who are demanding rights, but the humans who are conferring the rights on animals. So we humans, because we are a particular sort of biological organism, are turning round and saying that you cat, monkey, rat have particular sorts of rights. The argument, therefore, is not about the rights of animals, but about the duties of humans. And this is fundamentally different than the way the argument of rights is used in the context of political and social struggles. When the oppressed subjects of history (black people, women, gays and lesbians) rise up and demand rights they are speaking in their own name, and not having rights conferred upon them by some white middle class male elite. Rights are won in political struggle, by the subjects of history becoming articulate by arguing for themselves and making their own history. This is fundamentally different from the way the term rights is used by animals activists. I cannot accept the dishonest and hypocritical argument that animals have rights in the same sense that we use that term for social and political struggles.

What we have to examine is human duty, that is how we as human animals behave to other animals. I don't doubt that we have duties to other animals, and I don't dissent from the critique that modern capitalism is dominating, exploitative and deliberately destroys the sense of responsibility to the environment in which we live. We need to move towards a relationship between humanity and nature that is harmonious and less dominating. But that is a need which comes out of our own need as humans, and does not come out of some mythical concept of animal rights.

As a socialist and a Marxist I am uneasy with the whole concept of rights in this context. Rights are always posed in this debate as if they are some sort of absolute. That is, as if there is an absolute right to freedom of speech, absolute right of animals not to be molested and so on. But this is not the way the world works. Rights are constantly in conflict. The rights of one animal interfere with the rights of another (there is a problem about rights versus dinner!). This is a fundamental biological principle—all organisms exist simultaneously in competition and co-operation with all others. Even if you go naked and deny yourself not merely animal food but also remove all animal fibre from your body, your body is still an ecological battleground for many other organisms. Even if you lie down and die, a variety of different predators, from bacteria to scavenging mammals, will compete for the right to devour your flesh. This is the way biology works. One of my major criticisms of the animal rights movement and the ecology movement in general, is of their belief that somehow if you go back to a pre-industrial, pre-capitalist society you would live in a world where everything is bright and beautiful; that only man was vile, that the world was co-operative and non-competitive before human intervention. Yet before human beings existed in the world species were evolving; many organisms and entire species were dying out. This is a fundamental feature of evolution. The fact is that rights conflict, and because they conflict you cannot get out of the problem of making choices simply by saying that animals have rights. You have to make a value judgment about the value of human life against the value of non-human life.

At the moment the only way we know how to begin to develop a vaccine for AIDS is to work with chimpanzees—I wish there was another way, but there isn't. If we want an AIDS vaccine then chimpanzee research must go on. If you make a judgment that this research should not go on then you are making a judgment that will condemn many to a life of misery and, in many cases, death. That is a choice that is forced upon us not just by the nature of human existence but by the nature of life itself—it is not something that can be got out of by talking about rights.

The animal rights movement is a very complex conglomeration of forces both of the right and the left. Indeed it is an open secret that it has been systematically penetrated by many groups of the extreme right. In Milton Keynes, for example, members of the local animal rights group include supporters of an openly Nazi group calling itself the November 9th Movement, the date of Hitler's infamous Kristallnacht. The animal rights movement has been used as a cover for attacks on Jewish and Muslim style animal killings. It is worth remembering that the history of the movement is a fairly unsavoury one in a variety of ways. The only country ever to ban animal experiments completely was Nazi Germany during the 1930s. There is also an element within the animal rights movement, among so called 'deep ecologists', which is profoundly anti-human which would rather save chimpanzees and whales than humans.

To conclude. I have many criticisms of many aspects of science and its uses under capitalism. I insist that what we need to try and do is to create a science as well as a society which lives harmoniously with nature and understands that nature evolves, that eco-systems are complex and cannot be understood experimentally or appreciated in the crassly reductionist terms which modern science, as it developed under capitalism, has sponsored. But I also insist that we cannot avoid making moral, political and social choices by wrapping up arguments in cant about animal rights. If we want to save human lives, animal experimentation is still necessary.

Crime and class in the 18th century

A review of Peter Linebaugh, ***The London Hanged: Crime and Civil Society in the Eighteenth Century*** *(Allen Lane, 1991), £25*

JOHN CHARLTON

The following wretched condemned people were taken from Newgate Prison in the east of the City of London in an open cart, accompanied by ringing church bells (muffled) three miles across the busiest thoroughfares in town to Tyburn, on the edge of the modern Hyde Park. There they were strung up before crowds of their fellow Londoners, cut down when dead and seized by anatomists for dissection. Brian Cooley reaped hay in season. He stole a cane worth five shillings and was hanged in April 1743. His wife and children came over from Ireland to comfort him before his hanging. Bez Ozeland, a weekly servant, took some black warp silk on her birthday. She slept and worked in a single room. She was 42 years old. Her husband was at sea. She was found guilty and sentenced to death. Hannah Wilson was a Bethnal Green vendor of peas and beans. She was married at the Fleet, once at the age of 14 and once again at the age of 18. She was hanged at the age of 25 for stealing clothes worth 18 pence. George Purchase, a journeyman in Salisbury Court, was hanged in 1716 for shouting in a riot, 'No Hanoverian! No King George!' John Wilkins, a tailor, was hanged in 1747 for stealing a gown and a pair of breeches.

Even at 200 years remove these events remain deeply shocking. Brian, Bez, Hannah, George and John are just five of the 1,500 men and women hanged in London, mainly at Tyburn, between 1703 and 1772. The public nature of executions had a single purpose: the terrorising of the working population. The 'Murder Act' of 1747 stated, 'It is become necessary that some further Terror and peculiar Mark of Infamy be added to the Punishment'.[1]

It is a hideous story, but Peter Linebaugh has not set out to produce another ghoulish account of a gruesome 18th century public spectacle. What he has done is to use contemporary records of the hanged to create a quite superb anatomy of class relations in 18th century London; dock work on the riverside, silk weaving in Spitalfields, shipyard work at Deptford and the 'new' industrial suburbs of Clerkenwell and Shoreditch.

He goes beyond that, however, for what he produces is a remarkable account of the growth and consolidation of British capitalism from the years following the Stuart Restoration in 1660. Without making it explicit he totally refutes revisionists like J C D Clark, who deny the triumph of a bourgeoisie and who depicts England as a society governed by:

> *the religious dimension in which all moved...[and] traditional, hierarchical, deferential forms which were neither antiquated, tenuous survivals nor mere superstructures on a reality which was 'basically' economic, but substantive and prevalent modes of thought and behaviour in a society dominated still by the common people, by the aristocracy, and by relations between the two.*[2]

After stepping into Peter Linebaugh's courtrooms it is immediately obvious that here was a three class society in microcosm: aristocratic bench, bourgeois jury[3] and proletarian accused.[4]

Linebaugh charts the ruling class struggle to redefine the meaning of property, to standardise the uses of money and credit, to substitute money wages for customary rewards for labour, to grasp control of the labour process, and to subject vast tracts of the world to British domination. At the heart of this process was a violent class struggle and the victims of Tyburn were its exposed tip.

The aristocratic parliament devoted massive amounts of time to issues central to the concerns of the business classes. Linebaugh documents dozens of debates suggestive of considerable expertise among members and a pretty efficient lobbying system of merchants and representatives of trades such as watch making, silk weaving, coal and tea importing, poultry and meat handling, shipbuilding, and tailoring. For example, Sir Robert Walpole, the Prime Minister (1721-1742) took a close personal interest in the tobacco trade, mastering the most intricate technical details in an attempt to defeat both smugglers and operatives at all levels—from slaves on the plantations to London dockers who insisted upon a customary right to a share of the crop.

Linebaugh defines custom as 'a usage of a locality or trade, which by long continuance has acquired the force of law or right'.[5] It appears that virtually every trade had such rights or perquisites. In tobacco they were called 'sockings', in tailoring 'cabbage', in ship building 'chips', in shoemaking 'clicking', in hatmaking 'bugging', and in silk 'wastes'. They formed a substantial part of a worker's income and even contemporary opinion held that workers could not survive without this component. Such perquisites were at the very centre of class struggle in this period. Some had a long history reaching back to the pre-capitalist economy. Others were of more recent vintage reflecting both the strength of skilled workers and the survival of what Thompson called 'a moral economy' where workers' believed they had rights over at least part of the goods produced. With the growth of commodity production and intense competition employers wished to assert a new definition of property which totally excluded workers from any rights in the goods their labour produced. This was a struggle fought out over the whole period.

The new definition of property found its philosophical champion in the late 17th century in John Locke, who, as Director of the Council of Trade and Plantations, was very close to issues arising from the ownership of commodities. He wrote:

> *The chief and great end...of men's uniting into commonwealths...is the preservation of their property... Political power, then, I take it to be the right of making laws with penalties of death, and, consequently, all less penalties for the regulating and preserving of property, and of employing the force of the community in the execution of such laws...and all this only for the public good.*

However, if Locke's was the philosophical umbrella, the issues of property were fought out with much less finesse in parliament, the courts and the workshops. Almost without exception parliament and courts found for the employers and merchants rather than the workers.

As Linebaugh points out, the rulers had a twin strategy. Firstly, parliament tried to systematically eliminate customary practices by criminalising them. New policing agencies were instituted to spy upon workers and to apprehend offenders. The courts would then move with extreme savagery to jail, whip, brand, transport or execute transgressors against the new laws. Secondly, employers would increasingly use the money wage to gain greater control over labourers and to divide workers by skill and gender.

Though the rulers were to win these battles, the workers fought back. On a small scale individuals acted with superb courage in the face of the noose. The former apprentice locksmith and highwayman Jack Shepherd several times escaped the hangman and passed into workers' mythology as a champion of the poor. The author also documents several attempts by the Tyburn crowds to liberate prisoners from the tumbrils, an event which seemed to increase in frequency through the century.

Most significant, however, was the movement into collective action. There were four strikes of leather workers in the 1730s, and of sailors, coal heavers, glass grinders, shoemakers and tailors in the 1760s. But what really shook the ruling class were the two great insurrectionary movements, the Wilkes Riots of 1768 and the Gordon Riots of 1780. Although there were strong elements of crowd manipulation by middle class interests in both, what terrified the rulers was the blatant turn to class war, symbolised most dramatically in the total destruction by the crowd of Newgate Prison in June 1780 and by the liberation of hundreds of prisoners from jails and crimping houses (where the impressed were held[6]) across London. We get a definite sense that the rulers had grown to see workers en masse as a terrifying threat. There were calls for more policing and an end to the Tyburn procession:

> *In September 1781 the City of London argued to the Secretary of State that the official and ancient terror of a Tyburn procession no longer deterred wrongdoers, but openly hardened them in brutality... Edmund Burke... sought to avoid...*[a]*...massacre...at the gallows, for fear it would irritate rather than humble 'the lower and middling people'.*[7]

Executions went on of course, and still in public, but unannounced, in prison yards and even in the streets of the workers' districts.

In the latter part of the book Peter Linebaugh gives us a portrait of a section of the ruling class towards the end of the century, virtually obsessed by the problems of bringing their order to the workers' districts. Three figures stand out: Jeremy Bentham, his brother Samuel, and Patrick Colquhoun. Bentham is often characterised as an enlightened reformer. He was a utilitarian who preached that public policy should be aimed at 'the greatest happiness of the greatest number'. He wished to reform the prison system and was opposed to capital punishment, yet he was as barbarous as his associates when his own property was at stake. In 1780 he had his aged servant John Franks sent to the gallows for taking two silver spoons.

His brother Samuel became Inspector General of Naval Works in 1795 and devoted the rest of his life to wresting control away from the shipyard workers. It is easy to see why he needed to. It was estimated that only one sixth of the timber entering Deptford yard left it afloat![8] Bentham may be seen as an early forerunner of Frederick Winslow Taylor, the celebrated founder of 'scientific management', for, in addition to installing many labour saving technical innovations in the dockyards, he tried to outlaw 'chips', introduced a new wage structure, abolished the apprenticeship system and pioneered the principle of incessant work through 24 hour shifts and the measurement of tasks.

Patrick Colquhoun was a magistrate in Spitalfields, the silk dying district in the early 1790s. To the delight of the employers he introduced an effective network of spies and then dealt harshly with those apprehended. He moved on to the much greater task of cleaning up the sugar trade, which by the end of the century was at the very heart of British economic prosperity. Imports of sugar rose from 1 million hundredweight at mid-century to 3.7 million in 1800. The trade had been rocked by the revolution in Haiti in 1793 where black slaves had successfully repulsed both the British and French armies and navies. This campaign cost Britain £10 million and 100,000 casualties. Magistrates were given sanction to punish offenders by assigning them to replenish the colours, 'being Loose, Idle, Disorderly and fit to serve the King'.[9]

Sugar supplies and the profits of the merchants were threatened. Workers *traditionally* had rights over part of the crop. This had to be won back and Patrick Colquhoun led the attack. Colquhoun saw the working class as 'an epidemic...the mass of labourers are 'contaminated', one group of workers 'infect' another...[the Working Class is]...a military enemy whose various detachments and subdivisions...[form] the General Army of Delinquents'.[10] There were two strategies to deal with this problem. New secure wet docks were constructed to thwart the lightermen, lumpers, gangsmen and coopers. The workers were seen to need a military campaign of policing. The outcome was the formation of a Marine Police Force in 1798 which was to become the model for the Metropolitan Police 30 years later. It was there explicitly to protect merchants' property and discipline workers through spying, stop and search, compulsory dress codes and the threat of impressment. It was also the agency appointed to pay or withhold dockers' wages.

Peter Linebaugh demonstrates how a working class had taken shape, as the 18th century progressed, in a veritable crucible of class conflict. Readers reared on E P Thompson will perhaps find surprising his explicit use of the term 'working class' throughout the book to describe the various groups of labouring people and the London labourers collectively. It has usually been argued that the term has little relevance before the 1820s. So successfully does Linebaugh delineate conflict between working men and women and their masters and rulers that the term seems quite appropriate. Relations were crude, harsh and violent. Conflict was endemic. In the trades of riverside and suburban districts there are few signs of the stable 'conservative' artisans depicted in Prothero's book on John Gast, the shipyard carpenter.[11]

However, both views could be correct. The late 17th and 18th century tradesman and his 'moral economy' were an obstacle to nascent capitalism's drive to smash the values and practices of the ancient City Companies or Guilds. The new industrial suburbs free of guild restrictions acted like a vice on the established trades, forcing many workers into destitution and lives of crime whilst creating, for a few, opportunities to build their own enterprises. It could well be that this society of raw conflict produced a primitive sense of class consciousness. Indeed it is perfectly possible that this was precisely what Edmund Burke and his ilk were sensing in 1780 as they witnessed the sacking of Newgate, the liberation of prisoners and the growing hostility of the Tyburn crowds.

By the period of John Gast the workers' battle over custom was already virtually lost. The wages system with its inherent divisions and power to discipline was well established. Sectional craft union consciousness was a consequence. Although it was partially overcome in the struggles of the Chartists, it was to remain an obstacle to the development of independent working class action and organisation for much of the 19th century.

One of the book's remarkable features is the manner in which we are constantly reminded of capitalism's international dimension. The author writes:

> *London was the vortex of English imperialism, which began in the Irish Sea... The Thames was the jugular vein of the British empire. London, the largest city in the Western Hemisphere, containing by 1800 nearly a million souls, was both the capital of England and the centre of an empire that embraced the workshops of Bengal, the plantations of the Caribbean, the 'factories' of West Africa and the forests of North America.*[12]

The biographies of the hanged show that London had a cosmopolitan proletariat. Africans, Americans, Frenchmen, Danes and Dutchmen took the road to Tyburn as well as English, Scots and Welsh. But an inordinate number of Irish men and women went to the gallows. They were the subject of a contemporary proverb: 'The name of an Irishman was enough to hang him.' Following the massacres, displacements and settlements of Cromwell and William of Orange in the previous century, the Irish were already forced to the bottom of the labour market and were the major victims of crude prejudice.

Peter Linebaugh has written a splendid vigorous book which should become a classic of social history. He can really stir the emotions. I have felt myself raging at the horrific callous violence of those 18th century rulers and ideologues, some of whom, like the Benthams and Colquhoun, 'grace' the pages of so many books as rational modernisers who should engage our sympathy as fighters against archaic superstition. And I have been near to tears as I have followed those poor working people to the gallows, hoping each time that the author would be able to tell me that so-and-so escaped or at least got the lesser sentence. He has drawn life out of dry documents in a most impressive way, communicating the tenacity, vitality, exuberance, courage and real humanity of those men and women fighting to rise out of the appalling conditions in which they lived.

Notes

1 P Linebaugh, 'The Tyburn Riots Against the Surgeons', D Hay, P Linebaugh and E P Thompson, *Albion's Fatal Tree* (London, 1975), p76.
2 J C D Clark, *English Society 1688-1832* (Cambridge, 1986), p44.
3 Readers can find a fine account of this stratum in P Earle, *The Making of the English Middle Class* (London, 1989).
4 P Linebaugh, *The London Hanged* (London, 1991), pp77-79.
5 Ibid, p171.
6 The 'impressed' were usually poor men captured by press gangs and taken to service in the armed forces. During the Napoleonic Wars impressment was used by the courts as an alternative to other punishments.
7 P Linebaugh, op cit, p363.
8 Ibid, p381.
9 Ibid, p412.
10 Ibid, p428.
11 I Prothero, *Artisans and Politics in Early Nineteenth Century London* (London, 1979).
12 P Linebaugh, op cit, p411.

Revolution, reform and working class culture

*A review of Helmut Gruber, **Red Vienna, experiment in working class culture 1919-1934** (Oxford, 1991). £25*

JOHN REES

In the great argument between reform and revolution that has dominated the history of the socialist movement there have frequently emerged people who deny the terms of the debate. Their argument is this: we accept that pure electoralism leads to disaster and that socialism cannot be handed down from above by well intentioned MPs or councillors. We therefore reject traditional reformism. But we also reject the Marxist insistence that a revolution is necessary before workers can take control of their lives. We stand instead for a struggle which combines reformism and electoralism with extra-parliamentary struggle. We seek to change the culture of the working class, to build a bedrock of convinced socialist opinion at the grass roots. Then we will be able to rely on that same foundation to help fend off the attacks of the capitalists when we pass laws which seek to transform capitalism.

This argument was deployed by Eurocommunists, Bennites and supporters of Ken Livingstone's GLC in the 1980s. It is still at the heart of Boris Kagarlitsky's notion of reformist-revolution and of the *Militant*'s vision of social change. It is also a strategy that has already been implemented, with more determination than any of its more recent adherents have managed, by the Austrian Socialist Party (SDAP) in the 1920s and early 1930s. Helmut Gruber's *Red Vienna* is a first class account of this socialist experiment.

Vienna was controlled by a socialist administration from the end of the First World War until 1934. The SDAP was a reformist party, but it was far to the left of most modern reformist parties. Its leading theoreticians were known as the Austromarxists and the party was committed to finding a middle way between the bankrupt reformism of the old Second International and the Bolshevism of the Third International.

Although not in power nationally, the SDAP controlled the capital. It had significant tax raising powers and was convinced that Vienna could become a socialist laboratory, successfully experimenting in building a socialist culture. This muscular reformism had some real achievements to its credit. Over 63,000 new homes were built by the municipality between 1919 and 1934. This meant that every tenth dwelling was new. They housed some 200,000 Viennese workers. Rents were about 10 percent below the market price. The new blocks of flats often contained communal laundries, kindergartens and canteens.

Housing was the core of the SDAP's programme, but progress was made in other areas as well. Increased welfare provision brought the death rate down by 25 percent and the infant mortality rate down by 50 percent compared with pre-war levels. Welfare measures included school lunches, school medical and dental examinations, publicly funded vacations and summer camps and newly created after school centres.

These reforms were not seen merely as an end in themselves. The SDAP wanted to create a distinct working class culture which would underpin its bid for parliamentary power. Like many left reformists since, the SDAP accepted the Marxist critique of electoralism but rejected the revolutionary argument that it was therefore necessary to smash the state. Its alternative strategy was a parliamentary campaign plus a cultural struggle outside parliament.

The SDAP certainly had the support on which such a strategy could be based. In 1931-32 it organised a loose network of 40 cultural organisations with a total of some 400,000 members in Vienna alone. The scale of these organisations needs to be seen against the background of the 425,000 who were members of the SDAP, the 350,000 trade unionists and the 150,000 people who belonged to tenants associations. The SDAP's efforts ranged from publishing tabloid newspapers, through opening workers' libraries, to organising the 1931 Worker Olympics at the conclusion of which 'a huge gilt idol representing capitalism was overthrown by collective strength, and thousands of red flags carried by youth in white ushered in a socialist future'.[1] There was no area of life which the massive organisation of the SDAP did not try to influence: radio and cinema, childcare and sex, fashion and sport—none escaped the party's desire to mould a working class culture. Gruber spends considerable effort in outlining the SDAP's policy and practice in all these areas.

Gruber's sympathy for the aims of the SDAP makes his searching critique of its theory and practice all the more devastating. Without trying to deny the real changes that the Vienna municipality achieved, Gruber shows its strategy was inadequate to meet the needs of the workers. In every area the SDAP's politics were marked by paternalism and elitism. The party frequently exaggerated its achievements and sought to disguise an essentially bourgeois morality in the rhetoric of working class culture. Gruber rightly notes the similarity with the way in which ideas about working class culture were used by the Stalinists in Russia.

Even the core of the SDAP's achievements, its housing programme, was less impressive when judged by contemporary international standards:

> [The SDAP] *in their Olympian stance . . . failed to recognise or credit socialist housing programmes in other places. They did not take note that Hamburg also used a building tax to partly finance a larger number of worker flats; that the brilliant socialist architect and planner Ernst May developed a general housing plan for Frankfurt based on the harmony of form and function in a new design of worker urban living; that worker skyscrapers, and the suburban Parisian 'red belt' of worker housing had been constructed against great odds; or that worker housing in England was increased by one-third between 1919 and 1939, with massive slum clearing in London.*[2]

The Vienna housing programme was conservative in many respects. Architecturally it simply reproduced the pattern of traditional Viennese blocks. Worse still, the modern furniture recommended for the flats, much more compact than that owned by many Viennese workers, was too expensive for them to buy. But most fundamentally:

> *Throughout the two building periods from 1924 to 1933...the SDAP failed to conduct a single survey either at workplaces or in working class neighbourhoods about worker expectations and needs concerning the housing being created principally for them...* [This attitude] *stemmed from the transformational heritage of Austromarxism according to which workers had to be educated by the party to reach a higher state of being than their present precivilised or at best unformed state.*[3]

Hence, concludes Gruber, 'like virtually all interwar socialist parties, where the oligarchy "knew best" and always "acted in the common interest" of the party rank and file, the SDAP operated as a paternalist machine.'[4]

This top down organisation of workers' lives, all in the name of moulding workers into a new culture, developed an almost sinister edge when it came to aspects of workers' personal lives. Women were encouraged to create a supportive home atmosphere for male workers and warned of the dangers of adopting the trivialising fripperies of bourgeois fashion. More frighteningly familiar to those who have recently had to listen to feminist sermons about child abuse is Gruber's description of the welfare system:

> *The tendency of the welfare system to look upon the poor, the unemployed, those evicted, or those who consumed a glass too many, as deviants or at best as marginal families needing the full measure of social control to bring them up to normal standards, made welfare workers appear as hostile government agents in working class communities. Indeed, the removal of children to the diagnostic centre, as described by one social worker, resembled a police raid, with social worker and bailiff arriving unexpectedly to reduce the amount of parental resistance to what the parents considered a violation of their rights.*[5]

The same pattern of 'socialist' paternalism ultimately resulting in the uncritical imposition of establishment values reproduced itself in every area of the SDAP's work. In the educational sphere, for instance, the spokesman of the SDAP claimed that the new institutes and curriculum that had been introduced meant that 'Vienna can claim that proud title of "city of school reform".'[6] Yet the SDAP's fear of 'going too far' and upsetting the balance of power meant that they failed to really transform the school system, leaving all the old reactionary teachers in place. 'All the reform efforts were sabotaged by the teachers—either the former instructors of cadets, who as clericals and monarchists detested the republic, or relocated instructors from the German schools in Czechoslovakian cities who remained loyal to their Pan-Germanism down to supporting the Austrian Nazis in the early 1930s...workers were denounced as riffraff in the classroom, and Marxists were designated traitors.'[7]

The central point is this: there can be no middle way between a revolution from below, which allows workers to create their own institutions and thereby to control their own lives, and reformism which seeks to use the existing institutions of the capitalist state, and thereby ends up adapting establishment values and forcing them on a recalcitrant working class. We have seen enough municipal socialism in Britain over the last ten years to recognise this pattern only too clearly. The virtue of the Austromarxist example is that the self confidence and determination with which they held to their reformism gives their experiment a more extreme form than most.

Yet the whole Austromarxist theory was predicated on insisting that there was just such a middle way. Otto Bauer, the party's theorist, developed the idea that the Austrian republic which emerged after the war rested on a 'balance of powers' in which the right wing could not overthrow the parliamentary regime and the working class should not provoke them into doing so by stepping beyond the constitutional limits of the republic.

In fact this was simply a rationalisation of the SDAP's own bankrupt political strategy. Insofar as it had any purchase on reality this theory disguised that fact that the SDAP owed its ability to conduct its experiment in Vienna to the working class rising that was part of the great European revolutionary wave of the immediate post-war years—and to the fact that the SDAP itself had prevented a more revolutionary outcome. The ruling class tolerated it as the lesser evil, but only for a time. Gruber is admirably forthright on these questions:

> *The SDAP emerged as a mass party after the collapse of the old regime at the end of the war. Its future power and role were largely shaped during 1918-1919, when politics were in flux and the nature of the new republic was yet to be determined. The most dynamic political force at the time was the workers' councils, a partly organised mass movement of workers and demobilised soldiers with revolutionary aims that went beyond establishing a republic on a capitalist base. The councils were influenced by the Bolshevik revolution and the brief revolutionary regimes in Bavaria and Hungary. In Vienna, particularly, where a fledgling Communist Party was newly active, the councils threatened to become the directing force of the masses of workers... The SDAP, thus threatened from the left, adroitly manoeuvered the Vienna worker's council into accepting the principle of proletarian democracy, which allowed the socialists to bind the communists and other radical groups to decisions by majority rule. By the autumn of 1919, with the counter-revolution successful in Hungary, the councils were pushed to the sidelines. The Constituent Assembly, which had been elected in February, was able to function and secure the new republic without further threat of an alternative source of power.*[8]

But the cost of marginalising the workers' councils was high, even for the SDAP itself. The threat of the workers' councils had kept the right wing at bay and the mobilisation of the working class had given the SDAP its highest level of electoral support. The SDAP even failed to use this unique constellation of favourable factors to the full. It didn't push through thorough reforms, it didn't challenge the power of the Church and it let anti-semitic attacks, even on its own leaders, go unchallenged.

Indeed, the toleration of anti-semitism shows the SDAP's parliamentary cretinism at its most disgusting. Anti-semitism was rife, a constant refrain used against the SDAP which was supposedly part of the 'Jewish Bolshevik conspiracy'. Many SDAP leaders were Jews, yet 'the socialist leaders' response to the virulent anti-semitism directed against them and their party was either passive or perverse.' The SDAP leaders were at pains to avoid any identification with the Jews. They even answered anti-semitism with anti-semitism of their own:

> *The SDAP...played into the hands of the anti-semites by charging that they too were under the influence of or were pawns of Jewish bankers or Jewish capital... But at no time did the SDAP publish a full-scale rebuttal of anti-semitism or expose the close ties between the Pan-German and Christian Social exponents and the Catholic church and racist organisations.*[9]

On every key issue and at every decisive turning point the SDAP bowed to the power of the ruling class because its strategy of:

> *a class struggle on the two fronts of politics and culture was predicated on the neutral position of the republican state, with constitutional guarantees of political pluralism and democratic procedures. But the neutrality of the state was illusory.*[10]

The turning point came on 15 July 1927, when a frustrated mass of workers stormed the Palace of Justice, setting it ablaze. Police opened fire, killing many demonstrators. The SDAP was appalled at the workers' sudden eruption into self activity. One SDAP leader, Karl Renner, denounced the crowd as 'pitchfork revolutionaries'.[11] He went on to suggest that the SDAP go into coalition with the conservative Christian Socials in order to safeguard the republic. This was rejected, but after the events of 15 July the cultural politics of the SDAP, 'originally conceived as a major weapon in the armoury of the class struggle, more and more became a substitute for politics.'[12]

Otto Bauer's 'balance of powers' was predicated on his own party's usefulness to the ruling class. Once the right wing felt strong enough they were willing to unilaterally end the balance of power in their own favour. The final blow fell in February 1934 when reactionary Chancellor Dollfuss established an authoritarian regime, crushing a last desperate rising by the workers of Vienna. But in reality defeat had been prepared by the SDAP, as Gruber makes plain:

> *A tiny minority of workers had risen spontaneously by disregarding the wait-and-see policy of their leaders, who clung desperately to constitutional safeguards which had ceased to exist when Chancellor Dollfuss suspended*

parliament in March 1933. For more than a year the leaders of the SDAP had suffered the same paralysis of will which had immobilised the German left as Hitler rose to power. They repeatedly postponed the use of force to prevent the overthrow of the republic, although force had been a measure of self-defence in the SDAP programme since 1926. This policy of passivity in the face of the gradual demolition of republican safeguards was in effect capitulation to the corporate state projected by Dollfuss and the Christian Socials... Ultimately the insurrection of the few was only a desperate act in the face of a defeat that was already apparent; it was also directed against those socialist leaders who had cautioned and counselled against self-defence by the workers, and who were absent during the crucial hours from February 12 to 14.[13]

Helmut Gruber has done every socialist a valuable service by uncovering the history of Red Vienna. He is sometimes more concerned with the detail of cultural experiment than with historical context. Nevertheless, he has shown in an original and fascinating way the limits of municipal socialism, the weakness of even the most determined brand of reformism, the fact that a working class culture is an illusion (and, in these circumstances, a dangerous illusion) and that the need to smash the state is a key element in the struggle for workers' power.

Notes

1 H Gruber, *Red Vienna* (Oxford, 1991), p109.
2 Ibid, p64.
3 Ibid, pp52-53.
4 Ibid, p53.
5 Ibid, pp71-72.
6 Ibid, p77.
7 Ibid, p76.
8 Ibid, p181.
9 Ibid, pp26-27.
10 Ibid, p182.
11 Ibid, p108.
12 Ibid, p183.
13 Ibid, p4.

Blood simple

*A review of Chris Knight, **Blood Relations: Menstruation and the Origins of Culture** (Yale University Press, 1991) £40.00*

CHRIS HARMAN

Every generation of Marxists has to fight its battle against those who produce the latest proofs—strangely enough, always the same old proofs—that Marxism is finished. But we have also had, repeatedly, to fight another, even more tiresome battle against people who claim to be on our own side. Ever since Herr Professor Durhing beguiled half the intellectuals of the German socialist movement with his 'revolution in science' in the 1880s, Marxists have had to expose a series of intellectual quacks who have tried to present their pet systems of myths and half truths as the latest thing in scientific advance.

Chris Knight's book about the origins of human culture falls straight into the same tradition of quackery. Every chapter is headed by a quote from Marx. But the intellectual basis of the book owes little to Marx's insistence that social production is the key to the development of humanity. Rather Knight acknowledges his debt to: 'sociobiology's achievements' in seeing that 'what animates . . . the flesh and blood individual . . . are . . . genes . . . whose only law is to survive...'; to the mystical poets Peter Redgrove and Penelope Sharp, whose 'style and tone', he tells us, is 'Jungian'; to those 'involved in the Greenham Common anti-missile campaigns of the early 1980s' who refused 'to collaborate in the whole masculinist political set up . . . '; and to his 'political friends' which include prominent Labour MP Ken Livingstone and two lesser known luminaries of the London Labour left, Keith Veness and Graham Bash.

His politics are those of the Labour left of a decade ago—when Knight himself edited the 'personal politics' section of *Labour Briefing*, mixing Greenham Common feminism with municipal socialism—and his methodology is similarly eclectic. The resulting confusion leads to absurdities like speaking of a 'class conflict . . . between genders' among 'monkeys and apes'.

Most pop sociobiologists do not go beyond the 17th century mechanical materialist, Thomas Hobbes, who described life for humans in the 'state of nature' as 'nasty, brutish and short', with a 'war of all against all' making the development of civilisation impossible until people were forcibly compelled to behave themselves. Knight is no exception. He argues 'genetic imperatives' necessarily caused continual, bitter, bloody competition among our primate ancestors. Their behaviour, like that of present day primates, he describes as like 'primitive capitalists', their battles with each other as reminiscent 'of some of Lenin's descriptions of inter-imperialist rivalry'. And this prevented any real development of culture among our ancestors until about 50,000 or 60,000 years ago when co-operation replaced conflict.

His 'theory' is a Just So story about how such a change could have occurred—instead of telling how the elephant got its trunk, it claims to tell how humans got culture. It depends on adding a number of dubious claims to the initial postulate of endless conflict.

Firstly, males and females of all species are said to have different 'genetic imperatives' . Males can have innumerable offspring if they can squirt their sperm around widely enough, while females are restricted to those they carry inside their own bodies. So the genetically successful male will always be the one that fights other males for 'dominance' over as many females as possible and does nothing to help in the upbringing of progeny. But the genetically successful female will pay attention to rearing her offspring. In this way the motherly female and the philandering male are genetically fixed, and males, given the chance, will behave as parasites and oppressors, a 'leisured class', lording it over an exploited class of female reproducers. These, suffering from the incessant competition of animal society, have an interest in bringing about its revolutionary overthrow.

Secondly, human beings differ biologically from other primates in a way that alters the balance of power between the sexes, without changing the fundamental genetic disposition of either sex. The oestrus cycle, in which the female is only 'on heat' and of sexual interest to the male at the time of ovulation, is replaced by the menstrual cycle, with sex possible at all times—except, according to Knight, at the time of menstruation itself, when it is a fairly bloody business.

Thirdly, late on in human evolution women apparently discovered how to take advantage of this by synchronising their periods so as to deny men sex until they went out hunting and returned to share the catch with them. Such a 'sex strike' forced the innately competitive males to co-operate to the benefit of the females and of humanity in general.

Fourthly, all this allegedly triggered off the development of culture and language some 50,000 to 60,000 years ago.

Finally, the myths and taboos of 'traditional societies' are said to bear witness to this today. They re-enact elements of the sex strike by forbidding sex or cooking during menstruation, by banning hunters from eating their own kill, and by extolling the moon. Their tales of wondrous snakes or dragons are a celebration of women's power and solidarity, even if this has since been usurped by men. 'Such beliefs are in essence good science.'

This equation of myth with science is based on a linking together of half truths, false generalisations, unproven assertions and the occasional fact.

Take Knight's initial presupposition, the alleged, state-of-nature, bloody competition between male primates over food and females. Knight justifies himself by reference to Solly Zukerman's study of the chimps in London Zoo in the early 1930s. But there have been scores of further studies since, many based in the wild, which give a very different picture.[1] They reveal differences of social behaviour between different ape species as great as those between any of them and modern humans.[2] And in many cases there are far more instances of co-operation between individuals than conflict.

The social life of chimps, and still less gorillas, is certainly not one of endless battles by males to dominate females.[3] Cases of aggressive behaviour do occur among chimps—but they are not all pervasive and only occasionally end in fights.[4] Nor are there continual fights over food. When common chimpanzees make 'occasional forays into meat eating' they 'share out morsels among individuals who beg persistently enough'.[5] With pygmy chimpanzees, 'Food and feeding are a focus for social interactions . . . Plant food is frequently shared.'[6]

And any hunting is, itself, likely to involve co-operation between different members of the chimp group—and not only the males. It involves action that 'implies a lot of restraint, a good deal of co-operation, and not a little communication'.[7] So much for Knight's most basic sociobiological postulate, that co-operation was impossible until the 'sex strike'! With it his whole construction collapses. Every other point of his argument is similarly flawed.

i) 'Genetic success' for individual males does *not*, in all situations and at all times, depend upon males ignoring the interests of everyone else. To say the most successful genetic strategy will be to fertilise as many females as possible, rather than helping one female rear her offspring, is rather like saying a successful gambling strategy always involves putting small sums of money on many horses rather than the lot on a near certainty. Of course it doesn't. It all depends on the odds. If material conditions mean an unaided female will almost certainly lose her offspring to predators or through starvation, then any male who fails to help with child rearing will not be able to pass on his genes. 'Survival of the fittest' will then be the survival of the most fatherly. As Gigliari tells: 'In many species of mammals, the parental investment by males is considerable, and apparently enhances the reproductive potential of both sexes.' He refers to Callicebus monkeys, white handed gibbons, wild dogs, wolves, and Hartman Zebras.[8] I don't think Knight would want to argue a sex strike had to take place in all these cases!

ii) Human females are not unique in the replacement of the oestrus cycle by the menstrual cycle or in their readiness for sex at any point in the cycle. 'The menstrual cycle is a process common to old world monkeys, apes and men'[9] and, as a result, 'In anthropoid apes the sexual cycle is not expressed nearly as markedly as in other animals'.[10]

Among chimps 'mating may occur at any time during the female's cycle' although 'significantly more sexual behaviour occurs during the follicular phase',[11] 'orangutangs mate throughout the female's menstrual cycle without pronounced cyclical changes in behaviour,'[12] and gorilla 'females may present themselves to males throughout the cycle, but males accept a greater proportion when the female's labia are fully swollen'.[13] Among both chimps and gorillas, it can be either males or females who take the initiative sexually.[14]

Knight's picture of the philandering male, driven by an overpowering instinct to fight other males to fertilise as many females as possible, hardly matches up with the facts.

iii) Sychronisation of periods among females in close contact with each other is not, as Knight claims, an adaptive mechanism specific to humans which can explain some sudden invention of culture a few thousand years ago. It occurs among rats, gelada baboons, hamadryas baboons, rhesus monkeys and chimpanzees.[15]

What is more, it is certainly not a *conscious* mechanism, as is implied by talk of women choosing to synchronise periods to go on 'sex strike'. It is a completely unconscious process, arising as physical stimuli, probably of an olfactory nature, cause changes in hormonal balances.[16]

iv) There is overwhelming evidence for the existence of culture and language long before Knight's 50,000 to 60,000 years ago. Stone implements have been found that are more than 2 million years old[17] and by half a million years ago they were being designed according to common patterns. By the time of the neanderthals, 200,000 years ago, there is evidence of ritual burial. There was already a marked growth of the parts of the brain responsible for speech in modern man—Broca's and Wernicke's—in homo erectus 500,000 to 1,000,000 years ago (and possibly in homo habilis more than a million years before this),[18] while the vocal organs of the neanderthals would have been able to make most of the sounds we can.[19]

All this suggests there was a long drawn out development of symbolic culture and language out of rudimentary sounds and gestures similar to those used by chimps and gorillas today. There would have been all sorts of quantitative changes and qualitative leaps at different points during the 2 million years of this development, as humans evolved larger brains and learnt new ways of using them—archaeologists have long distinguished between the different 'cultures' that characterise tools to be found at different times in this long history. But this does not at all mean that humans accidentally managed to quadruple the size of the primate brain over a 3 or 4 million year period before suddenly 50,000 to 60,000 years ago discovering how to use it.

v) Among many surviving hunter-gatherer societies—those closest in their lifestyle to our ancestors of 50,000 to 60,000 years ago—myths and taboo are not all what Knight's model demands. He himself admits, 'It is certainly not the case that [Australian] Aboriginal women everywhere synchronised their periods with one another or with the moon in the recent pre-contact period', and that 'we have little hard evidence for either the presence or absence of real menstrual synchrony among the hunter-gatherer peoples of Africa'.

Nor are menstrual taboos by any means universal in such societies. The Mbuti pygmies of the central African rainforest ignore the strict menstrual taboos that prevail among their agricultural Bantu neighbours,[20] while the Kung regard menstruation as a relatively minor event.[21] So desperate is Knight for evidence that he claims painting the body red has menstrual significance. Does he apply that to all women who use makeup? As for his other great taboo, the 'first kill' one, Knight himself writes that it is 'not always rigidly adhered to', that 'it is in fact systematically evaded or undermined in a multiplicity of historically determined ways'. Put more simply: it does not apply universally as he claims!

What we are faced with in this book, then, is a series of phoney facts linked together by an intricate cobweb of speculation and then dressed up as 'Marxism'. This is particularly regrettable since there has developed, in recent years, a body of evolutionary theory among a minority of archeologists and anthropologists that fits in with what genuine Marxists have long argued.[22]

The starting point of this approach is to recognise that in certain situations natural selection favours groups whose genetic make up enables them to learn from each other, co-operating to get a livelihood.

This happened some millions of years ago among certain ape like creatures. Faced with climatic changes different groups of this species responded differently. While the ancestors of the gorilla and the chimp adapted to forest and woodland life, our ancestors were able to survive in savannah (open grassland dotted with clumps of trees) because three characteristics present in all African apes became more marked in them—the ability to stand upright, the ability to co-operate in gathering food and the ability to make rudimentary tools.

Their mode of existence gave selective advantage to traits—both biological and cultural—that only exist in embryonic form in other primates: co-operation, the use of the hand to make and carry tools, the development of communication through gesture and voice, the detailed observation of animal life to be hunted and plant life to be collected, increased concern with the socialisation of the young while they learnt from their elders, the establishment of friendly links with other groups through intermating.

What we have here is the beginnings of a labour theory of human origins and of culture, something which then enables us to begin to explain other epochal changes in human existence, like the rise of agriculture, the growth of a surplus, and the origin of classes, the state, systematic warfare and women's oppression. A few of those who practise this approach are conscious Marxists. Most are not. But they are driven to materialist conclusions by the desire to explain the factual material they have discovered about the history of humanity. We can learn a lot from them—providing we are not put off the whole topic by Knight's menstrual moonshine.

Notes

1 See, for instance, J Goodall, *The Chimpanzees of Gombe* (Cambridge Mass, 1986). For a list of 25 field studies of chimpanzees, see N M Tanner, *On Becoming Human* (Cambridge, 1981) p62. For a summary of other evidence, see V P Alexeev, *Origins of the Human Race* (Moscow, 1986), p275.

2 A point made, for instance, by MF Gadika and G Teleki, in *Current Anthropology*, June 1981.

3 RE Leakey and R Lewin, *Origins* (London, 1977), p64, AF Dixson, *The Natural History of the Gorilla* (London, 1981), p128 and N M Tanner, op cit, pp93-103.

4 See the evidence from N Sugiyama, M Reynolds and M Reynolds, quoted in N M Tanner, op cit, p102.

5 R E Leakey and R Lewin, op cit, p76.

6 A L Zihlman, 'Common ancestors and uncommon apes', in J R Durant, *Human Origins* (Oxford, 1989,) p98.

7 R E Leakey and R Lewin, op cit, p154, 156, and B J Williams, *Evolution and Human Origins*, (New York, 1979), p. 155 and J Goodall, op cit, p304.

8 M P Ghiglieri, *The Chimpanzees of Kibale Forest* (New York), p179.

9 A E Dixson, op cit, p141.

10 V P Alexeev, op cit, p272.

11 A E Dixson, op cit, p. 148. See also the abstract of J F Dahl's paper, 'Sexual aggression in pygmy chimpanzees' in the *International Journal of Primatology*, 1987, p451, and also J Goodall, op cit.

12 R Nadler's findings, reported in A F Dixson, op cit, p150.

13 A F Dixson, op cit.

14 R Nadler, as reported in A F Dixson, ibid, p145, and N M Tanner, op cit, p97.

15 'The synchrony of oestrus swelling in captive group living Chimpanzees' J Wallis, *International Journal of Primatology*, vol 6, No 4, 1985, pp330, 342.

16 See the discussion on its causes, in ibid.

17 R Leakey, *Recent fossil finds in Africa*, in J R Durant, op cit, p60.

18 The archaeologist P V Tobias argues that these areas were already developed in homo habilis, up to a million years earlier than this.

19 According to P Lieberman, *On the Origins of Human Language*, (New York, 1975).

20 For a full account of the Mbuti, and the way they make fun of many of the taboos of their neighbours, see C Turnbull, *The Forest People*, (New York, 1962). Knight himself quotes the example, but he then goes on to try to turn the truth on its head by claiming it reinforces his case!

21 M Showstack, *Nisa: The Life and Words of a !kung Woman*, (London, 1990), pp353-4, see also pp239 and 362.

22 See, for instance, R E Leakey and R Lewin, N M Tanner, V P Alexeev, op cit.

The Socialist Workers Party is one of an international grouping of socialist organisations:

AUSTRALIA: International Socialists, GPO Box 1473N, Melbourne 3001

BELGIUM: Socialisme International, Rue Lovinfosse 60, 4030 Grivengée, Belgium

BRITAIN: Socialist Workers Party, PO Box 82, London E3

CANADA: International Socialists, PO Box 339, Station E, Toronto, Ontario M6H 4E3

DENMARK: Internationale Socialister, Ryesgade 813, 8000 Arhus C, Denmark

FRANCE: Socialisme International, BP 189, 75926 Paris Cedex 19

GERMANY: Sozialistische Arbeitergruppe, Wolfsgangstrasse 81, W-6000 Frankfurt 1

GREECE: Organosi Sosialisliki Epanastasi, c/o Workers Solidarity, PO Box 8161, Athens 100 10, Greece

HOLLAND: International Socialists, PO Box 9720, 3506 GR Utrecht

IRELAND: Socialist Workers Movement, PO Box 1648, Dublin 8

NORWAY: Internasjonale Socialisterr, Postboks 5370, Majorstua, 0304 Oslo 3

POLAND: Solidarność Socjalistyczna, PO Box 12, 01-900 Warszawa 118

SOUTH AFRICA:
International Socialists of South Africa, PO Box 18530, Hillbrow 2038, Johannesberg

UNITED STATES:
International Socialist Organisation, PO Box 16085, Chicago, Illinois 60616

International Socialism 2:40 Autumn 1988
Phil Marshall: Islamic fundamentalism—oppression and revolution ★ Duncan Hallas: Trotsky's heritage—on the 50th anniversary of the founding of the Fourth International ★ Ann Rogers: Is there a new underclass? ★ Colin Sparks: The origins of Shakespeare's drama ★ Mike Gonzalez: Introduction to John Berger on Picasso ★ John Berger Defending Picasso's late work ★ Alex Callinicos: The foundations of Athenian democracy ★ Norah Carlin: Reply to Callinicos ★

International Socialism 2:39 Summer 1988
Chris Harman and Andy Zebrowski: Glasnost, before the storm ★ Chanie Rosenberg: Labour and the fight against fascism ★ Mike Gonzalez: Central America after the Peace Plan ★ Ian Birchall: Raymond Williams ★ Alex Callinicos: Reply to John Rees ★

International Socialism 2:36 Autumn 1987
Dave Beecham and Ann Eidenham: Beyond the mass strike—class, state and party in Brazil ★ Chris Bambery :The politics of James P Cannon ★ Norah Carlin: Was there racism in ancient society? ★ Paul Kellogg: Goodbye to the working class ★ Lutte Ouvrière: A critique of the SWP Analysis of the French railway workers' strike ★ Gareth Jenkins: A reply to Lutte Ouvrière ★ Ian Birchall: A comment on Colin Sparks on film theory ★

International Socialism 2:35 Summer 1987
Pete Green: Capitalism and the Thatcher years ★ Alex Callinicos: Imperialism, capitalism and the state today ★ Ian Birchall: Five years of *New Socialist* ★ Callinicos and Wood debate 'Looking for alternatives to reformism' ★ David Widgery replies on 'Beating Time' ★

International Socialism 2:31 Winter 1985
Alex Callinicos: Marxism and revolution In South Africa ★ Tony Cliff: The tragedy of A J Cook ★ Nigel Harris: What to do with London? The strategies of the GLC ★

International Socialism 2:30 Autumn 1985
Gareth Jenkins: Where is the Labour Party heading? ★ David McNally: Debt, inflation and the rate of profit ★ Ian Birchall: The terminal crisis in the British Communist Party ★ replies on Women's oppression and *Marxism Today* ★

International Socialism 2:29 Summer 1985
Special issue on the class struggle and the left in the aftermath of the miners' defeat ★ Tony Cliff: Patterns of mass strike ★ Chris Harman: 1984 and the shape of things to come ★ Alex Callinicos: The politics of *Marxism Today* ★

International Socialism 2:27 & 28
Special double issue published in conjunction with Socialist Worker ★ Alex Callinicos and Mike Simons on ★ The Great Strike: the Miners' Strike of 1984-5 and its lessons ★

International Socialism 2:26 Spring 1985
Pete Green: Contradictions of the American boom ★ Colin Sparks: Labour and imperialism ★ Chris Bambery: Marx and Engels and the unions ★ Sue Cockerill: The municipal road to socialism ★ Norah Carlin: Is the family part of the superstructure? ★ Kieran Allen: James Connolly and the 1916 rebellion ★

International Socialism 2:25 Autumn 1984
John Newsinger: Jim Larkin, Syndicalism and the 1913 Dublin Lockout ★ Pete Binns: Revolution and state capitalism in the Third World ★ Colin Sparks: Towards a police state? ★ Dave Lyddon: Demystifying the downturn ★ John Molyneux: Do working class men benefit from women's oppression? ★

International Socialism 2:18 Winter 1983
Donny Gluckstein: Workers' councils in Western Europe ★ Jane Ure Smith: The early Communist press in Britain ★ John Newsinger: The Bolivian Revolution ★ Andy Durgan: Largo Caballero and Spanish socialism ★ M Barker and A Beezer: Scarman and the language of racism ★

International Socialism 2:14 Winter 1981
Chris Harman: The riots of 1981 ★ Dave Beecham: Class struggle under the Tories ★ Tony Cliff: Alexandra Kollontai ★ L James and A Paczuska: Socialism needs feminism ★ reply to Cliff on Zetkin ★ Feminists In the labour movement ★

International Socialism 2:13 Summer 1981
Chris Harman: The crisis last time ★ Tony Cliff: Clara Zetkin ★ Ian Birchall: Left Social Democracy In the French Popular Front ★ Pete Green: Alternative Economic Strategy ★ Tim Potter: The death of Eurocommunism ★

International Socialism 2:12 Spring 1981
Jonathan Neale: The Afghan tragedy ★ Lindsey German: Theories of patriarchy ★ Ray Challinor: McDouall and Physical Force Chartism ★ S Freeman & B Vandesteeg: Unproductive labour ★ Alex Callinicos: Wage labour and capitalism ★ Italian fascism ★ Marx's theory of history ★ Cabral ★

International Socialism 2:11 Winter 1980
Rip Bulkeley et al: CND In the 50s ★ Marx's theory of crisis and its critics ★ Andy Durgan: Revolutionary anarchism in Spain ★ Alex Callinicos: Politics or abstract thought ★ Fascism in Europe ★ Marilyn Monroe ★

International Socialism 2:10 Autumn 1980
Steve Jeffreys: The CP and the rank and file ★ Ian Birchall: A short history of *NLR* ★ Nigel Harris: Crisis and the core of the system ★ Cuba ★ English Civil War ★

International Socialism 2:9 Summer 1980
Callinicos/Rogers: Southern Africa after Mugabe ★ Chris Harman: Theories of the crisis ★ Pete Goodwin: *Beyond the Fragments* ★ Debate on Cuba ★ Raymond Williams & Co ★